Hero On the Western Front

Hero On the Western Front

Discovering Alvin C. York's Great War Battlefield

By
Michael Kelly

Thomas J. Nolan. PhD
Brad Posey
James B. Legg

FRONTLINE
BOOKS

First published in Great Britain in 2018 by
Frontline Books
an imprint of
Pen & Sword Books Ltd
Yorkshire - Philadelphia

ISBN 978 1 52670 075 9

A CIP catalogue record for this book is
available from the British Library

Printed and bound by
Replika Press Pvt. Ltd.

Pen & Sword Books Ltd incorporates the Imprints of Aviation, Atlas,
Family History, Fiction, Maritime, Military, Discovery, Politics, History,
Archaeology, Select, Wharncliffe Local History, Wharncliffe True Crime,
Military Classics, Wharncliffe Transport, Leo Cooper, The Praetorian Press,
Remember When, Seaforth Publishing and Frontline Publishing.

For a complete list of Pen & Sword titles please contact
PEN & SWORD BOOKS LTD
47 Church Street, Barnsley, South Yorkshire, S70 2AS, England
E-mail: enquiries@pen-and-sword.co.uk
Website: www.pen-and-sword.co.uk
Or
PEN AND SWORD BOOKS
1950 Lawrence Rd, Havertown, PA 19083, USA
E-mail: Uspen-and-sword@casematepublishers.com
Website: www.penandswordbooks.com

Contents

List of Plates

List of Maps

Dedication

To my late parents, Jack and Mary Kelly, who imbued me with the values of history, honour and perseverance.

Introduction

By Ed Bearss, Chief Historian, U.S. National Park Service

I have always been lucky. I was born on June 26, 1923, weeks before the death of President Warren G. Harding. I grew up on my grandfather's multi-acre cattle ranch, an easy horseback ride from the site of Chief Sitting Bull's Sundance two weeks before the Battle of the Little Big Horn. I went to a one-room school house in Sarpy, Montana, for three years, riding a horse to school each day. Starting when I was nine in 1935, I used a large National Geographic map of Europe to track (using colored push pins and yarn) the movements of armies in the Italo–Ethiopian War, the Spanish Civil War and World War II before Pearl Harbor.

In our neighbourhood lived the Barnards, one of whose children, Florence, was born on Armistice Day 1918, and her parents named her Florence Peace Barnard. Another neighbour was Clarence Roberts, who was with the 'Lost Battalion' of the 77th Division at the Meuse-Argonne. A cousin named 'Hiking' Hiram Bearss was a 1st Battalion commander at Belleau Wood. A Marine Corps hero, he was transferred by General John J. Pershing to command the 102nd U.S. Infantry Division and was awarded the Army's Distinguished Service Cross at St Mihel and led one of the Yankee Division's two brigades at Meuse-Argonne. So, by the time I was in the first grade, I was interested and through my relatives and friends, felt an involvement in the Great War.

Following the attack on Pearl Harbor, I enlisted in the U.S. Marine Corps and in mid-November 1943, I had my first indirect connection with Alvin York. A USO show visited Oro Bay on New Guinea. This show included Gary Cooper. We had recently seen Cooper star as Lou Gehrig in *Pride of the Yankees* and *Sergeant York*. On the Sunday after the show, a friend and I arranged to fly in a C-47 from the nearby Dobadura airstrip 200 miles north to Dumpu. The same plane was taking the USO show with Gary Cooper, who also grew up shooting game from horseback in Montana as I had. It turned out my grandmother was a close friend of Cooper's parents, so on our three-hour flight I spent ninety minutes recalling our Montana childhoods and his role as Sergeant York. Cooper had met with York before he made the film, so I was one removed from the man.

On 2 January 1944, I was scouting for my platoon when I fired at Japanese soldiers across what we marines would dub Suicide Creek at Cape Gloucester, New Britain. During this engagement, I was shot four times by a Japanese machine gun, Laying just six inches below continued machine gun tracer fire, I was saved by two heroes who dragged me out by my shoulders, who then laid flat and pushed us out using their toes. It was then that the critical importance of terrain in combat – that mere inches meant life or death for me and, as I would come to learn, many others – meant success or failure in battles. For this reason, the location of Alvin York's success was also critical, different terrain could have led to a vastly different outcome than depicted in *Sergeant York*. After twenty-six months recovering from my wounds, I was discharged from the Marine Corps and ultimately graduated from Georgetown University in Washington DC. In 1955 I went to work for the U.S. National Park Service at the Vicksburg National Military Park as a park historian. Here I supported many projects uncovering history, including the discovery and recovery of the USS *Cairo* and the earthworks at Grand Gulf among others.

In the National Park Service, we were confronted by the situation where historians and archeologists were involved in interpretation. The historians championed use of documents and the archeologists emphasized the importance of artifacts and evidence found in the ground using spades and since World War II, handheld metal detectors, including those by Fisher, that have become increasingly capable. Indeed, the man who first hired me in September 1956 was J.C. 'Pinky' Harrington. Harrington is recognized as the 'Father of Historical Archeology' in the U.S. When he excavated George Washington's Fort Necessity site in Pennsylvania in the mid-1930s, he found that the fort's ground profile was circular and not rectangular as presumed by historians unaided by archeology.

As another example of the importance of proper archeology in historical interpretation, consider its impact on understanding the reality of the Battle of the Little Big Horn between Sitting Bull's warriors and George Armstrong

Custer's 7th Cavalry. A 1983 range fire within the battlefield burned off more than 600 acres of sage brush and deep-rooted prairie grass. Park management knew that records maintained at nearby Fort Custer documented that, since its establishment in 1877, there had not been any range fire that had seriously impacted Park lands. Consequently, senior NPS management sought authority to undertake an extensive archeological survey of the burned-cover area.

The survey would be supervised by NPS professionals to include Douglas D. Scott and Richard A. Fox. The grunt work of undertaking the survey would be done by volunteers employing the most recent metal detectors. The use of metal detectors had become popular by U.S. Civil War buffs by the mid-1960s. These buffs lusted at an invitation to work on the Little Big Horn archeology projects by Scott and Fox. Insofar as known, the only archeology on site had been performed by Park historian Don Rickey before the fire and people with metal detectors sneaking into the park at night. Proper archeological supervision in 1984 and 1985 seasons had flagged (location), registered and bagged cartridge cases. In the base of each cartridge, its firing by a specific weapon left a distinctive impression of its firing pin. This information demonstrated that the warriors fought as individuals, not subjected of course to U.S. military discipline and concomitant tactical practice. They often used different weapons and returned to their local lodges when 'the spirit moved them'.

I have served as an historian at several NPS organizational levels, starting at Vicksburg, Mississippi, throughout my forty-two years as an employee of the NPS. In my last thirteen years into 1995, I served as the Chief Historian, which included close review of park field reports including the landmark archeological research at the Little Big Horn Battlefield. Therefore, I have directly relevant and time-proven nationally recognized knowledge and experience in both documental and critical archeological integration in the science of historical interpretation. After my 1995 retirement, I have worked as a tour leader for such prestigious organizations as the Smithsonian Institution, National Geographic and South Mountain Expeditions among others, providing historical expertise at dozens of military parks and sites in the U.S. and World War I and II battlefields in Europe.

In October 2017, I worked with Michael Kelly on a two-week tour of Great War sites in France and Belgium. A highlight of our tour was a visit to the Meuse-Argonne, where Kelly shared his encyclopaedic knowledge of the York sites concerning York's heroic actions on October 8, 1918. Familiar with my credentials, Kelly invited me to review and evaluate his forthcoming book entitled *Hero on the Western Front; Discovering Alvin C. York's Great War Battlefield*, with contributions by Thomas J. Nolan, PhD., Brad Posey and James Legg.

Like most combat veterans of World War II and long-time employee of the U.S. NPS, I was familiar with the complexities of determining the specific location of tactical actions in combat when returning to the battlefield. As at the Little Big Horn, archeologists could trace a warrior's movements, but not necessarily those of a specific individual.

My review of Kelly's manuscript demonstrates it is a tour-de-force and measures up to the highest standards of research and scholarship. I can do no better than to cite the objectives that Kelly includes in his Foreword, where he identifies serious problems with the 'SYDE' that compromise the validity of their claims that they had located the York sites. Better yet, I urge readers to carefully read Chapter 28 entitled 'Analysis of SYDE Claims', and I assure them that they will agree with the location of the York sites as identified by the Nolan Group.

Ed Bearrs,
Chief Historian Emeritus,
United States National Park Service.
December 2017

Acknowledgements

That this book exists at all is attestation not to any abilities of its author but to the benevolence, dedication, and persuasion from several people, some whom are my dearest friends and colleagues.

Over the years, they have worked on behalf of the Nolan Group researching and gathering evidence, be it historical, geospatial or archaeological, to discover the true location where Alvin C. York earned the Congressional Medal of Honor in 1918. They have been tireless in their efforts; Brad Posey, who was working at the same time on another project involving the Lost Battalion and, amid his toils had to return to the U.S. from Germany to seek a new job, is responsible for much of the work in this book, and the Group is extremely grateful to him. Doctor Tom Nolan, the project leader, has annotated many of the maps that are contained within, and his expertise on spatial technology has resulted in an elephantine library of artefact records that can be drawn on for study purposes for all time. The methodology of search was devised by him, and it has been through his guidance, leadership, and scientific prowess that the project arrived at a most satisfactory conclusion. I am grateful to him in allowing me unadulterated access to his PhD dissertation. The team archaeologist, James Legg, has long experience working in that environment; his knowledge and meticulous application to detail allowed the project to arrive at the best result it could have ever hoped for. The Dutch investigative journalist and historian Stephan van Meulebrouck, relentlessly pursued and interviewed some important players in this invigorating story, revealing some important facts in pursuit of the truth behind the York fight location in the Argonne Forest.

For more than ten years many people have played a part in the York story. Special mention should be made of Mons. Yves Desfossés, of the French Regional Department of Archaeology. It was he in the first place who granted the necessary permission to conduct an archaeological survey, and then authorised and supplied backhoe equipment and manpower to assist further in the search. He has been forthright in his opinion of both groups of investigators that appear in this book, and his comments will manifest later. Professor Michael Birdwell of Tennessee Tech and the curator of the York papers, a member of the Nolan Group and an attendee during the first two phases of exploration, has continued to offer support and advice. Frédéric Castier, of Saint-Quentin assisted with landowner permissions in the first instance and then as a translator in the field. David Currey, a film-maker and historian from Tennessee, made a record of the first phase. He is responsible for the logistics of the excellent Sergeant York Exhibit, based in Tennessee.

Grateful thanks are due to Professor Ed Lengel for his review and endorsement of this book, he is also a cousin of Alvin C. York. I thank Professor John McQuilton, late of the University of Wollongong, Australia, for his advocacy, and to Doctor Matthew Kelly, the highly experienced Australian forensic archaeologist, for his support. I am obliged to Lieutenant-Colonel Russell Linwood, ASM, retired Australian Army, and to Second World War Pacific veteran and historian Ed Bearss of the United States for their welcome contribution. Robert Desourdis is to be congratulated for his spirited willingness to assist in the evaluation of this book.

I am grateful to Kim Hassel for her assistance in German translations, Colin Fiford for his eagle-eyed editing skills, Ian Cobb and Eddie Browne for their energy and avidity in their skilful metal detecting, Harry Rupert for his assistance on the ground in Châtel-Chéhéry. To Martin Mace for giving me the opportunity to publish the true story behind the discovery of the site where Alvin C. York fought in the Argonne Forest in 1918, and to Mark Khan who pointed me in the right direction. Thanks also to Jim Deppen, Gordon Cummings and Margie Nolan for their work behind the scenes and their enthusiastic support. I am indebted to Doctor Jennifer Roberts, University of Wollongong, for her advice. I should also thank Doctor Lucien Houlemare and his wife, Annicke, for the hand of friendship they have extended to me, my wife and the Nolan Group over many years in the village of Châtel-Chéhéry. Grateful appreciation is extended to the then Mayor of Fléville, Damien Georges, and the then Mayor of Châtel-Chéhéry, Roland Destenay. Carol Schulties, a relative of Maryan Dymowski, and Karen Johnson, cousin of Carl Swanson, have been stalwarts in support of the Nolan Group and I am grateful for their permission to reproduce information on their relatives. Bob D'Angelo, the spokesman for the group called 'The Other Sixteen', has graciously allowed me to use antecedent information from his website based upon the other members of the patrol, and has been especially enthusiastic for their biographies and stories to be published. Finally, I thank my wife, Pauline, who has accompanied me and tolerated my efforts to discover the truth on my many research visits to France over the last fifteen years. Without her support, this book would not have been possible.

Foreword

Is there a common denominator in determining who is a hero? Can bravery in the field of conflict ever be described of as part or total foolhardiness? Providing answers to these questions is not easy. There are many heroes in battle, some would say *all* participants are heroes; the majority of those heroes remain unknown, their actions not witnessed by those in a position of rank able to provide the necessary recommendation. Those who are recognized, and who, had they been living a peaceful life at home, would probably have gone about their trifling business with the world none the wiser of their existence. In the period of training and bonding with their fellow men, they became soldiers, some who, in the heat of battle, could cast fear away, putting to one side their natural instinct for survival. They launched themselves into a maelstrom of death and destruction, and finding themselves capable of performing amazing feats of derring-do, no matter if they died or survived, they emerged as heroes. The survivors are decorated for their valour, the world as they knew it would never be the same again. They emerge into a new light, bathed in iconic, hero worship. Some profit from their bravery, receiving a pecuniary advantage by writing their story. They all discover a new status in life, but most are shy and retiring, preferring to avoid public attention and downplaying their role, whilst praising those who were with them at the scene of action.

The Reverend Theodore Bayley Hardy was one such man. Decorated for his bravery on the Western Front during the Great War for going out into the open and giving succour to the wounded, he would softly say to the wounded man, 'It's only me.' Here was a man who, when he was told he would receive his nation's highest accolade, first refused it, and it was eventually with great reluctance he accepted the award. When talking to his beloved soldiers, he would embarrassedly cover the Victoria Cross medal ribbon on his tunic with his arm. He was killed out in the open tending to wounded soldiers. Many decorated heroes went home with the horrors of battle first and foremost in their minds; scenes that could never be erased from their memory. Post-Traumatic Stress Disorder (PTSD) was prevalent in the Great War it was hardly ever recognized, certainly amongst the ordinary ranks. Shell-shock was even considered a form of cowardice, and many in the British Army paid a heavy price. After the war had ended, men returned home to an uncertain future. Despite the horrors of war, they at least had been fed, watered and clothed, which was more than many would have had they remained at home. Some men became violent, beating their wives, and they quarrelled and fought in the streets and bars. They turned to criminal activities and others became alcoholics, whilst many more lost their sanity. Major Charles Whittlesey who had commanded elements of the United States 77th Division, to be ever remembered in the annals of history as the 'Lost Battalion', could not erase his memories of war, particularly the suffering and losses of his men at Charlevaux Mill in 1918. In his anguish after the war, he jumped to his death from a ship en route to Havana, never to be seen again.

These officers and men came from a variety of backgrounds, from families of wealth, some of whom were at the very pinnacle of their social class, whilst others came from the depths of poverty. Both Alvin C. York during the Great War and Audie Murphy from the Second World War came from similar backgrounds; Murphy from penurious circumstances in Texas, York from humble beginnings in backwoods in the Cumberland Gap in Tennessee. Murphy became the highest decorated American soldier during the Second World War, earning the Congressional Medal of Honor for his action in staving off a concentrated German attack, and in the process, killing around fifty of the enemy. York, twenty-six years earlier in the Argonne Forest, had single-handedly killed twenty-one Germans and taken 132 prisoner. The similarity between the men ends here; Murphy had volunteered for service, York had not. After wrestling with his conscience, York did fight but the spectre of doubt, based upon his religious affirmations, was always in his mind.

There is no distinction in class system when it comes to the act of bravery. Some men are born and raised into a strict environment of military tradition; they join the regiment to achieve distinction; and they yearn to be decorated in battle. It is drummed into them from an early age, to cherish the Flag and to doggedly pursue their duty no matter the consequences. Whilst others, like Murphy and York, although their patriotism was never doubted, would not have harboured such grand thoughts. They fought with a love for their country, believing in what they were doing was right, despite York's initial doubts based upon his religious beliefs. Both were imbued with a pride in their unit, and the desire never to let their comrades down. This was, and still is, an enduring characteristic amongst fighting men. York was thrown into a firefight situation and, without consideration for all grandiose thoughts of military doctrines, he reacted to the circumstances in which he found himself, doing what came to him naturally. Alvin C. York was a shining example of a soldier who found himself in a dangerous situation to which he responded immediately, without fear of, or if ever thinking of, the possible consequences. Afterwards, if they survived, there would follow promotion and decoration; they would be revered for the rest of their lives. But could anyone understand their troubled minds? Only those who had borne witness to the horrors could have an inkling of what they all shared. They would not talk of what they had seen, simply because those horrors were such that no one would understand let alone believe that man could be so capable of inflicting such inhumanities on his fellow man. Their experiences would remain with them, locked away in the inner sanctum, some never to be shared for all time. We know of the sadness that York felt at the loss of his great friend, Murray Savage, who, like York, possessed a deep religious belief. Perhaps York, on a star-filled night in Tennessee, years after the conflict had ceased, would reflect on those comrades he had known in France who had not returned, believing that maybe somewhere the music of their voices lingered. In fellowship and camaraderie, they had followed resolutely the dark highway of death. They had heard the beating of the wings of the Angel of Death, but, unrepiningly, their sense of duty prevailing, they unflinchingly and without hesitation, trod that dark path, pursuing their destiny and passing into the oblivion beyond.

After the war, Alvin C. York resisted all offers that would bring him into the limelight. He turned away from proposals that would have made him a very rich man. His religious beliefs were to him of paramount importance, and when he gave permission for a movie to be made about his story, it was in the knowledge that the money would be used to build a Bible school in his home village in Pall Mall, Tennessee. The movie, with Gary Cooper in the starring role, a film largely inaccurate, told the whole world the story of York's courage.

These pages will give only a brief biography of York; his life story has been comprehensively written on over the years. The objective of this book is to, by demonstrating the use of sound research and professional application, highlight the discovery of the *true* site in the Argonne Forest where York fought on 8 October 1918.

By use of historical documentation, official unit histories, both American and German, personal accounts and maps of the time, you will be taken by the Doctor Nolan Project team (Nolan Group) every step of the way to discover the archaeology, the use and science of geographic information science (GIS), and how, when coupled with history and archaeology, this resulted in some amazing artefact discoveries from the site of a firefight in a forested ravine in France that took place almost 100 years ago.

The methods employed were relatively new to battlefield technology. With thanks to the expertise of Doctor Tom Nolan, of Middle Tennessee State University (MTSU), a specialist in the field of GIS, the team integrated historic maps, reports and documentation into a spatial database that enabled them to model the landscape as it would have appeared in October 1918. It was hoped that this methodology would help lead the Nolan Group team to the site of the York fight.

To gather the information on the ground, metal detectors were used to locate artefacts, and at the end of the exploration the most probable location of where the fight took place has been determined.

In the United States, GIS systems were first used in battlefield exploration by the National Park Service. Over a period, its use has included a cultural resources inventory at Fredericksburg-Spotsylvania National Military Park and the creation of a historic landscape as it was during the American Civil War in more than 88,000 acres at the Petersburg National Battlefield. GIS was introduced at the Chickamauga National Military Park to map monuments and orientation tablets. The database also allows the staff to direct visitors who are searching for where their forebears fought during the battle to a specific location.

One of the better-known battlefield interpretations where GIS played a huge part was with Doctor Douglas C. Scott Jnr and his explorations at the Little Bighorn National Monument in Montana. At the time, in the 1980s GIS was very much in its embryonic form but even so, the purpose and procedures carried out at the Little Bighorn set the tone, and Scott's ground-breaking procedures have much in common with the research as applied by the Nolan Group in France.

As the result of a fire that swept over the Little Bighorn battlefield in 1983, relics were exposed and it provided a unique opportunity for the battlefield to be surveyed. Metal detectors were used and each relic that was found was mapped and photographed. The patterns that emerged from the location of the artefacts enabled the researchers to gain an insight, hitherto not available in the historical documentation alone, into individual combatants and actions that had been previously overlooked in the written accounts of the battle.[1]

Like the Little Bighorn Battlefield, the location where the York patrol fought, near the sleepy little French village of Châtel-Chéhéry, the fighting took place on one day only, 8 October 1918. It was at a location on the left flank of the main American attack. The fact that it was a one-day action was a great asset for the Nolan Group; it meant that most artefacts discovered were from that engagement alone.

The foreword started with questions, it will conclude with a question. Why is it necessary to go to extreme lengths to ascertain the *actual* site of a battle? Does it really matter? In this case we know that York fought close to the village of Châtel-Chéhéry, is that not sufficient detail? What difference does it make that the confrontation took place on the western or the eastern side of a hill, 600 metres apart or a mile apart in either direction? A memorial has been erected to remember the exploits of York, and it will remain as a lasting tribute to him, but I believe, as a historian that we should endeavour to ascertain, employing our best efforts, where a point of history was made. The site of an American Civil War battle or the hill on Iwo Jima where the U.S. Marines raised the flag in the Second World War are equally important to *try* and establish, wherever possible, the location of the action. Imagine the marker stone of the 'Lost Battalion' from October 1918 being a kilometre down the road from where it is known the fight took place, or that the Omaha Beach landings were a beach or two farther along from the actual landings.

That one battle should be considered historically more important than another is of no matter, the importance lies with the criteria for ensuring the interpretation of that battle is accurate, and that criteria should be applied to all historical events.[2] Of late, there has been much debate as to the true site of the

Battle of Hastings, with two schools of thought involved, although is doubtful if the true location will ever be ascertained 1,000 years on. But in the York case the site of his bravery has been located with a high percentage of certainty. You will read later of people in high places who glibly ask the question, what differences will the knowledge of where York fought make to history? The answer is simply this: if the current understanding of what took place is allowed to stand, the American official history of the battle in this area on 8 October 1918 would have to be rewritten. The Nolan Group will, within these pages, put forward a strong case enabling all to see what took place and where on that October morning in 1918. The reader will arrive at his own conclusions, based upon unbiased, sound, meticulous, historical research, and scientific application. In addition, the six American patrol members who lost their lives, and the twenty-one Germans who were killed in the fight, are deserved of Remembrance. They were all players in the deadly end game that was the Great War. To them all, the survivors and the dead, we owe a great debt.

Michael Kelly

Grimsby, Lincolnshire, England 2017

Author's Notes

It is a fact that the affidavits and testimonies contained within the book by Tom Skeyhill *Sergeant York. His Own Life Story and War Diary*, cannot be found in any archive. They exist only in that book, which was published in 1928 by a New York publishing company who are no longer in business. However, and to allow me to use extensive quotes from those important documents, Professor Michael Birdwell and the Sergeant York Foundation, who hold copyright, have allowed me to use Skeyhill's working manuscript of the book. For this I am extremely grateful.

The purpose of this book is to locate the true site of York's fight in the Argonne Forest in October 1918. It is in no way intended to downplay the heroism displayed by Alvin C. York, or indeed any other members of that patrol. Another research team claim to have discovered the site, which is in a different location more than 600 metres away. The Sergeant York Discovery Expedition (SYDE) led by Colonel Mastriano, United States Army, state that with 100 per cent certainty they were in the right place. The Nolan Group dispute the claim and will demonstrate within this book the case for recognition of the true fight site. No professional entity involved in a serious archaeological exploration can ever claim to be 100 per cent certain of their conclusive findings, unless there is outstanding evidence that can be corroborated.

Quotes from American sources are reproduced in the spelling form in which they were written. Otherwise spelling is in British English.

Abbreviations and Meanings:

LIR	Landwehr Infantry Regiment
RIR	Reserve Infantry Regiment
LDW	Landwehr Division
CMH	Centre of Military History
Mineur	Sappers
SYDE	Sergeant York Discovery Expedition

PART I

Events in the Argonne Forest

It's not the size of the dog in a fight, it's the size of the fight in the dog.

Mark Twain

Chapter 1

The Hero

Alvin Cullum York was born in Pall Mall, in the Valley of the Three Forks of the Wolf River, Tennessee, on 13 December 1887. Alvin was the third son of William and Mary and came after the arrival of Henry and Joe. He was followed in turn by Sam and Albert, his sister Hattie, brothers George and James, sister Lillie, brother Robert and sister Lucy in that order.

The hardships of living in the outback of Tennessee meant that York plied a meagre existence from farming. York became a hunter and, resultantly, a great marksman.

Regional history was smattered with acts of violence. During the American Civil War it attracted the unwanted attentions of Civil War Union bushwhackers and Confederate guerrillas, during which time the population suffered fearfully, including York's family; his maternal grandfather was murdered by Union bushwhackers. Survival in such a harsh environment was paramount and it provided the foundation that was to shape York's life.

His marksmanship was such that he won many shooting contests. These would comprise of turkey shoots, where the unfortunate animals were tied behind logs with only their heads showing. The competitors would shoot from a standing position, 60 yards away. They would pay ten cents a shot and if they had a hit they would get the turkey.

York's crack shooting was going to be of great benefit in the war that was to come and, without doubt, was to save his life in the Argonne Forest and ensure him a place in the annals of American history.

In his early days, York lived a high life of drinking, gambling and fighting in the border bars of Tennessee and Kentucky known as 'Blind Tigers'. In 1914, his best friend, Everett Delk, was killed in a bar fight in Static, Kentucky. The realisation that this death was completely senseless had a profound effect on York.

He thought long and hard. He was taken to going on long walks in the mountains and eventually he decided to finish with the life he was leading. In that same year, he went to the Wolf River church, where he'd listen to the Reverend H.H. Russell from Indiana. He so impressed York that he gave up smoking, drinking, swearing and fighting and joined the Church of Christ in Christian Union (CCICU).

York's religious beliefs remained with him for the rest of his life: his conscription into the Army, his period at war in France and for the four decades he survived after the First World War.

Gracie Williams was one of thirteen children born to Mr and Mrs Frank Williams, who owned the farm adjoining the York place. Gracie and her parents strongly disapproved of Alvin's wild behaviour and reform was the only path that might lead him to a successful courtship. Alvin was thirteen years' older than Gracie and her father considered him too old for her. Despite the obstacles, Alvin and Gracie's relationship grew until the autumn of 1917, when the distant war in Europe intruded on the isolated valleys of the Cumberland Plateau and Alvin was summoned to report for induction by the Fentress County Draft Board in Jamestown on 15 November. He departed for basic training at Camp Gordon, Georgia, the next day. At their last meeting before he departed, Gracie promised to marry him when his military service was over.

York suffered deep mental anguish about becoming a soldier. David Lee says that the violence he had seen in the borders reinforced York's religious objection to fighting and it had:

> ... left him with a difficult choice. Taught that both religion and patriotism were virtues, he was now troubled and uncertain because they seemed to indicate such opposite courses of action.[1]

In addition, York's family ancestors, who had fought for their country since the Revolution, felt a close kinship with such frontier greats as Andrew Jackson, Davy Crockett and Sam Houston. All these things weighed heavily on his mind as his drafting date drew ever closer:

> One moment I would make up my mind to follow God and the next I would hesitate and almost make up my mind to follow Uncle Sam.[2]

With the persuasion and assistance of his Pastor, Rosier Pile, York applied for the conscientious objector status based on his religion. David Lee has stated the Fentress County Draft Board refused his application and dismissed subsequent appeals because the CCIU had no doctrine other than the Bible. York reluctantly joined the Army.

After basic training at Camp Gordon, York was assigned to Company G, 2nd Battalion, 328th Infantry, 82nd (All American) Division. He was labelled as a conscientious objector by his fellow soldiers[3] and made few friends in his unit. However, he was extremely fortunate in having Captain Edward Danforth as his company commander and George Buxton as his battalion commander. These men were both well educated, had strong religious faith, and appreciated York's beliefs, recognising York was suffering some mental turmoil.

Through a combination of pastoral counselling and education they helped him reconcile the conflict between patriotic and religious duty. Tom Skeyhill, who would later write York's *Own Life Story*, felt that he consoled himself with the belief that American military intervention was the only hope for peace in Europe and his role was that of a 'peacemaker'.

The 82nd Division arrived in France during the latter part of May 1918. After trench warfare training the division was in place in the line in the Saint-Mihiel sector by June. The Saint-Mihiel Offensive began on 12 September 1918 and was the first completely American military operation of the Great War. York emerged from the offensive promoted to corporal and squad leader. The Meuse-Argonne Offensive followed on 26 September. The 82nd Division was initially kept in reserve and was not committed until 6 October. It was ordered into action as part of an assault designed to rescue elements of the 308th Infantry, 77th Division, a unit that would be forever remembered as 'The Lost Battalion' that had been cut off and surrounded since 2 October.

The mission of the 2nd Battalion, 328th Infantry, in this operation was to attack west from Hill 223 just outside the village of Châtel-Chéhéry and sever the narrow gauge Decauville railway that was the supply line of the German troops surrounding the 'Lost Battalion'.

York's Company G was assigned on the extreme left of the 2nd Battalion, who attacked a little after 0600 on 8 October and came under heavy rifle and machine gun fire from the front and both flanks that stopped the advance at the bottom of Hill 223. Platoon Sergeant Harry Parsons realised the attack had stalled and ordered Sergeant Bernard Early to take three squads, including that commanded by York, and move to the left, in an attempt to outflank and silence the machine guns.

Early's sixteen men made a wide circle to the south and west, and they had gone about a mile or so in the dense forest when they encountered two Germans wearing Red Cross armbands. The German medics fled down a path and Early deployed his men in a skirmish line and pursued them. The Americans broke into a clearing and surprised a group of Germans, who quickly surrendered. As the Americans were organising the prisoners, a machine gun opened fire. The German prisoners immediately dropped to the ground and in seconds Sergeant Early was hit multiple times in the body, Corporal Cutting was hit three times in the arm and Corporal Savage was killed, as were five more of the patrol.

This left York as the senior non-commissioned officer with seven unwounded privates. York was so close to the German prisoners that the machine gunners had to expose their heads to aim the gun and avoid hitting their comrades. York engaged the German gunners with rapid, accurate rifle fire and shot any who exposed themselves to aim their weapons. A German lieutenant tried to resolve the impasse by leading several enlisted men in a bayonet charge. The Germans realised that York's rifle had a maximum capacity of five rounds and would run out of ammunition before he could shoot them all. York killed all the enlisted men and wounded the lieutenant in the stomach with his .45 calibre Colt automatic pistol.

The method of his disposal of the charge by the enlisted men showed York's calmness under fire. It is said he shot them sequentially from the rearmost man to the officer at the front leading the charge. This prevented the survivors realising their mounting losses and stopping to fire their rifles.

At this point, a German officer in the group of prisoners offered to surrender his remaining men. York and the surviving Americans lined the prisoners up and marched them toward the American lines. Several groups of Germans were encountered on their way and they were taken prisoner. They were taken to the 2nd Battalion Command Post (CP), where 132 were counted.

York was ordered to escort them to Brigade Headquarters in Varennes 10km away. For his actions on 8 October, Alvin C. York was promoted to sergeant and awarded the Medal of Honor. His citation reads:

Rank and organisation: Corporal, U.S. Army, Company G, 328th Infantry, 82nd Division. Place and date: Near Châtel-Chéhéry, France, 8 October 1918.

Entered Service at: Pall Mall, Tenn. G.O. No.:59, W.D., 1919. Citation: After his platoon had suffered heavy casualties and 3 other non-commissioned officers had become casualties, Corporal York assumed command. Fearlessly leading 7 men, he charged with great daring a machinegun nest which was pouring deadly and incessant fire upon his platoon. In this heroic feat, the machinegun nest was taken, together with 4 officers and 128 men and several guns.[4]

Chapter 2

Welcome Home Alvin

An article in *The Saturday Evening Post* in April 1919 by George Pattullo brought the exploits of Alvin York to the attention of the public. Newspapers picked up on the story and by the time York arrived in New York from France on 22 May he was famous. He was greeted by a ticker tape parade, cheering crowds, and a formal banquet hosted by the Tennessee Society of New York. From New York, he travelled to Washington D.C., where he was the guest of Cordell Hull, his congressman from Tennessee. York received a standing ovation from the House of Representatives, met with the Secretary of War Newton Baker and visited the White House. By 28 May he was on his way to Fort Oglethorpe to be discharged and return home. On 29 May York was back in his beloved valley and it wasn't long before he married Gracie Williams. One week and a day after his return from the war, on 7 June 1919, she became Mrs Alvin C. York. The Tennessee Governor, Albert Roberts, officiated at the wedding.

Attempting to settle down in Fentress County with his new wife, York found himself the recipient of countless offers in return for his endorsement. Newspapers, the entertainment industry and manufacturers were willing to pay him hundreds of thousands of dollars for his cooperation. York was adamant in his refusal to capitalise on his wartime experiences. The only gift he did accept was an offer of a house and farm in Pall Mall as a tribute from the Nashville Rotary Club. Instead of personal profit, York chose to devote himself to the service of his community.

York's military experience made him painfully aware of his lack of education and the disadvantages children in the Upper Cumberland laboured under from the lack of good schools. He concluded that the most beneficial educational project for the region would be a vocational school to provide job skills for local students. He formed the Alvin C. York Foundation and embarked on a national speaking tour to raise money. He also lobbied state government for support.

By 1929 the York Agricultural Institute was established in Jamestown and York named as the first president. Unfortunately, York lacked the business acumen to make a success of running the school. Conflicts with local political leaders, the Fentress County School Board and the State Board of Education led to his resignation as president of the York Institute in 1936, although he still retained the honorary title of president emeritus. York was forced to turn his energies elsewhere.

He dreamed of creating a Bible school to instruct students on the skills necessary to live a Christian life. He lacked the financial resources for such a project and when Jesse Laskey, a film producer working for Warner Brothers, renewed his offer to make a film of York's life story, he was tempted for the first time to profit from his fame.

In his book Michael Birdwell says that Laskey had first become interested in a film on York when he witnessed his 1919 reception in New York from his office window.[1] Laskey had repeatedly tried to interest York in the project but it was not until 1940 that he finally relented and gave him permission for the film to be made under the condition that it cover his whole life and not concentrate on his combat experiences. York planned to use his proceeds from the movie to fund his Bible school. Laskey considered Warner Brothers the best studio to produce the movie and had chosen the company for several reasons, in particular Harry Warner had helped him financially when he lost his job and house during the Depression.

By the mid-1930s, York had concluded that American sacrifices in the Great War had accomplished little of lasting value. Indeed, many American soldiers returning home were of the impression that they had taken part in a conflict that was not of their making, that they should not have played any part in it and that those they had fought for, the French were ungrateful, inhospitable and profiteering.[2] With Europe drifting ever closer to war, York advocated preparedness but favoured isolation over intervention. Michael Birdwell has said that during the filming of *Sergeant York*, Alvin came to believe that Hitler was not only a military threat to the United States, but an evil that threatened the entire world. York became the spokesman for the *Fight for Freedom Committee*, which advocated interventionism and was formed to counter the influence of the isolationist, anti-Roosevelt, anti-Semitic *America First Committee*, represented by Charles Lindbergh. York and Lindbergh debated on the radio, in the newspapers, and in public speeches until the Japanese attack on Pearl Harbor settled the issue.

Birdwell further states that the movie premiered in July 1941, but was withdrawn in August due to a Senate investigation of Hollywood, instigated by Senator Gerald Nye of North Dakota and Bennet Clark of Missouri. The two senators, strong supporters of the *America First Committee*, believed that movies such as *Sergeant York* violated the official neutrality of the United States and amounted to pro-war propaganda. The investigation ended with America's entry into the war in December 1941 and the movie was re-released in 1942.[3]

Another consequence of the making of *Sergeant York* was a revision of the original stories by the surviving members of the York patrol. Shortly after the battle, the participants made sworn statements describing their part and their individual actions during the engagement. David Lee says that these statements formed the basis for subsequent descriptions of the event.[4] Since the movie depicted people who were still living, it was necessary for the studio to obtain their permission before including them in the film. All seven survivors eventually gave their permission in return for payment, but it was felt that Corporal Cutting[5] used the occasion to launch a personal effort to discredit Alvin York.[6] Furthermore, Cutting maintained it was he who captured the prisoners, and he and the rest of the members of the patrol should be recognized for their heroism. The survivors went even further by publishing a letter in the *Boston Globe* on 14 July 1941 disputing the movie version of events and impugning York's courage under fire. Their efforts were largely ignored but it does initially muddy the water for students of the battle. York opened his Bible school with the movie proceeds but it closed within a year when the Second World War absorbed all the potential students. York remained active in Fentress County after the war but his final years were marred by a battle with the Internal Revenue Service over his accounting of the movie profits and declining health. A major stroke in 1954 left him bedridden and he died on 2 September 1964. More than 8,000 people attended his funeral at the small, white frame church in Pall Mall where he had once taught Sunday school. The State of Tennessee acquired the York house, farm and adjacent grist mill as a park after the death of Gracie. It serves as a lasting memorial to Alvin York's life and works. The 'old sergeant' was once asked how he should be remembered.

He replied that he had wanted people to remember how he tried to improve basic education in Tennessee because he considered a solid education as the key to success.[7] It is true that most people do not remember him as such, but that he is forever associated with Gary Cooper's laconic screen portrayal of the mountain hero and the myth surrounding his military exploits in the Argonne Forest in 1918.

Chapter 3

The Meuse-Argonne Offensive

The American First Army carried out its first offensive on 12 September 1918 in the St Mihel Salient, south-east of Verdun. The attack was designed to straighten and to 'pinch out'[1] the bulge in the line. In less than forty hours the Americans had achieved their objectives. All the time that this attack was being planned, another larger offensive was being worked on in the Meuse-Argonne sector. This was to be along a front of 24 miles and the most intricate of battle plans were put into place. These involved the French troops remaining in their outposts until the last possible moment before withdrawing to allow the massive movement of 600,000 American troops to move in. The ability of the U.S. Army to undertake such a massive task bears witness to first-class planning and application by skilled staff. What is more, the movement by the Americans, some from their success at St Mihel, was never detected by the Germans. On the eve of battle, nine American divisions were poised to go 'over the top'. Only five had seen service in offensive combat and only four of the nine were supported by divisional artillery, with which they had never served.[2]

The Germans had plenty of time to organise their defences adequately. They had been in occupation since 1914 and over the period they improved them, so they were extremely formidable. The three major belts of defensive lines ran from east to west, each named after a witch from the operas of Richard Wagner.[3] The first major line was the Etzel-Giselher Stellungen, 3 miles behind the initial front lines, with the high point of Montfaucon laying within its boundaries. Four miles to the north was the second and most formidable line of them all, the Kriemhilde Stellung, taking in the high ground around Cunel and Romagne, and the village of Grandpré.

Five miles to the north of that was the weakest line, the Freya Stellung.[4] This system was indicative of a revised German tactic of offensive within defensive. The lines were designed to have elasticity; assaulting troops would overcome

Map 1: The Meuse-Argonne Offensive, 26 September 1918. (American Armies &
Battlefields in Europe) Centre of Military History, Washington

the front lines, the defenders would move back, and at the time when offensive troops thought they were making some good forward movement, they would be confronted by a German line that would snap back upon them like an elastic band, enveloping them from the front and the sides.

The American objectives were simple on paper, it was the 'doing' that would prove more difficult. It was to be an attempt to drive the Germans northwards towards the River Aisne and to sever the German arterial railway supply on the Lille–Metz line in the region of Mézières-Sedan.[5] The offensive began on 26 September 1918. There was an artillery barrage by 105mm and 155mm heavy guns, a large naval armament, and the superb quick-firing French-made 75mm gun, which was so effective and so highly thought of that the French had christened it, 'God the Father, God the Son, and God the Holy Ghost'.[6] The American First Army, alongside the French Fourth Army, commenced their attack at dawn. They pushed slowly forward, taking their first objectives, but the Germans resisted strongly and on 29 September the Americans took to the defensive to reorganise. The Argonne Forest is spread like the haunches of a huge beast. It is a vast area of wood with many tree-lined slopes and it proved to be extremely difficult terrain for the Americans to make any forward movement. It had never been intended for them to fight in the forested areas in the first place, the preference being to skirt them but, inexorably, the Americans had to resort to forest fighting as the Germans had strong defences within them.

After consolidating, a second assault commenced on 4 October, and on 7 October the American 82nd Division reached the small village of Châtel-Chéhéry. This village, nestled amongst picturesque rolling hills, had been occupied by the Germans for four years. The seizure of the village by the Americans on 7 October was to be followed by the occupation of the forest beyond, and the capture of the German Decauville railway, all to be the objectives of the 82nd Division in the early morning attack on 8 October 1918.

The story that will unfold in this book takes place outside this sleepy little village. The forest now bears little witness as to what took place on 8 October 1918, although the amount of forestation is roughly much the same. There was just a little over one month until the war would finish, and at the end of this offensive, which lasted only eight weeks, there were more than 122,000 casualties, about 77 per cent of them fatal.

Chapter 4

The Americans at Châtel-Chéhéry

The Meuse-Argonne Offensive commenced on 26 September 1918. The 82nd Division, less one infantry brigade, attacked on 7 October, and, working with the 28th Division on the left, assaulted the east flank of the Argonne Forest at Châtel-Chéhéry. By the end of 7 October the 82nd had advanced 1km. The following day the attack continued and on 9 October the remaining infantry brigade of the 82nd Division passed through the 28th Division and executed a turning movement to the north, while the brigade on the right attacked north.[1]

This was the Second Phase of the Meuse-Argonne Offensive (4–30 October) and it was to prove the hardest because the terrain was almost unsurmountable.[2]

The 82nd Division under the command of Major-General George. B. Duncan had entered the Meuse-Argonne Offensive on 6 October 1918, planning for the attack on the following day, having previously being held in reserve. Their infantry order of battle was thus: 164th Infantry Brigade comprised of the 325th, 326th, 327th and 328th Infantry Regiments.

By 6 October the advance of the 1st Corps was halted in a line from Fléville, Apremont, Le Chêne Tondu and Binarville. The Germans held strong positions in the Argonne Forest and on the high ground at Châtel-Chéhéry and Cornay.

The 82nd Division Summary of Operations as prepared by the American Battle Monuments Commission in 1944 states that from the above positions the enemy were delivering destructive flanking fire on both the 1st and 28th Division. Therefore, and to reduce the situations around Châtel-Chéhéry and Cornay, the First Army ordered the 1st Corps under the command of Major-General Hunter Liggett to attack in a westward direction on 7 October. The 1st Corps issued field orders at 6 pm on 7 October. The following morning at 5 am, along the front held by the 28th Division, the attack was launched. Fléville and Cornay, Hill 223 and Hill 244 were, among others, to be the first objective.

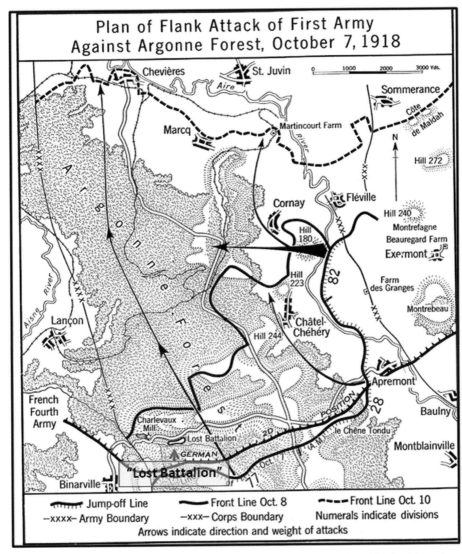

Map 2: *The Argonne Forest. Plan of flank attack 7 October 1918. (American Armies and Battlefields in Europe) Centre of Military History, Washington*

The 82nd Division infantry was instructed to relieve the 28th Division on the Fléville front, and the 164th Infantry Brigade attack instruction was that the 327th on the *right* was to take Cote 180, Cornay and the high ground to the east of the village. The 328th on the *left* was to capture Hill 223.

The Americans used French 1918 Fôret d'Argonne, 1:20,000 map sheets. Contour lines gave the names to hills. If there wasn't a contour they gave it

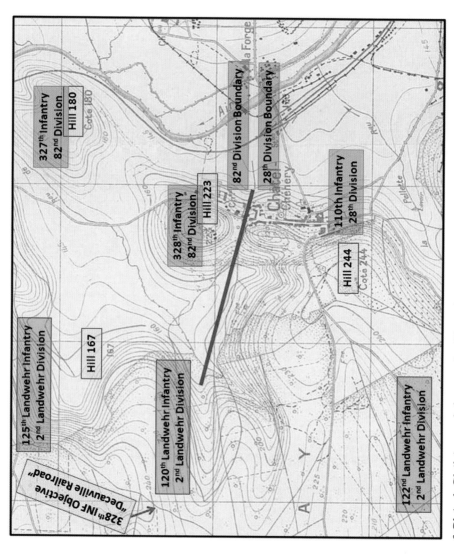

Map 3: Overview of Châtel-Chéhéry and the attack. (Posey)

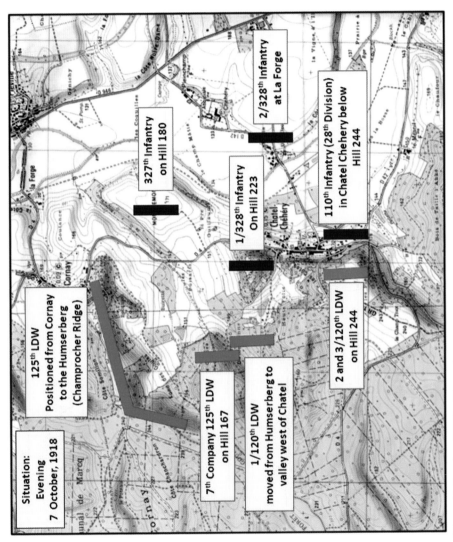

Map 4: Unit dispositions, 7 October 1918. (Posey)

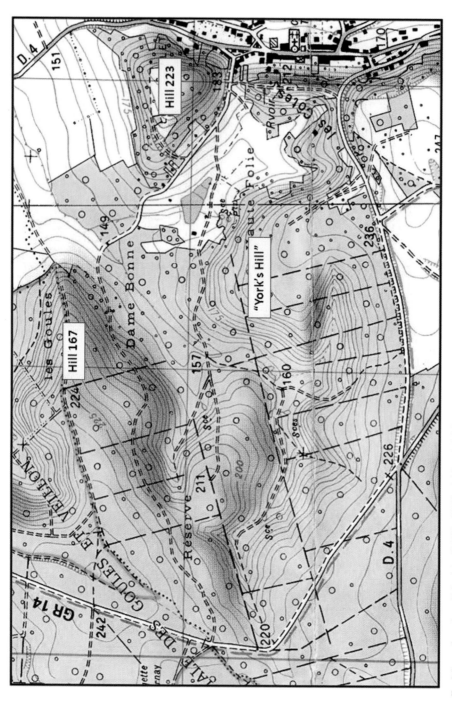

Map 5: Map showing 'York's Hill', Hills 167 & 223. (Posey)

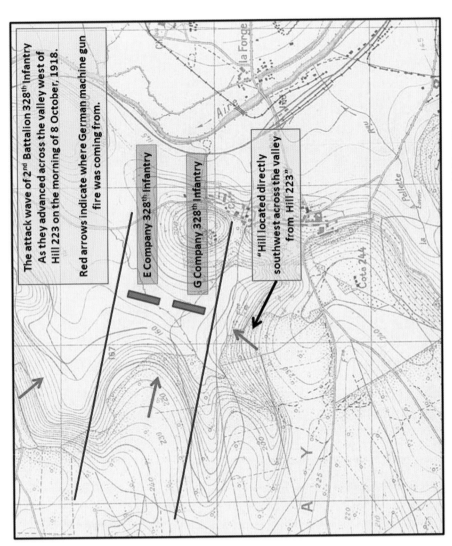

The attack wave of 2nd Battalion 328th Infantry As they advanced across the valley west of Hill 223 on the morning of 8 October, 1918.

Red arrows indicate where German machine gun fire was coming from.

E Company 328th Infantry

G Company 328th Infantry

"Hill located directly southwest across the valley from Hill 223"

Map 6: The 2nd Battalion, 328th Infantry, attack. Early morning 8 October 1918. (Posey)

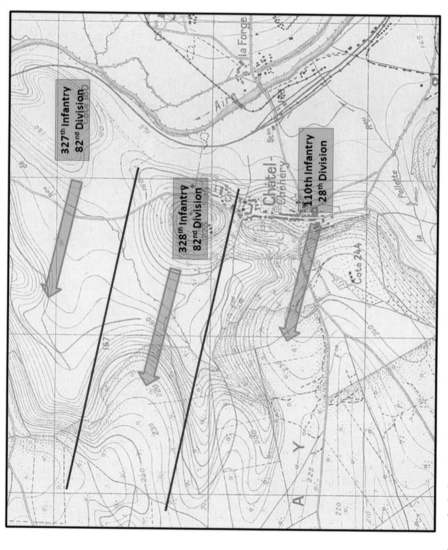

Map 7: Line of attack, before the change of direction. (Posey)

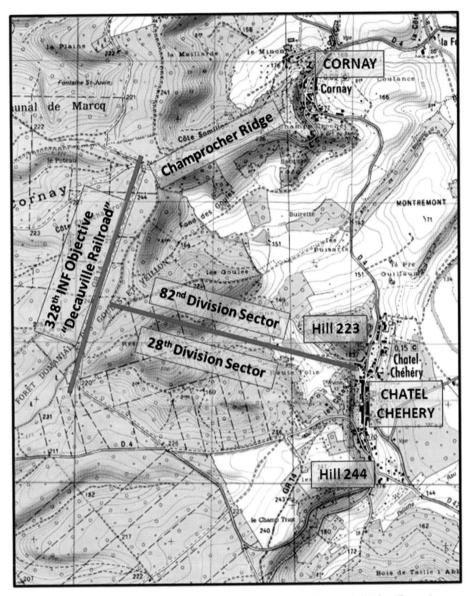

Map 8: Divisional sectors at the time of the attack, 8 October 1918. (Posey)

the nearest French name for that terrain feature. The battlefields to the west of Châtel-Chéhéry have three hills, Hill 223, Hill 167 and Hill 244 (See Map 4). There was one more piece of high ground that bore no contour features and it became known as 'York's Hill' (See Map 5).

Corporal Alvin C. York was an N.C.O. in G Company of the 328th Infantry of the 2nd Battalion, 82nd Division. In Major General George B. Duncan's 1919, *Official History of the 82nd Division*, Duncan wrote:

> In the 328th Infantry, the 2nd Battalion had moved west across the Aire River with orders to pass the lines of the 1st Battalion on Hill 223 and jump off at 6 hours, October 8, 1918, with a compass direction ten degrees north of west. Their objective was the Decauville railroad, two kilometers away. The 328th Infantry Machine Gun Company and the one-pounder and trench mortar platoons, also of the 328th Infantry, were moved to Hill 223 and Châtel-Chéhéry for the purpose of supporting the attack.[3]

It is important to note the compass direction 'ten degrees north of west'. The attack initially was to be oriented along a compass direction of 10 degrees north of west and this order was given but was changed to northwards before the attack commenced. All assault formations, except for the 2nd Battalion, 328th Infantry, received this message. The 328th attack continued along the original bearing. The runner bearing the message had been killed and it was not until later in the morning before the note in his pocket was found and delivered to Major Tillman, the 2nd Battalion commander who was in the process of clearing Hill 167.[4] This resulted in a 1km gap between the 327th and 328th, thus exposing the right flank of the 328th. This was due to the failure of the 28th Division to advance beyond Hill 244 by the time the attack had commenced.[5]

The history of the *Three Hundred and Twenty Eighth Regiment of Infantry* states:

> At 1:15 on the morning of the 8th the Battalion and Company Commanders of the 2nd Battalion were ordered to the Regimental P.C. and were given detailed instructions to execute a passage of the lines and continue the advance to the Corps objective. The Battalion moved out at 2:00 and advanced across the river and intervening valley to Hill 223 and the ground immediately north of that point. During this preparatory advance, the enemy artillery registered a direct hit on

the only bridge across the river and it was necessary to ford the badly swollen stream. Despite this hardship and numerous casualties due to heavy shelling, the troops executed the passage of the lines in good order and were in position ready to advance at the zero hour, which was 6:00 o'clock. From right to left in the front line were 'E' Company under Capt. [then First Lieutenant] Hopper and 'G' Company under Major [then Captain] Danforth.[6]

Sam K. Cowan in his 1922 book *Sergeant York* says that at the front of Hill 223, on the way to Germany [toward the German lines] were three more hills. 'The one in the centre was rugged, those to the right and left more sloping, the one to the left – which the people of France have named "York's Hill" turns a shoulder toward Hill No. 223. The valley which they form is only two to three hundred yards wide.' The hills that Cowan describes are Hill 167 in the centre, the Champrocher or Cornay Ridge to the right and the hill that the 82nd Divisional history says was located directly south-west of Hill 223. It was behind this hill in the ravine where the York fight took place.

In Tom Skeyhill's manuscript of *Sergeant York, His Own Life Story and War Diary* this is York's company commander, Captain Danforth's account of what transpired:

> At 6 a.m. on the morning of October 8, 1918, the 2d Battalion, 328th Infantry, attacked from Hill 223 in the direction ten degrees north of west, with is objective, the Decauville Railroad, about three kilometers away … I was in command of Company G of this battalion … I deployed my company for assault in two waves, two platoons in the front wave and two platoons in the supporting wave. The left support platoon was commanded by Sergeant Harry M. Parsons, one of his corporals being Alvin C. York.[7]

As they advanced down the hill to cross the valley, there was a steep wooded hill to their immediate front. E Company of the 328th Infantry was on their right, and on the left, Unit 5 of the 28th Division. Captain Danforth and his company reached the centre of the valley but were halted by withering machine gun fire from the unscalable heights of the Champrocher Ridge[8] on their right and from a heavily wooded hill on the left.[9]

During this period of the attack, Lieutenant Kirkby P. Stewart was killed leading one of the assault platoons. Losses along the line were heavy and the withering machine gun fire prohibited any forward movement. Seventeen men of G Company under the leadership of Acting Sergeant Bernard Early were designated to make their way around the left rear to silence enemy guns on the left flank.[10]

The patrol consisted of the following men:

Sergeant Bernard Early (wounded)
Corporal Savage's Squad:
Corporal Murray Savage (killed)
Private Maryan Dymowski (killed)
Private Ralph Weiler (killed)

Corporal Cutting's Squad:
Corporal William Cutting (wounded)
Private Fred Wareing (killed)
Private Feodor Sok
Private Michael Saccina
Private Patrick Donohue
Private George Wills
Private William Wine (killed)

Corporal York's Squad:
Private Carl Swanson (killed)
Private Mario Muzzi (wounded)
Private Percy Beardsley
Private Joe Konotski
Private Thomas Johnson

Understanding American and German Historical Maps:

It is important to fully understand the contemporary names used by both the American and German armies to identify terrain features and places on the battlefields. This has in the past, confused other researchers, causing them to show inaccuracies in their interpretation of key features. To accurately interpret what the American and German historical records tell us, we need first to establish common names for the terrain features each army references in their individual reports, war diaries and field messages. Here you can see both the American map and the German maps.

You can see that the Germans called the Champrocher Ridge, Humserberg Hill. What the Americans named Hill 223 was called The Schlossberg (223m above sea level), and Hill 244, the Hohenbornhoehe (244m above sea level). Grid Square 1429 and contour index 153 will be discussed in detail later. The modern IGN topographical map shown will serve as the standard map to illustrate the information found in the historical documents.

When Doctor Nolan was transposing the early maps from 1918, both American and German, on to modern topographic maps from the French Institut Geographique National (IGN), Varennes-en-Argonne topographic map

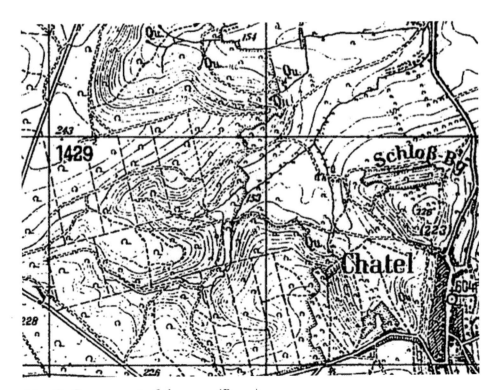

Map 9: German map of the area. (Posey)

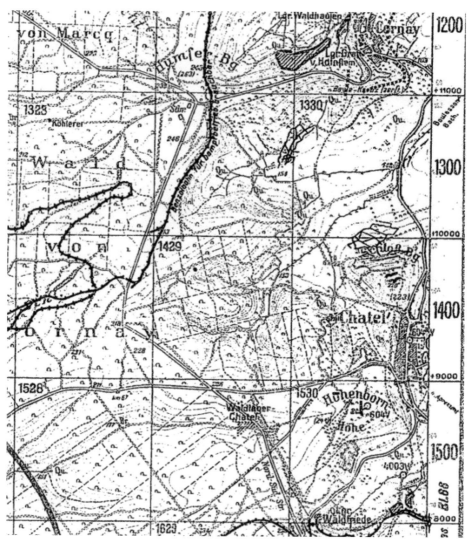

Map 10: German map with more detail. (Posey)

sheet, he discovered that there were discrepancies in contour interval and the exact contour profile of terrain features, depicted on both the contemporary topographic maps in relation to the modern map. The discrepancies, however, are not significant when it comes to identifying or plotting on the modern landscape the location where events happened or the location of terrain features. For instance, Hill 223 is depicted in the same location on both contemporary maps and the modern IGN map. All the hills and terrain features are consistent

Comparison of Contour Lines From
Scanned Georeferenced Image of French 1:20000 Map
With Contour Lines Digitized From IGN 1:250000 Map

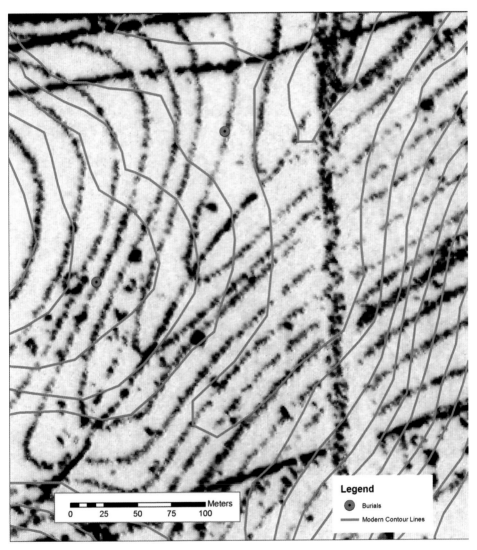

Map 11: German map with contour line comparison. (Nolan)

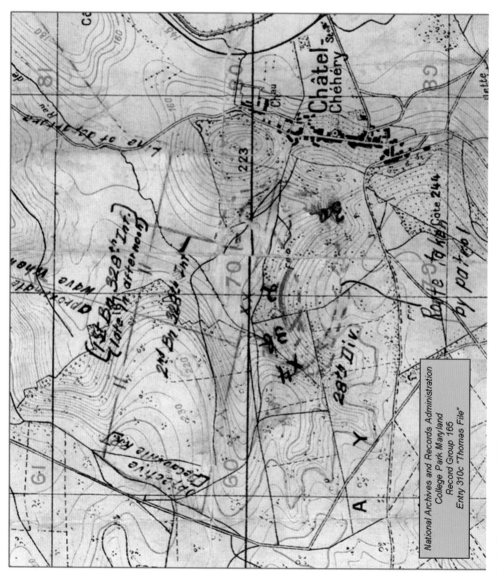

Map 12: Danforth/Buxton map, 1929.

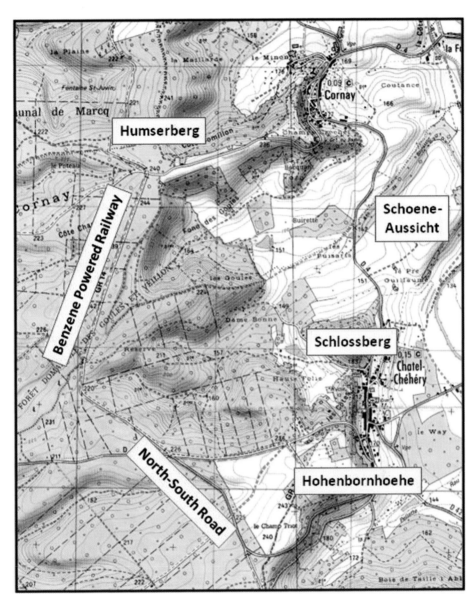

Map 13: Modern map with German names. (Posey)

with each other on all the maps. There are no grounds for contention of where these terrain features are located, based on the discrepancies between the contemporary maps and the modern map. The same applies to the contemporary and modern cardinal orientation of significant terrain features as they are referred to in the historical accounts and compass directions reported by the participants.

Prominent Landmarks
German Names in RED American Names in BLUE

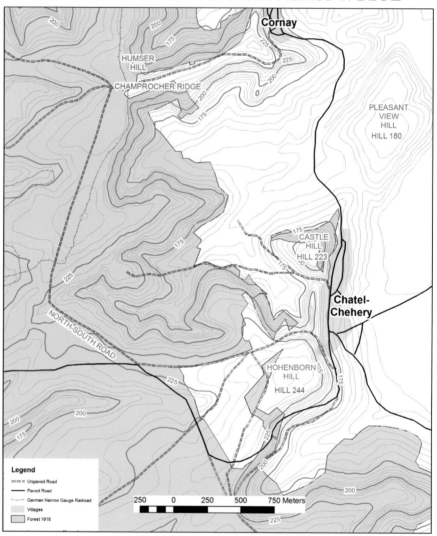

Map 14: Landmarks – German & U.S. names. (Posey & Nolan)

In other words, 'the hill located directly south-west of Hill 223' is still the same hill on today's topographic map and an azimuth of '10 degrees north of west', or a compass reading of 270 degrees. It is the same today as it was in 1918 as seen through an Army issue contemporary or modern lensatic compass. Nor have the hills, streams and valleys moved from where they were in 1918.

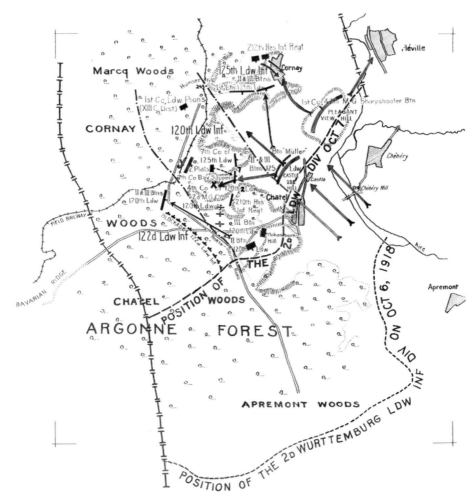

Map 15: German rebuttal Map, 1929.

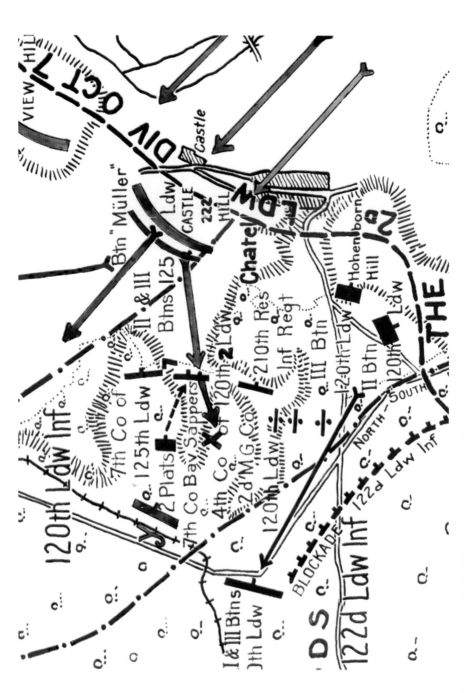

Map 16: Closer view of the German rebuttal map, 1929.

Chapter 5

A Man for All Seasons

We take up the story as it unfolds with Alvin C. York using the working manuscript of Tom Skeyhill's *Sergeant York, His Own Life Story and War Diary.* In this document, York reproduces the official version of the fight as he gave it at divisional headquarters shortly afterwards. York admitted to Skeyhill that, against all regulations, he kept a diary whilst in France. The diary has not been seen for many years, and the only record of this and of the statements and affidavits made by the York patrol are in the pages of Skeyhill's book. York, through Skeyhill, states that the diary was sent to the War Department in Washington.[1] What follows are both York's record written in Skeyhill's manuscript in 1928 and the official statement made by York shortly after the fight.

Manuscript:

> … we got around on the left and in single file advanced forward through the brush towards where we could hear the machine gun fire. We done went very quietly and quickly. We had to. We kept well to the left and deep in the brush … Without any loss and in right smart time we done skirted the left side of the valley and were over on the hill somewhere near where the German machine guns were placed. The heavy brush and the hilly nature of the country hid us from the enemy.[2]

In his official statement, York records:

> … we turned our course slightly to the left, thereby working around on the right flank of the machine guns and somewhat to their rear which caused us to miss these forward guns [pointing at the map]. As we gained a point about here [pointing at the map and designating a point somewhat in the rear of the machine guns].[3]

By this time, the patrol was nearly 300 yards to the left and in front of the American front line. They were on the ridge held by the Germans. After some deliberation; some wanted to attack from the flank, Early and York felt it the best option to carry on until well behind the German front line:

Manuscript:

> Then suddenly swing in and try to jump them from the rear ... we opened up in skirmishing order and sorter flitted from brush to brush using all the cover we could and pushing on as fast as possible. We had now sorter encircled the German left end and were going away in deep behind them without them knowing anything about it.[4]

The official statement reads:

> As we advanced we saw two Boche with Red Cross bands on their arms. We called them to halt, but they did not stop and we opened fire on them. Sergeant Early was leading and I was third ... We immediately dashed down a path, along which the Boche were running, and crossed this stream [pointing at map]. The Boche then turned to the right and ran in the direction from which we had come. When we reached the point where they turned, we stopped for half a second to form a skirmish line. I jumped about four paces away from a sergeant and we told the other men to scatter out because we thought there was going to be a battle and we did not want to be too close together. As soon as we formed our skirmish line we burst through the bushes after the Boche.[5]

Corporal Savage's squad was in the lead, then York's and then Cutting's. Sergeant Early was in the front leading. As they came out of the brush there was a little stream of water.[6] Across the stream on the other bank were several Germans who immediately threw up their hands. York thought it might have been a headquarters. He saw orderlies, stretcher bearers and two officers sitting or standing around a sort of small wooden shack. He saw the Germans had just had breakfast with preserves, jams and loaf bread all around. They were not armed except for the major, [Lieutenant Vollmer] it was a total surprise, for both

American and German soldiers.[7] The Americans told them to put their hands up, and to show they meant business, a few shots were fired. The Germans threw up their hands in surrender. Sergeant Early passed the order to hang fire but keep them covered while the Germans were searched. As he gave this order some machine guns upon on the hill in front and between them and the American lines opened fire. Sergeant Early was struck by five bullets through his lower body and one in the arm. Corporal Savage was killed, York reckoned he must have had a hundred bullets in his body, and most of his clothes had been shot off.[8] Corporal Cutting was wounded and six of the patrol were killed or wounded. The German prisoners immediately fell to the ground, as did the survivors of the American patrol. York survived the withering machine gun fire because he like other patrol members were next to the prisoners and the German guns did not wish to fire on their own men. In his official statement, York states:

> This little stream of which I spoke runs through a gulch into the valley. On either side of the stream there was a little stretch of flat level ground, about twenty feet wide, which was covered with extremely thick bush. On the east bank of the stream was a hill having an exceedingly steep slope. This hill was somewhat semi–circular in shape and afforded excellent protection to anyone behind it. Along the top of the hill were the machine guns firing across the valley at our troops.[9]

York continues in the 1928 record:

> I was caught out in the open, a little bit to the left and in front of the group of prisoners, and about twenty-five yards away from the machine guns which were in gun pits and trenches upon the hillside above him.[10]

York was now in charge of the patrol, although he was unable to give any orders as the noise of battle prevented him from doing so. Right in the firing line of the German prisoners, York adopted a position lying down, giving the Germans even less of a target. His great marksmanship abilities ensured that each time a German head showed York shot him. The shooting continued and, because of their elevated position, the Germans had to show their heads to see where York was below them. At 25 yards, York would not miss his target. When he was able, he stood up and continued to shoot from his favourite position, off-hand.[11] He was using his rifle and several clips were expended. His barrel was getting hot and rifle ammunition running low, or it was in his pack where he couldn't get to it. In the middle of the fight, a German officer [Lieutenant Endriss] and five men jumped out of a trench and charged York with their bayonets fixed. They were just twenty-five yards away. York had half a clip left in his rifle but he could get to his pistol and then calmly and collectedly he shot the German soldiers. [The rifle stripper clip would have contained five .30-.06 cartridges, the .45 calibre M1911 pistol seven cartridges per clip.] York shot the sixth man first, then the fifth, the fourth, the third and so on. This way the Germans were not aware they were losing their numbers and did not take to ground to shoot at York. This probably saved York's life. The officer was shot and mortally wounded in the stomach. Returning to using his rifle, York continued to shoot the Germans while shouting at them to surrender. By this time he had killed more than twenty Germans.[12]

In his official report, York said:

> In this first fire, we had six killed and three wounded. By this time, those of my men who were left had gotten behind trees, and two men sniped at the Boche. They fired about half a clip each. But there wasn't any tree for me, so I just sat in the mud and used my rifle shooting at the Boche machine gunner … The lieutenant with eight or ten Germans armed with rifles rushed toward us. One threw a little grenade, about the size of a dollar and with a string that you pull like this when you want to explode it, at me, but missed me by a few feet, wounding, however, one of his own men.[13]

During the fight, York heard a pistol firing from the midst of the German prisoners; it transpired it was the German commander shooting as he was the only one armed with a pistol. York checked his weapon later and all the clips were empty. When the machine guns stopped firing, the German

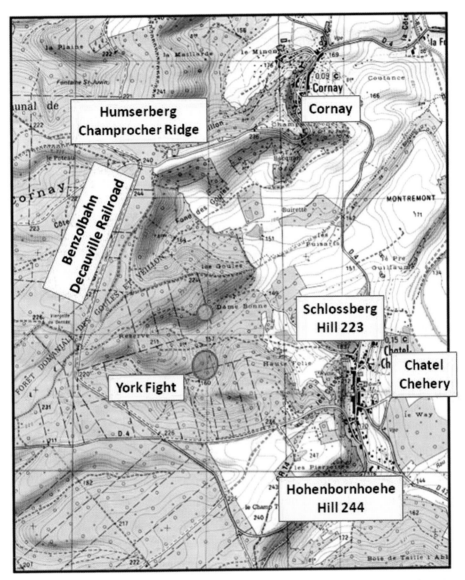

Map 17: Map showing Nolan Group (blue) & SYDE (yellow) fight locations.
(Posey)

commander walked to York and told him that if he stopped shooting he would tell his men to surrender. York agreed and on the German officer's command the Germans threw down their arms and equipment and came down the hill.

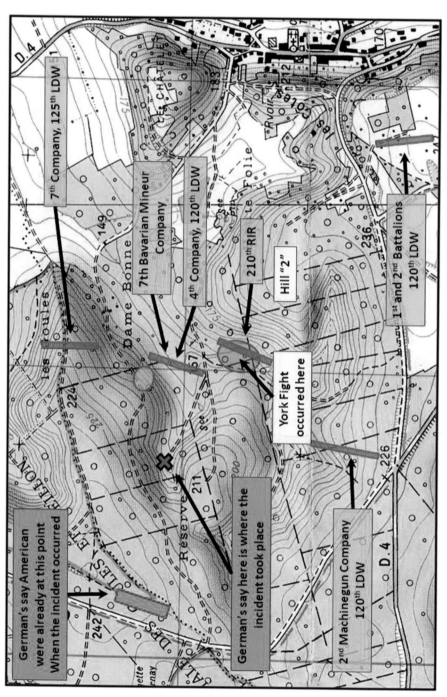

Map 18: Map showing German positions and scene of York's Fight. (Posey)

The remnants of the American patrol came together and they searched the German prisoners.

> … We had about 80 or 90 Germans there disarmed and had another line of Germans to go through to get out. So, I called for my men and one of them answered from behind a big oak tree and the others were on my right in the brush so I said lets [sic] get these Germans out of here.[14]

The German major (Lieutenant Vollmer) had worked in Chicago before the war and could speak English and asked York how many men he had. York told him that he had plenty and told the major to line his men up in columns of two keeping his hands up. Corporal Cutting showed York his wound. He had been shot in the arm and all the buttons had been shot off his uniform and there was a great big 'X' shot in his helmet. The prisoners were ordered to pick up the American wounded, amongst them the badly wounded Sergeant Early. The German major wanted to take the column down the gully, but York knew that was the wrong way.

> The Boche commanding officer wanted to line up facing north and go down through the valley along the road which runs by the foot of the hill, but I knew that if they got me there it would be as good as they wanted on account of the machine guns on the opposite slope, so I said, 'No, I am going this way,' which was the way I had come and which led through the group of machine guns placed here [pointing at the map], which seemed to be outpost guns. We had missed this machine gun nest as we advanced, because we had gone further to the left.[15]

York scattered his men along the column and at the rear, telling them to stay well back whilst he led the group from the front. He took the commanding officer and the two other officers and put one in front of him and one on each side. York pointed out on the map a further machine gun nest that they encountered on the way back. The German major told these elements to surrender and as they did so they joined the ranks of prisoners. When he reached the Battalion

P.C. the prisoners were counted by Lieutenant Woods and Lieutenant Garner. There were 132 of them.[16] York, in an additional statement to the 82nd Division, said that he had 'roughly counted them and thought there were about 146'.[17] Another group of prisoners were added to this number and York received orders to march them back to Brigade Headquarters at Varennes, by which time York had 208 prisoners, others being added to the column en route. The Brigade commander, Brigadier-General Lindsay, said to York, 'Well, York, I hear you have captured the whole damned German army.'[18]

During the night of 7/8 October, the 'Lost Battalion', under the command of Major Charles Whittlesey, was relieved on the left flank of the 77th Division after five days of hard fighting at the Charlevaux Mill. Whittlesea had led a force of nearly 700 men into the Charlevaux Ravine on 2 October, where they were cut off in a narrow pocket on the steep slopes and for five days resisted all attacks and snubbed any requests for surrender. When they were eventually relieved, just 194 survivors returned to their lines. Their relief has been attributed in part to the attack by the 328th Infantry on 8 October at Châtel-Chéhéry.

York stated that he got permission the following day from Captain Danforth to return to the scene of the fight as he felt there may still be wounded lying out in the open. So, with stretcher bearers, he went back to the place. He noticed that the Salvage Corps had been busy; they had already been and cleaned up the place.[19] He states he found the dead had been buried, both American and German. The ground around was much disturbed, and there was an old canteen lying within a few inches of where York stood. He counted eighteen bullet holes in it. A shrapnel helmet lay close by that had bullet holes in it, just like a 'pepper box'. York thought these items had been damaged by German machine gun fire during his fight. (There are clues that these items may have been the subject of American target practice by York in his 1919 visit to the site. This will be discussed later.) He surmises that the German machine gunners fought like a heap of wild cats, inferring that the other Germans did not.[20] The latter were from the 1st Battalion 120th Wuerttemberg Landwehr Regiment. On the slope where the machine gun fire was coming from was the 7th Bavarian Mineur Company, who were much more willing to fight. They were commanded by Lieutenant Thoma.

Reports and affidavits were made not only by members of the patrol, but by others who were not present at the fight. Some give invaluable information as to the route to, and the site of, the encounter. Captain Danforth, York's company commander, wrote an account that is produced in Skeyhill's book:

At 6 A.M. on the morning of October 8, 1918, the 2d Battalion, 328th Infantry, attacked from Hill 223, in the direction of ten degrees north of west, with its objective, the Decauville Railroad, about three kilometers away. The battalion had moved into the Argonne sector with other units of the 82d Division on the night of October 6th and 7th. All day of October 7th we lay along the main Army road, running from Varennes to Fléville, and watched the attack of the 1st Battalion, which in the early afternoon gained the height of Hill 223. About 3 A.M. October 8th, the regimental commander sent for the company commanders of the 2d Battalion and issued instructions for the attack of the battalion to be made from Hill 223 at 6 A.M. I was in command of Company G of this battalion and immediately upon receiving these instructions began moving my company across the Aire River to the designated jump-off line on Hill 223.

I reached this hill at 5:50 A.M. and deployed my company for assault in two waves, two platoons in the front wave and two platoons in the supporting wave. The left support platoon was commanded by Sergeant Harry M. Parsons, one of his corporals being Alvin C. York. At zero hour we began the advance, moving down the slope of Hill 223 and across the five-hundred-yard open valley toward a steep wooded hill to our immediate front. On our right was E Company, 328th Infantry; on our left Unit 5 of the 28th Division, though throughout the entire day we had no contact with these troops on our left.[21]

Danforth continued that they were stopped by concentrated machine gun fire when in the centre of the valley from the unscalable heights of the Champrocher Ridge on their right. Danforth was with the assault waves and he states that he gave no orders for the support platoons, who were following at 300 yards distant, to be employed. Captain Danforth continued with the main assault. The Decauville Railroad was taken by companies from the 2nd Battalion. They consolidated their position and held it through the night of 8/9 October.

Danforth was not to hear of York's feat until 9 October, stating:

> On the morning of October 9th at about ten o'clock Corporal York with seven men reported to me on the railroad. Corporal York, when questioned about his whereabouts and activities during the previous day's fighting, said that he had been sent with a detachment to silence some machine gun nests on the left of the valley, that this detachment had become heavily engaged, losing half its strength, and that he had captured about one hundred and fifty prisoners. He stated that all non-commissioned officers of the detachment had been killed or wounded, that he had taken command and had shot a number of Germans during the engagement and that he had carried his prisoners from headquarters to headquarters, finally delivering them to the military police many miles to the rear. His statement to me on the morning of October 9th was the first time I knew anything of his fight on our left flank and offered the best explanation of why the fire from that point had slackened on the morning of the 8th, after coming out of the lines I fully investigated this detachment's fight and recommended Corporal York for the Distinguished Service Cross and later, after a more careful study, for the Medal of Honor.[22]

Danforth's comment is noteworthy. He was in the main assault force of the 2nd Battalion going over the ground where the SYDE maintains the York fight took place. Clearly, he remarks about York's fight on the 2nd Battalion's left flank, putting the York patrol in the place where the Nolan Group say the fight took place, to the left side of the main infantry assault. It should also be noted there is no mention by Danforth of York asking him if he could return to the scene of the fight on the day following the fight as York has stated in his diary.

Chapter 6

The Official History of the 82nd Division

T he author of the history of the 82nd Division, Major-General George Edward Buxton, was commander of that division from May to 10 October 1918. The history gives the most definitive account of what happened on that morning of 8 October 1918. It also highlights clearly where the York action took place; this will be defined in detail later in this book. A great deal of effort was taken to ensure that the history was correct:

> Immediately after the Armistice, General Buxton directed every Company, Battalion and Regimental Commander to prepare a written statement of the history of his unit, following the completion of this work, four large parties of officers were taken to the Meuse-Argonne battlefields.[1]

Colonel Richard Wetherill was designated to examine the movements and actions of the 328th Infantry. Buxton states that overnight on 7/8 October 1918 the Headquarters of the 1st Corps changed the compass direction of the assault units, ordering the attack to be directed to the north rather than in a north-westerly direction. The change only reached the front battalion at 6.30 am and it was, with some difficulty, able to correct the course. However, the change of course did not reach the 328th Infantry until 10.30 am. A dead runner[2] was discovered carrying the change of course message in his pocket. By this time, the assaulting battalion of the 328th Infantry had been fighting its way 10 degrees north of west for four and a half hours, with both flanks wholly unprotected.[3] Buxton refers to the opening stages of the attack, where he says the 2nd Battalion of the 328th Infantry came under steady and intense machine gun fire from the north-west and south-west[4] (See Maps 6 and 7).

This battalion maneuvered down the long western slope of Hill 223, crossed the five hundred yards of open valley, fought its way through a kilometer of heavy woods which covered the precipitous spur protruding into the center of the valley from the west, and dug in along the Corps objective, the Decauville Railroad, at 17 hours that afternoon. It had not liaison with the troops attacking to the north of Hill 180, over a kilometer away. For most of the day, it was without contact with units of the 28th Division, also attacking in a westerly direction from Chatel-Chehery. By nightfall this battalion had taken some 270 prisoners and left more than one hundred dead Germans on the ground. It had captured the astonishing total of 123 machine guns, a battery of four field pieces, two trench mortars, a set of electrical field signal equipment complete, four anti-tank guns and a quantity of German small arms and ammunition of several varieties.[5]

An entry in the Official History clearly gives the route of the attack:

A force of four non-commissioned officers and thirteen privates was sent from the left support platoon of G Company to encircle the hill and silence the enemy guns. This detachment, under Acting Sergeant Early, encircled the hill from the southeast and by very skilful reconnaissance passed through the heavy woods on the east crest and descended to the wooded ravine on the west side of the hill. The detachment in working through the underbrush came upon a German battalion estimated to contain about 250 men, a considerable number of whom were machine gunners. Orders taken later from the pocket of the German battalion commander proved that the mission of this battalion was to launch a counter-attack against the left flank of our attack at 10 hours 30 minutes. About seventy-five Germans were crowded around their battalion commander, apparently engaged in receiving final instructions. A force of machine gunners and infantrymen, however, were lying in fox holes fifty yards away on the western slope of the hill. Other machine gun detachments were located on the north and northeast slopes of this same wooded hill ...[6]

It is important to note that all the historical accounts, both American and German, as will be discovered, indicate the fight took place on the western slope of a hill. The history goes on to describe the fight and then, in another clue as to the direction of extraction from the site with his prisoners, Duncan records:

> On his [York's] way back over the hill he picked up several additional prisoners from the north and northeast slopes of the hill.[7]

The SYDE site is on an east-facing slope, again reinforcing the fact that their location is in the full face of the main 2nd Battalion infantry assault, a most unlikely area to be infiltrated by a patrol. The Germans captured by the York patrol were going to attack the American 2nd battalion at 10.30 hours on their left flank, according to the orders seized from the German battalion commander.

Chapter 7

The York Diary, Sergeant York and his Own Life Story

When one compares the account of the fight that follows with the rest of the Skeyhill book, the expression is different to the mountain dialect that is predominant throughout the rest of the text. As Nolan Group member Brad Posey has noted, it was not unusual for summaries to be written by someone else and often the adjutant or another officer would record the affidavits.[1] Many of the men in the Army were immigrants who could hardly speak English, let alone write it. Many were illiterate and their signatures are often just recorded with an 'X'.

York's official 1919 statement contains important observations that he made. Hitherto, his comments within Skeyhill's book as York's war diary are those made a long time after the war in 1928. However, those observations York made in the 1919 statement are taken whilst still fresh in his mind and, importantly, before he was elevated to hero status. Some parts have been reproduced earlier in the book, and although it is a long passage it is so important that it should be replicated in full. This is the preamble to his statement as it appears in the working manuscript:

> … On the 8th of October 1918, York was a corporal in G Company, 328th Infantry. This company was the left assault company of the 2d Battalion which jumped off from the crest of Hill 223 just north of Chatel Chehery and attacked due west, with its objective, the Decauville Railroad, two kilometers due west. The success of this assault had a far-reaching effect in relieving the enemy pressure against American forces in the heart of the Argonne Forest. The local success achieved by this battalion was, in itself, of outstanding proportions. About 300 prisoners were taken and nearly 200 dead Germans left on the ground and material captured which included four 77's, a trench mortar

battery, a complete signal outfit and 123 machine guns. The attack was driven through in spite of resistance of a very savage character and most destructive enemy machine gun and artillery fire. The battalion suffered enfilade fire from both flanks.

The part which Corporal York individually played in this attack is difficult to fully estimate. Practically unassisted, he captured 132 Germans [three of whom were officers], took about 35 machine guns and killed no less than 25 of the enemy, later found by others on the scene of York's extraordinary exploit. York is well known in his section of Tennessee for his remarkable skill with both rifle and pistol. The following story has been carefully checked in every possible detail from headquarters of this division and is entirely substantiated.

Although Sergeant York's statement tends to under estimate the desperate odds which he overcame, it has been decided to forward to higher authority the account given in his own words:

York's statement:

'Sergeant Harry M. Parsons was in command of a platoon of which my squad was a part. This platoon was the left support platoon of G Company, my squad forming the extreme left flank of the platoon. The valley was covered by machine gun fire from the right, [pointing at the map], from the front, and from the left front. Machine guns from the left front were causing a great deal of damage to our troops advancing across the valley. Sergeant Parsons was ordered to advance with his platoon and cover our left flank. As the fire was very hot in the valley, we decided to skirt the foot of the hill on our left and thereby gain some protection.

'We had advanced a little ways up to about here [pointing at the map] when we were held up, by machine guns from our left front here [pointing at the map]. Sergeant Parsons told Sergeant Bernard Early to take two squads and put these machine guns out

'We advanced in single file. The undergrowth and bushes here were so thick that we could only see a few yards ahead of us, but as we advanced, they became a little thinner. In order to avoid frontal fire from the machine guns, we turned our course slightly to the left, thereby working around on the right flank of the machine guns and somewhat to their rear, which caused us to miss these forward guns [pointing at the map]. As we gained a point about here, [pointing at the map and designating a point somewhat in the rear of the machine guns], we turned sharply to the right oblique and followed a little path which took us directly in rear of the machine guns. As we advanced we saw two Boche with Red Cross bands on their arms.

'We called to them to halt, but they did not stop and we opened fire on them. Sergeant Early was leading and I was third. As I said before, we were proceeding in single file. We immediately dashed down a path, along which the Boche were running, and crossed this stream [pointing at map]. The Boche then turned to the right and ran in the direction from which we had come. When we reached the point where they turned, we stopped for half a second to form a skirmish line. I jumped about four paces away from a sergeant and we told the other men to scatter out because we thought there was going to be a battle and we did not want to be too close together. As soon as we formed our skirmish line we burst through the bushes after the Boche.

'This little stream of which I spoke runs through a gulch into the valley. On either side of the stream there was a little stretch of flat level ground, about twenty feet wide, which was covered with extremely thick bush. On the east bank of the stream was a hill having an exceedingly steep slope. This hill was somewhat semi-circular in shape and afforded excellent protection to anyone behind it. Along the top of the hill were the machine guns firing across the valley at our troops.

'We burst through the undergrowth and were upon the Germans before we knew it, because the undergrowth was so thick that we could see only a few yards ahead of us. There was a little shack thrown together that seemed to be used as a sort of a P.C. by the Germans. In front of this, in a sort of a semi-circular mass, sat about seventy-five Boche, and by the side of a chow can, which was near the P.C., sat the commanding officer and two other officers. The Boche seemed to be having some sort of conference. When we burst in on the circle, some of the Boche jumped up and threw up their hands, shouting "Kamerad." Then the others jumped up, and we began shooting. About two or three Germans were hit, none of our men fell.

'Sergeant Early said: "Don't shoot anymore, they are going to give up anyhow," and for a moment our fire ceased, except that one German continued to fire at me, and I shot him. In the meantime, the Boche upon the hill with the machine guns swung the left guns to the left oblique and opened fire on us. I was at this time just a few paces from the mass of Boche who were crowded around the P.C. At first burst of fire from the machine guns, all the Boche in this group hit the ground, lying flat on their stomachs. I, and a few other of our men, hit the ground at the same time. Those who did not take cover were either killed or wounded by the Boche machine gun fire, the range being so close that the clothes were literally torn from their bodies. Sergeant Early and Corporal Cutting were wounded, and Corporal Savage killed.

'In this first fire we had six killed and three wounded. By this time, those of my men who were left had gotten behind trees, and two men sniped at the Boche. They fired about half a clip each. But there wasn't any tree for me, so I just sat in the mud and used my rifle, shooting at the Boche machine gunners. I am a pretty good shot with the rifle, also with the pistol, having used them practically all my life, and having had a great deal of practice. I shot my rifle until I did not have any more clips convenient and then I used my pistol.

'The Boche machine gun fire was sweeping over the mass of Germans who were lying flat, and passing a few inches over my head, but I was so close to the mass of Germans who were lying down that the Boche machine gunners could not hit me without hitting their own men. There were about fifty Boche with the machine guns and they were under the command of a Lieutenant. By this time, the remaining Boche guns had been turned around and were firing at us, and the Lieutenant with eight or ten Germans armed with rifles rushed toward us. One threw a little grenade about the size of a dollar and with a string that you pull like this when you want to explode it, at me, but missed by a few feet, wounding, however, one of his own men.

'I just let the Boche come down the hill and then poured it into them with my pistol, and I am, as I said before, a pretty good shot with the pistol. I shot the lieutenant, and when he was killed the machine gun fire ceased. During the fight, I kept hearing a pistol firing from the midst of the Boche who were lying on the ground. This was evidently the commanding officer shooting as he was the only one in the crowd armed with a pistol, and all of his clips were empty when I examined them later. When the machine guns ceased firing the commanding officer who spoke English, got off the ground and walked over to me. He said: "English?" I said: "No, not English." He said: "What?" I said: "American." He said: "Good Lord." Then he said: "If you won't shoot anymore, I will make them give up." And I said: "Well, all right, I will treat you like a man," and he turned around and said something to his men in German, and they all threw off their belts and arms and the machine gunners threw down their arms and came down the hill.

'I called to my men and one of them answered me from over here, another from over here, and another here (they were pretty well scattered), and when they all come to me, I found there were six left besides myself. We searched the Boche and told them to line up in columns of twos. The Boche commanding officer wanted to line up facing north and go down through the valley along the road which runs by the foot of the hill, but I knew if they got me there it would be as good as they wanted on account of the machine guns on the opposite slope, so I said, "No, I am going this way," which was the way I had come, and which led through the group of machine guns placed here [pointing at the map], which seemed to be outpost guns. We had missed this machine gun nest as we advanced, because we had gone further to the left.

'When we got the Boche lined up in a column of twos, I scattered my men along and at the rear of the column and told them to stay well to the rear and that I would lead the way. So I took the commanding officer and the two other officers and put one in front of me and one on each side of me, and we headed the column. I did that because I knew that if I were caught on the side of the column, the machine gunners would shoot me, but that if I kept in the column, they would have to shoot their officers before they could kill me. In this manner we advanced along a path and into the machine gun nest which is situated here. [pointing at the map]

'The machine gunners, as I said before, could not kill me without killing their officers, and I was ready for them. One aimed a rifle at me from behind a tree, and, as I pointed my pistol at him, the commanding officer said: "If you won't shoot anymore, I will tell them to surrender." He did and we added them to our column. I then reported with the prisoners to the Battalion P.C. They were counted there and there were 132 of them. I was there ordered to deliver the prisoners to Brigade Headquarters, which I did, and returned to my company the next morning.'[2]

It is believed that the passage was written or dictated by someone else, and it is also felt that those in the following affidavits have also been composed by another person. This statement by York is likely to be a summary of what he reported to Buxton in an interview conducted only a few months after the fight. The recollections of York in the Skeyhill book are from ten years later in 1928.

Tom Skeyhill became aware of Sergeant Alvin C. York in New York City in the spring of 1919. He witnessed the enthusiastic fervour of the many thousands of people who had turned out to welcome him home from France. Skeyhill describes the ticker tape occasion with:

Mobs everywhere, with banners, bands, bells, whistles, singing, screaming, clanging, whistling, and in every other way acclaiming the big hero of the day.[3]

Skeyhill was an Australian. Born in Terang, Victoria, he had been wounded in Gallipoli fighting with the Australian Army.[4] He was at first sceptical about the exploits of Sergeant York; it sounded a little too far-fetched, an almost unbelievable feat. Doubtless Skeyhill had been drawn to York by Pattullo's article because he repeats nearly word for word the latter's claim for the authenticity of York's action. Much later, in spring 1927, Skeyhill tried to visit York, as he said, to enquire after his welfare; the idea of writing a book was not in his mind at that time. However, he was to be disappointed as York had travelled to Florida. Skeyhill elected to write to York instead and after a series of exchanges, he was invited to Pall Mall, Tennessee. Over time the two became friendly and York told Skeyhill about his war diary. He was so hard-pressed for funds to build his new school he had been willing for it to be published. However, the publishers had told him that the diary was too short and they wanted him to build the story of his life around it.[5] The war diary was kept in a bank vault, the intention being to keep it there until his death. He had once taken it out to show two reporters, but despite his request for them not to publish it, much to York's chagrin they did. Eventually, York backed down and showed the war diary to Skeyhill:

> Well, I kept a little notebook in America jes [sic] to remind me of places I had been. When I got to France I bought one of them little black French notebooks. I carried this little diary in my pocket. Every night I put down what happened. I wrote in it in camp, on the ships and in the fox holes and trenches at the front. I wrote in it every night. Of course I knowed [sic] no soldier in the American army was permitted to keep a diary. It was against the rules and anyone caught carrying it with him was subject to be court-martialled ...[6]

After a further period of contemplation, York finally gave the go ahead for Skeyhill to write the book. York gave him the diary and his autobiography that he had begun to write, plus some private letters.[7] York insisted that the truth be told and gave Skeyhill a letter to the War Department granting permission for Skeyhill to get access to York's personal records. Skeyhill also set off to trace the other members of the patrol, realising the importance of their statements and affidavits. From the eight survivors, Skeyhill was successful in tracing seven of them.[8] In addition, nine other affidavits were taken from eleven other personnel connected with the incident.

Skeyhill makes an important statement in the book when he writes:

> This story is told in York's own way. Great care has been taken to preserve his mountain dialect, though it must be remembered that during the past ten years the Sergeant has read many books and has met people all over the country, all of which has made his speech more literary than that of the average mountaineer ...[9]

If one studies the facsimile copy of the handwritten pages from York's diary, it may be seen that he wrote in the mountain dialect.

Chapter 8

American Statements and Affidavits

Two affidavits were taken from Private Percy Beardsley just three weeks apart. This is his first taken on 26 January 1918.

On the 8th day of October 1918, I was a member of Corporal York's squad in G Company, 328th Infantry. When we were sent under acting-Sergeant Bernard Early to clean out the machine guns on our left, I was following behind Corporal York. I saw two Red Cross Germans and when they started to run, we fired at them. One of them stopped and gave himself up. We followed after the other Germans and about twenty paces from where we had first sighted these two Red Cross Germans, we ran into a bunch of Germans all together in an underbrush on the slope of the hill. When we appeared, Germans came running out of the brush and machine gun trenches in every direction. There seemed to be about one hundred of these Germans. Some of them held up their hands and shouted 'Kamerad' and gave themselves up. A few shots were fired at us and a few men on our side fired back. After this, all the Germans in sight stopped firing and came in around us, having thrown down their arms and equipment.

Before we could line them up in column and move them out, German machine gunners, whom we had not seen before this, commenced firing down the hill at our men. This fire came mostly from opposite our own right flank. We had six men killed and three wounded in a very short time.

I was at first near Corporal York, but soon after thought it would be better to take cover behind a large tree about fifteen paces in rear of Corporal York. Privates Dymowski and Waring were on each side of me and both were killed by machine gun fire. When the machine gun fire on each side of my tree stopped, I came back to where the Germans

were and fired my pistol two or three times. I saw Corporal York fire
his pistol repeatedly in front of me. After I came back from the tree
I saw Germans who had been hit fall down. I saw German prisoners
who were still in a bunch together waving their hands at the machine
gunners on the hill as if motioning for them to go back. Finally the
fire stopped and Corporal York told us to have the prisoners fall in
columns of twos and for me to take my place in the rear.

This statement was read to Private Beardsley after being taken, and he
stated the same was correct. I certify that the above is statement made
by Private Percy (1,910,246) Beardsley, Company G, 328th Infantry,
to which he made oath before me.[1]

G. EDWARD BUXTON, Jr.

Major, Inf., U.S.A.

Division Historical Officer

This is the second official affidavit of Private Percy Beardsley.

2d Bn. 328th Inf.

82d Div. American A.E.F.

Frettes, France, Feb 21, 1919

Affidavit of Private Percy (1,910,246) Beardsley.

Personally appeared before me the undersigned, Private Percy
(1,910,246) Beardsley, first being duly sworn according to law, says
that he was present with Sergeant Alvin. C. York, northwest of Chatel
Chehery on the morning of October 8, 1918, and testified to the
distinguished personal courage, self-sacrifice, and presence of mind
of Sergeant Alvin C. (1,910,426) York as follows:

On the morning of the 8th of October, 1918, Sergeant York was a
corporal in G Company, 328th Infantry and I was a member of his
squad. Our battalion, the 2d Battalion of the 328th Infantry, was
attacking the ridge northwest of Chatel Chehery. The battalion had
to manoeuvre across the valley under heavy machine gun fire which

came from our right and left as well as in front of us. Very heavy fire came from a hill on our left flank. Sergeant Parsons was our platoon leader and he told acting Sergeant Early to take three squads and go over and clean out the machine guns that were shooting at our left flank. He circled the hill first in a southerly and then in a south-westerly direction until the noise of the machine guns sounded as if the guns were between us and our battalion. We went down the west slope of the hill into a ravine filled with heavy underbrush and there found two Germans and fired at one of them when he refused to halt. We were following the one who ran and came onto a battalion of Germans grouped together on the bottom and slope of the hill. Those nearest us were surprised, and, thinking they were surrounded, started to surrender, but a lot of machine gunners halfway up the hill turned their machine guns on us, killing six and wounding three of our detachment.

All three of our other non-commissioned officers were shot and there was left only Corporal York and seven privates. We were up against a whole battalion of Germans and it looked pretty hopeless for us. We were scattered out in the brush, some were guarding a bunch of Germans who had begun to surrender, and three or four of us fired two or three shots at the line of Germans on the hillside.

The German machine gunners kept up a heavy fire, as did the German riflemen on the hillside with the machine gunners. The Germans could not hit us without endangering the prisoners whom we had taken at the very first. A storm of bullets was passing just around and over us. Corporal York was nearest the enemy and close up to the bottom of the hill. He fired rapidly with rifle and pistol until he had shot down a German officer and many of his men. The officer whom Corporal York shot was leading a charge of some riflemen with bayonets fixed down the hillside towards us.

Finally, the German battalion commander surrendered to Corporal York, who called the seven privates remaining up to him and directed us to place ourselves along the middle and rear of the column of prisoners, which we assisted him in forming. When we moved out some Germans on a near-by hill continued to fire at us. Corporal

York was at the head of the column where he placed two German officers in front of him. A considerable number of German prisoners were taken on our way back over the hill. Corporal York made them surrender by having the German battalion commander call to them to give themselves up.[2]

PRIVATE PERCY BEARDSLEY.

Sworn to and subscribed before me
At Frettes, France, this 26th
Day of February 1919.
Edwin A. Buckhalter.
1st Lieut. 328 Inf, Bn. Adjt.[3]

Of all the statements made, Beardsley gives the most detailed account in both his January and February statements. The fact that his February statement is the same as the other February statements taken from other men is perhaps not as important as the differences between his January and February testimonial.

Let us examine the differences more closely. In his January statement, Beardsley says that he took cover behind a tree, fifteen paces to the rear of York. Both Dymowski and Waring were killed on either side of him. After the machine gun fire stopped, he returned to where the captured Germans were and fired his pistol two or three times. He saw York in front of him firing his pistol repeatedly. He saw Germans fall and the German prisoners waving their hands to try and stop the machine gunners firing. The firing stopped and York had the prisoners line up in columns of twos and took his place in the rear of the column.

However, in the February affidavit Beardsley says that when the Germans on the hill started to fire, the patrol was scattered about the brush, he said that three or four of them fired two or three shots at the Germans on the hillside. He said York was closest to the enemy and 'close up to the bottom of the hill'. York fired rapidly with rifle and pistol until he had shot down a German officer and many of his men and that the officer was leading some riflemen with fixed bayonets down the hillside towards the Americans. Then Beardsley says the German battalion commander surrendered to York. As they marched the prisoners off, other Germans on a nearby hill continued to fire at them and they picked up a considerable number of prisoners on their way back to the American lines.

Now let us examine the statements made by Private George W. Wills. His first statement was made on 26 January 1919:

On the 8th day of October 1918, I was a member of Corporal Cutting's squad in G Company, 328th Infantry. When we were sent under acting-Sergeant Bernard Early to clean out the machine guns on our left, I was following behind Corporal Cutting. I saw two Red Cross Germans and when they started to run, we fired at them. One of them stopped and gave himself up. We followed after the other Germans and about twenty paces from where we had first sighted these two Red Cross Germans, we ran into a bunch of Germans all together in an underbrush on the slope of the hill. When we appeared, Germans came running out of the brush and machine gun trenches in every direction.

There seemed to be about one hundred of these Germans. Some of them held their hands up and shouted 'Kamerad' and gave themselves up. A few shots were fired at us and a few men on our side fired back. After this, all the Germans in sight stopped firing and came in around us, having thrown down their arms and equipment. Before we could line them up in column and move them out, German machine gunners, whom we had not seen before this, commenced firing down the hill at our men. This fire came mostly from opposite our own flank.

We had six men killed and three wounded in a very short time. When the heavy firing from machine guns commenced, I was guarding some of the German prisoners. During this time I only saw Privates Donohue, Saccina, Beardsley and Muzzi. Private Swanson was right near me when he was shot. I closed up very close to the Germans with my bayonet on my rifle and prevented some of them who tried to leave the bunch and get into the bushes from leaving. I know that my only chance was to keep them together and also to keep them between me and the Germans who were shooting.

I heard Corporal York several times shouting to the machine gunners on the hill to come down and surrender, but from where I stood, I could not see Corporal York. I saw him however, when the firing stopped and he told us to get along the sides of the column. I formed those near me in columns of twos.

This statement was read to Private Wills, after being taken, and he stated that same was correct.

I certify that the above is statement made by Private George W. (1,910,418) Wills, Company G, 328th Infantry, to which he made oath before me.

G. EDWARD BUXTON, JR.
Major, Inf., U.S.A.
Division Historical Officer.

Wills' second statement was taken on 6 February before Major Buxton and is word for word that of Private Beardsley's, taken on the same day.

Wills has said in his first statement that he was very near to Corporal Savage when he was hit; he adds that he could see Privates Donohue, Saccina, Beardsley and Muzzi. He says he could hear York shouting to the Germans on the hill to surrender, but he could not see him from his position.

In his February statement, Wills agrees with Beardsley that a German officer led a group of riflemen with fixed bayonets and York shot the officer and many of his men. Neither Wills nor Beardsley have mentioned this in their January statements.

The charge by the officer and men is a significant event in the fight. Only York has mentioned this in his statement. One has therefore to be sceptical about the affidavits and statements and their content should be viewed with some caution.

This is the affidavit of Private Joseph Konotski, who signed with his 'X' mark, and was taken on 6 February 1919:

On the morning of October 8, 1918, west of Chatel Chehery, Sergeant York performed in action deeds of most distinguished personal bravery and self-sacrifice. His platoon had been sent to the left flank of the assaulting wave, which was then exposed, to clear out some machine guns. Encountering a large machine gun nest, all but seven men of his platoon were killed or wounded and all non-commissioned officers, except Sergeant York kept his usual balance and self-control. He rallied the men and closed in on the enemy, using his rifle as long as he could conveniently reach his ammunition. He then resorted to his pistol with which he killed and wounded no less than fifteen of the enemy.

After this intense fight Sergeant York succeeded in taking prisoner the battalion commander. Then, instructing his seven men he took the remainder of the enemy prisoners in an exceedingly tactful manner. In lining the prisoners up preparatory to taking them to the Battalion P.C., Sergeant York displayed decided decision by placing the officers at the head of the column with himself next in line and the remaining men distributed in the line, making it impossible for the enemy to kill any of his men without killing a German.

On the way in to the Battalion P.C. a number of the enemy made their appearance and were taken prisoners. When Sergeant York arrived at the Battalion P.C. he turned over 132 prisoners of whom three were officers, one being a field officer.[4]

JOSEPH KONOTSKI (his X mark)

Subscribed and sworn to before me at Frettes, France, this 6th day of February 1919.
Edwin A. Burkhalter,
1st Lieut. 328th Inf., Bn. Adjt

And the sworn affidavit of Private Donohue:

Hq. 82d Div., American E. F., France.
26 January, 1919.

Private Patrick (1,910,305) Donohue, Company G, 328th Infantry, being duly sworn made the following affidavit:

On the 8th Day of October 1918, I was a member of Corporal Cutting's squad in G Company, 328th Infantry. When we were sent under acting-Sergeant Bernard Early to clean out the machine guns on our left, I was following behind Corporal Cutting. I saw two Red Cross Germans, and when they started to run, we fired at them. One of them stopped and gave himself up. We followed after the other German, and about twenty paces from where we had first sighted these two Red Cross Germans, we ran into a bunch of Germans all together in an underbrush on the slope of the hill. When we appeared, Germans came running out of the brush and machine gun trenches in every direction. There seemed to be about one hundred of these Germans.

Some of them held up their hands and shouted 'Kamerad' and gave themselves up. A few shots were fired at us and a few men on our side fired back. After this, all the Germans in sight stopped firing and came in around us, having thrown down their arms and equipment. Before we could line them up in column and move them out, German machine gunners, whom we had not seen before this, commenced firing down the hill at our men. This fire came mostly from opposite our own right flank.

We had six men killed and three wounded in a very short time. During all this shooting, I was guarding the mass of Germans taken prisoners and devoted my attention to watching them. When we first came in on the Germans, I fired a shot at them before they surrendered. Afterward I was busy guarding the prisoners and did not shoot. From where I stood, I could only see Private Wills, Saccina, and Sok. They were also guarding prisoners as I was doing. Later, we were moving prisoners out of the woods, I saw Private Moreau, but I do not know where he was or what he was doing during the fight. The men I have mentioned above were all members of Corporal Cutting's squad, and our squad had each fired at least one shot when we first saw the Germans and before Corporal Cutting told us to stop shooting. I was wounded slightly on the shoulder at the first aid station, to which I helped Corporal Early, and continued on duty until that night, when the doctor evacuated me.

This statement was read to Private Donohue after being taken, and he stated that same was correct.

I certify that the above is statement made by Private Patrick (1,910.305) Donohue, Company G, 328th Infantry, to which he made oath before me.[5]

G. Edward Buxton, Jr.
Major, Inf., U.S.A.,
Division Historical Officer.

Captain Joseph Woods made two affidavits, the first of them on 27 January 1919:

I certify that I personally counted the prisoners reported to the P.C. of the 2d Battalion, 328th Infantry, by Corporal Alvin C. York, Company G, 328th Infantry, on Oct. 8, 1918 and found them to be 132 in number.[6]

Jos. A. Woods,
1st Lieut., Inf., U.S.A.
Asst. Div. Inspector.

The second was taken on 21 February 1919:

2d Bn. 328th Inf.,
82d Div., American E.F.
Frettes, France, Feb. 21, 1919

Affidavit of 1st Lieut. Jos, A. Woods, Inf., U.S.A. personally appeared before me … who made the following affidavit:

On the morning of Oct. 8, 1918, I was battalion adjutant, 2d Battalion, 328th Infantry. The Battalion P.C. had been moved forward from Hill 223 to a hillside across the valley and just west of Hill 223, the jumping-off place. We heard some heavy and almost continuous firing on the other side of our hill and in the direction taken by Sergeant Early, Corporal York and their detachment. Sometime later, I personally saw Corporal York and seven privates returning down the hillside on which our P.C. was located. They had 132 prisoners with them, including three German officers, one a battalion commander. I personally counted the prisoners when Corporal York reported the detachment and prisoners. Corporal York was in entire charge of this party and was marching at the head of the column with the German officers. The seven men with Corporal York were scattered along the flanks and rear of the column. Sergeant Early and Corporal Cutting both severely wounded, were being assisted at the rear of the column.

Jos. A. Woods.
1st Lieut. Inf., U.S.A.

Sworn to and subscribed before
me at Pratthay, France, 23 Feb., 1919
R.L. Boyd, Maj. A.G.D.,
Adjutant 82d Div.

Captain Bertrand Cox made an affidavit in which he describes the battlefield after the fight:

2d Bn., 328th Inf.,
82d Div., American E.F.
Frettes, France, February 21, 1919

Affidavit of Capt. Betrand Cox, 328th Inf.

Personally appeared before me the undersigned, Capt., Bertrand Cox who made the following affidavit:

On the morning of October 8th, I commanded a support platoon of F Company, 2d Battalion of the 328th Infantry. Shortly after Corporal York and his detachment of seven men succeeded in capturing the greater part of a German battalion, I advanced with my platoon and passed the scene of the fight, which took place before this capture was accomplished. The ground was covered with German equipment and I should estimate that there were between 20 and 25 dead Germans on the scene of the fight.

BERTRAND COX
Captain 328th Inf.

Sworn to and subscribed before me
At Frettes, France, this 26th day of February 1919
Edwin A. Burkhalter,
1st Lieut. 328th Inf. Bn. Adj.

The affidavits are not source documents. They are produced in *Sergeant York, His Own Life Story and War Diary*, edited by Tom Skeyhill. They do not exist outside the diary, hence the many references to Skeyhill's manuscript. The affidavits are all very closely matched in detail as to what took place, some are identical and it is suspected that they were written by someone else, in the presence of the soldier; this would be the officer taking the statement. They were taken after the war. Private Percy Beardsley made two statements, on 26 January 1919 and 6 February 1919.

On this day, Major Buxton took affidavits from Lieutenant Woods, Private Beardsley, Private Wills, Private Donohue and Private Saccina. It is not known if he took affidavits from any of the other survivors since none of these statements exist outside of Skeyhill's book. Why was this information taken so late in the proceedings? The war was over, it had been four months since the action, thoughts of peace and home and the return to normality were abundant, and under any other circumstance the fight in the forest would have been forgotten. York had been promoted to sergeant as a direct result of the conflict, his award of the Distinguished Service Cross had been approved, but then the circumstances and the criteria for the award of the Congressional Medal of Honor were further examined by Captain Danforth, who made his recommendation to higher authority. An Army investigation into the incident was formed and a visit was made to the ravine by persons on that board on 7 February 1919. The officials present during this visit were Brigadier-General Julian R. Lindsey, York's brigade commander, Alvin York, Major Buxton, Captain Danforth, George Pattullo, and the Army photographer from the Signal Corps, Private 1st Class F.C. Phillips, together with Major Tillman.[7]

Undoubtedly, by this time, the decision had been taken that York should be awarded the Congressional Medal of Honor, and to meet the criteria it was necessary for the higher command to invest in a little embellishment to ensure that the best possible scenario would be presented.

This is not to say that York was not deserved of the high award. It is not the intention of the Nolan Group to belittle York's part in this firefight; his action in the ravine undoubtedly saved the patrol. Without his stance, the result would have been much different. He was a man of the mountains, an excellent marksman, totally cool, calm and collected, who was cast into a situation to which he reacted with great bravery. It would not have been his idea to revisit the scene in 1919, but of those who wished to propel him forward for the Congressional Medal of Honor.

When Skeyhill was researching for his book in 1928, he sought out the patrol members who had not given a statement in 1919. These were the patrol leader, Acting Sergeant Bernard Early, and the man who ordered the patrol, Sergeant Harry M. Parsons. It is probable that statements were not taken from them at the same time as the others because the severity of their wounds had necessitated their removal to hospital.

There now follow the sworn affidavits of the missing two. First, Sergeant Harry M. Parsons:

> State of New York,
> County of Kings.
> Harry Parsons of the City of New York and County of Kings, State of New York, being duly sworn, deposes and says:
>
> I was the platoon sergeant of the 1st Platoon, G Company, 2d Battalion, 328th Infantry, 82d Division; we had no commissioned officer, and I was in charge of the platoon. The platoon was made up of Greeks, Slavs, Swedes, Jews, Irish, Germans, and Italians, all American citizens, of course. There were also a number of farmers and a few mountaineers, one of whom was Alvin C. York. On the morning of October 8, 1918, we marched the town of Chatel

Chehery, and up on to Hill 223, where we waited for the zero hour. Without artillery support we went over the top at about daylight. Our platoon was upon the extreme left flank of the division, and was in the second wave, about one hundred yards in the rear of the first. The Germans quickly opened on us with machine guns, securely entrenched in the ridges and brush on our front and left flank. Our first line was mowed down; Lieutenant Stewart was killed ... [8]and the survivors forced to dig in.

The machine gun fire was something terrible. If the advance was to be continued, somehow or other the machine guns would have to be put out; and I knew the advance had to be continued at all costs. Our company commander, Captain Danforth, was over on the right on the other side of the hill, fighting against desperate odds. I had no opportunity of getting in touch with him and he had no chance of getting over to us. But I figured at all cost the machine guns had to be silenced. It was an awful responsibility for a non-commissioned officer to order his me to go to what looked to be certain death. But I figured it had to be done. I figured they had a slight chance of getting the machine guns. So I made the decision – and I now know that it was the wisest decision I ever made.

I ordered the left half of my platoon, what remained of four squads, to deploy through the heavy brush on the left and work their way over the ridges to where the German machine guns were firing – and then attack the machine guns and put them out of commission. Sergeant Early was in charge of the four sections, and Corporal York, Corporal Cutting and Corporal Savage were in charge of the squads. The thirteen private soldiers were, privates. Dymowski, Wiley, [sic], Waring, [sic] Wins, [sic] Swanson, Muzzi, Beardsley, Konotski, Sok, Johnson, Saccina, Donohue, and Wills. Lead by Sergeant Early, as ordered, the men immediately advance through the brush on our left flank and disappeared. A few minutes later we heard heavy firing from the direction which they had taken; and shortly after the German machine gun fire ceased. It was after this that Corporal York and seven privates returned with 132 German prisoners. Corporal York marched in front of the prisoners and was in absolute command. Unquestionably, the silencing of these machine guns played a tremendous part in our success in finally reaching our objective.[9]

HARRY MASON PARSONS.

Subscribed and sworn to before me

This the 1st day of May 1928.

Bessie M. Swan, Notary Public

My commission expires on the 29th day of March 1929.

Then the affidavit of Bernard Early:

Bernard Early of the City and County of New Haven, State of Connecticut, being duly sworn, deposes and says:

As senior non-commissioned officer in charge of the left half of 1st Platoon, G Company, 2d Battalion, 328th Infantry, 82d Division, on the morning of October 8, 1918, I led what remained of our squads, totalling seventeen men, from the valley under Hill 223 in the Argonne Forest around our left flank in an attempt to silence German machine guns which were holding up my battalion's advance to the Decauville Railroad which was our objective.

My command was on the extreme left of our division. I led my men through the thick undergrowth about half a mile toward where we figured the German machine guns were. Then I decided to swing in behind and attack them from the rear. On account of the nature of the country the Germans were unable to see us, just as we were able to see them. So far we had no casualties. When we were well behind the German lines, we surprised a German stretcher bearer who immediately ran and we trailed him through the undergrowth deeper in behind the German lines.

We jumped a little stream and suddenly unexpectedly discovered the headquarters of a German machine gun regiment. There must have been at least one hundred Germans, including three officers and several non-commissioned officers. They were having breakfast and we completely surprised them. We fired several shots to intimidate them and rushed them with fixed bayonets. I was out in front leading them and, seeing the Germans throwing up their hands, I ordered my men to cease fire and to cover and close in on them. I then ordered my men to line them up preparatory to marching them back to our P.C. In the act of turning around issuing this order, a burst of machine gun bullets struck me. I fell with one bullet through my arm, and five through the lower part of my body. I called on Corporal Cutting to take command and get the prisoners out and if possible later on come back and get me.

A little later Corporal Cutting was wounded and Corporal York took command. I was carried back with the German prisoners to our first aid station. There I was operated on and some of the bullets were taken out and I was sent to the hospital.[10]

This statement was read to Bernard Early after being taken and he stated the same was correct.

BERNARD EARLY.

State of Connecticut}
County of New Haven} *ss.*
New Haven, April 11, 1928.

I certify that the above is the statement made by Bernard Early of said City and County of New Haven, State of Connecticut, to which he made oath before me.

LEWIS L. FIELD,
Commissioner of the Superior Court
For New Haven County.

STATEMENT/AFFIDAVIT CHART		
Name of Soldier	**Date of Affidavit**	**Additional Detail**
Captain E.C.B. Danforth	Unknown	Letter to Buxton 25 August 1929
Sergeant H.M. Parsons	1 May 1928	
A/ Sergeant B. Early	11 April 1928	
Private P. Beardsley	26 January 1919	Further affidavit made on 21 February 1919
Private M. Saccina	26 January 1919	Same as Sok, Donohue, & Konotski
Private G. Wills	26 January 1919	Same statement as Beardsley, 21 February
Private P. Donohue	26 January 1919	Same as Saccina, Sok & Konotski
Private J. Konotski	6 February 1919	Same as Saccina, Sok & Donohue
Private T. Sok	6 February 1919	Same as Saccina, Konotski & Donohue
1st Lieutenant J.A. Woods	26 January 1919	
Captain B. Cox	21 February 1919	

Chapter 9

The Saturday Evening Post

The news of Sergeant York's action was brought to the attention of the world when, on 26 April 1919, *The Saturday Evening Post* in Philadelphia produced an article entitled '*The Second Elder Gives Battle*'. Written by George Pattullo, it gives a remarkable insight into the action, and Pattullo had the distinct advantage that he accompanied York over the ground on which the patrol had travelled and on to the site of the fight. He accompanied the enquiry team that went with York to the scene. It contains some glaring passages of glorification that undoubtedly was intended to stir the hearts of the American public, but it also has some very interesting first-hand information.

Pattullo writes:

> The battalion had to cross a valley several hundred yards in width. On the left rose a considerable hill from which the boches sprayed them machine gun fire; straight ahead towered the elevation known as 167, a steep ridge, from which came a withering fire; Cornay Ridge on their right, sounded like a thousand steel hammers at work. In other words, the Americans were caught by fire from three directions; York was on the extreme left of the advance, his platoon being the support platoon of the left assault company. 'See that little rise just where the slope of the hill comes down? Well it looked like we couldn't get beyond that. The line just seemed to melt away when it reached theirs.' [York said.] ... . As the little party started up the hill which they proposed to clear of boches, machine guns peppered them from the Cornay Ridge at their backs; but the trees and brush were very thick and they escaped beyond observation without losing a man, the nests they were after lay on the other side of a slope; the boches were

firing at the infantry in the valley, and were wholly unconscious of the detachment bent on circling round behind them. The Americans went stumbling upward through the leafy jungle, bullets whipping the branches above and round them.

None were hit, however, and soon they gained above the fire. It was a stiff climb. I went up that hill later without a pack and free from anxiety, and found it hard going. What must it have been with full equipment, machine guns blazing at them, and the enemy ahead in unknown strength. About two-thirds of the way up they came upon an old wide trench, probably built by the French early in the war.[1] They entered this and followed it.

The clamor of the fight on the other side of the hill now grew less. The trench led over the crest.[2] Going warily in single file … the detachment penetrated upward through the dense woods and began to descend the other slope … Still they saw no Germans, they could hear firing off to their right, they could hear it ahead; but not a sign of the enemy did they see. Finally, they debouched upon a path, and in there in the wet earth were fresh footprints. They crossed the path and continued the descent, veering to the left to make sure they should get behind the enemy. A few minutes, and they entered another path – well worn, full of new footprints. 'Which way had we better take?' whispered Sergeant Early to Corporal York. 'Let's right-oblique.' Answered the mountaineer; and they right-obliqued and went downward along the path. It dipped steeply to a cuplike valley amid the hills. A puny stream flowed through this valley; everywhere was trees and bushes and tangles of undergrowth. Suddenly, they espied two Germans ahead of them in the path. Both wore the Red Cross brassard, and both started to run at the first glimpse of the Americans. Some shots were fired, and one stopped. He surrendered; the other disappeared.[3]

'It looked like a battle was coming,' said York, 'so we went into skirmish order.' They scattered out amid the riot of brush and pushed forward. Presently the leaders of the party arrived at the stream. [They have crossed the stream already, now they are going to cross again in an easterly direction] There on the other side were about twenty or thirty Germans, gathered near a small hut that was evidently some kind of P.C.[4] At any rate, several officers were holding a conference, and a number of the men were squatted on the ground apparently about to eat.

The Americans instantly let fly. A few of the enemy returned the shots, but the majority dropped guns and equipment and threw up their hands, shouting 'Kamerad!' What had happened? How came the enemy behind them? 'Don't shoot,' ordered Sergeant Early. 'They are going to surrender.' Surrender they did, the whole outfit, including the major in command of the battalion. [Lieutenant Vollmer] 'What are you? English,' He asked. 'Americans,' answered York. 'Good Lord!' said the major. Early's detachment now made preparations to take them out. But before they could move all hell broke loose.

Along the steep slope of the hill facing them, not thirty yards away, was machine gun after machine gun, snugly placed in fox holes, but pointing in the other direction. The Boches manning them swung these guns round and opened up a fusillade on the attackers. The valley became a chattering, shrieking bedlam. Some Heinies on a hill far to the rear of the Americans sensed a new menace and opened up wildly against their own position, but their fire was many yards high and merely seared the tops of the trees.

At the first burst of fire every Heinie prisoner dropped flat on his stomach and hugged the ground. The Americans followed their example. Some took refuge behind trees, others burrowed amid the underbrush; but six were killed. Sergeant Early was shot through the body; Corporal Cutting had three bullets through the left arm; Private Muzzi had a wound in the shoulder; Private Beardsley, who had an automatic, and was crouched down near Corporal York when the trouble started, crept back to a big tree for protection.

On one side of him lay Private Dymowski and on the other Private Wareing. Both were riddled with bullets – shot all to pieces. Beardsley told me afterwards that he considered the situation hopeless and could not operate his gun.

Pattullo continued that six of the detachment were killed almost immediately after the German machine guns opened fire, three were wounded including the N.C.O. in command. This left York and seven privates.

> Of these, Private Beardsley could do nothing from his position while the enemy fire kept up, for it raked both sides of his tree from close to the ground to a height of four feet. Private Michael A. Saccina says in his statement: 'I was guarding the prisoners with my rifle and bayonet on the right flank of the group of prisoners, so close to them that the machine gunners could not shoot at me without hitting their own men. This saved me. During the fighting I remained on guard, watching these prisoners and unable to turn round and fire myself for this reason. From where I stood I could not see any of the other men in my detachment.' … Private Donohue, a game little Irishman: 'During all this shooting I was guarding the mass of Germans taken prisoners and devoted my attention to watching them. When we first came in on the Germans I fired a shot at them before they surrendered. Afterwards I was busy guarding the prisoners and did not shoot. From where I stood I could see only Privates Wills, Saccina and Sak [Sok].' They were also guarding prisoners. Private George W. Wills: 'When the heavy firing from machine guns commenced I was guarding some of the German prisoners. During this time I saw only Privates Donohue, Saccina, Beardsley and Muzzi. Private Swanson was right near me when he was shot. I closed up very close to the Germans with my bayonet on my rifle and prevented some of them who tried to leave the bunch and get into the bushes from leaving. I knew that my only chance was to keep them together and also to keep them between me and the Germans who were shooting. I heard Corporal York several times shouting to the machine gunners on the hill to come down and surrender, but from where I stood, I could not see Corporal York. I saw him however when the firing stopped and he told us to get along the sides of the column.

This is the column of German soldiers who would be marched out to the American lines. Pattullo continues:

My purpose in quoting the statements of these men is to show by elimination what York did, in order to convince the skeptical. Every man except the second elder is now accounted for; we know from their own lips what the survivors of the first blasts did in the fight that ensued. But somebody killed more than twenty boches on the slopes of that hill and put thirty-five machine guns out of action. Who was it?[5]

Pattullo must have enjoyed the theatrical. This was a wonderful scoop. He knew he could enthrall the world through his newspaper. This story would rate amongst the best he would ever write and he would have been in his element, in the presence of York and the senior Army officers and following in the footsteps of a hero. Pattullo would have been aware too, that the purpose of the visit to the battle scene in 1919 was to exemplify credibility to pave the way for the approval of the Congressional Medal of Honor to York, that was probably the reasoning behind his invitation, and he did an admirable job.

The comment regarding thirty-five machine guns being put out of action is, at the very least, wayward. The Germans would not have thirty-five machine guns in an isolated position at the rear, particularly when they are facing a major frontal attack. As we will see, the German accounts totally refute this claim with good tactical cause.

York told Pattullo that he dropped to the ground along a narrow path that led to the German machine guns, directly in front of him lay the German prisoners. The position of the prisoners and York's low profile undoubtedly saved him from the vicious machine gun fire. York started to fire back. The enemy guns were less than 30 yards away from him, but from his prone position he could see the heads of the Germans who had to elevate themselves to see their target. This was where York came into his own. He sighted the Germans as he had done in the turkey shooting contests back home. He brought down an enemy with every shot apart from one, where he showed Pattullo he had creased the trunk of a tree. York continued that he fired a couple of clips or so:

Things were moving pretty lively, so I don't know how many I did shoot – and first thing I knew a boche got up and flung a little bomb at me about the size of a silver dollar. It missed and wounded one of the prisoners on the ground, and I got the boche – got him square.[6]

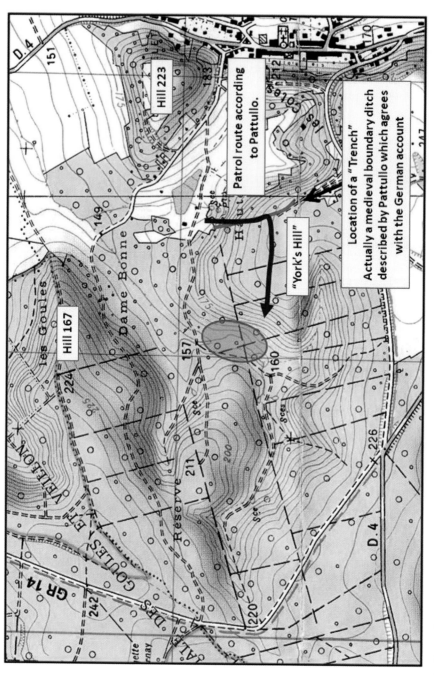

Hill 223

Patrol route according to Pattullo.

Location of a "Trench"
Actually a medieval boundary ditch described by Pattullo which agrees with the German account

"York's Hill"

Hill 167

Map 19: Patrol route according to George Pattullo. (Posey)

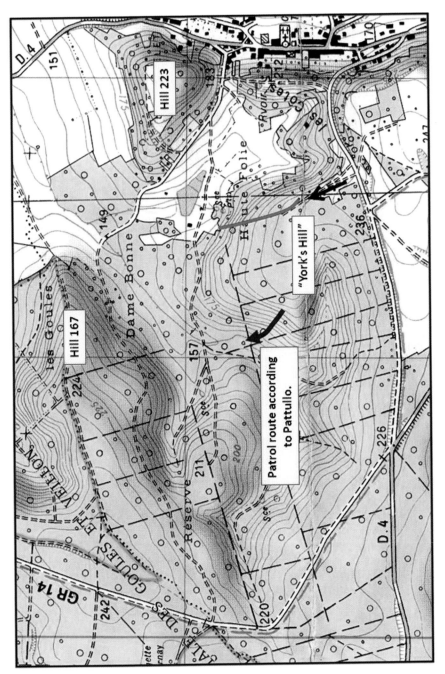

Map 20: Patrol route – sequence. (Posey)

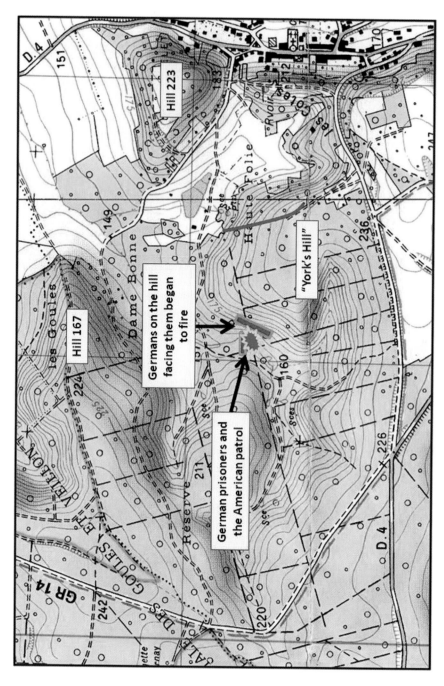

Map 21: Patrol route – sequence. (Posey)

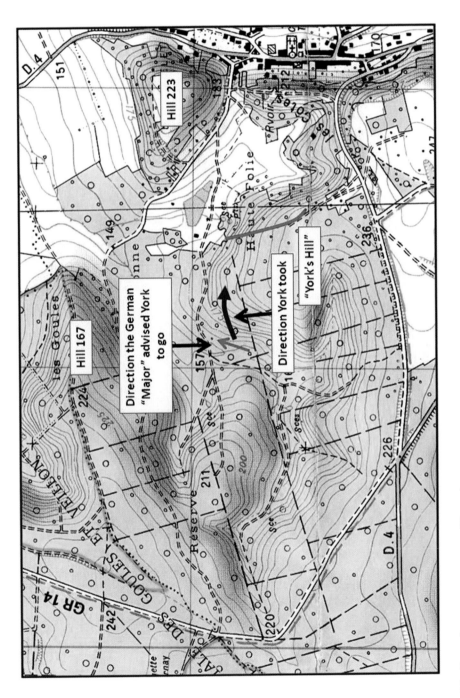

Map 22: Patrol route – sequence. (Posey)

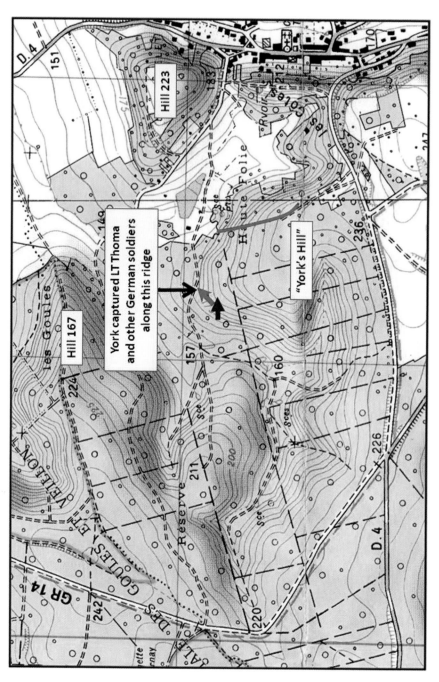

Map 23: Patrol route – sequence. (Posey)

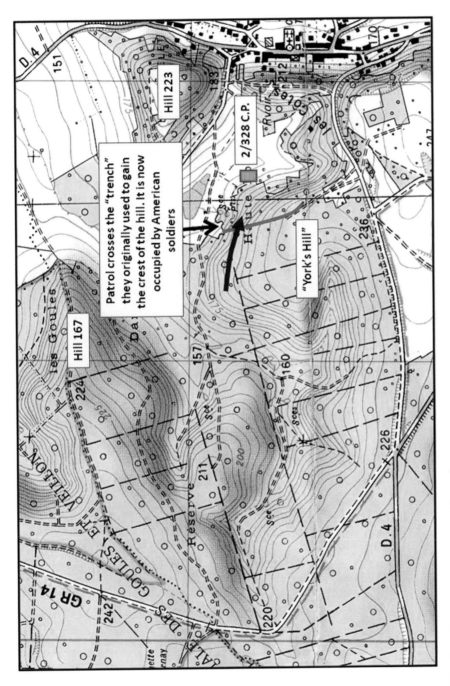

Hill 223

2/328 C.P.

Patrol crosses the "trench" they originally used to gain the crest of the hill. It is now occupied by American soldiers

Hill 167

"York's Hill"

Map 24: Patrol route – extraction. (Posey)

York shot the German dead. The next thing, York saw a lieutenant rise up from around the back of one of the German machine guns. The officer had seven men with him and they rushed him from their position:

> I had my automatic out by then, and let them have it. Got the Lieutenant right through the stomach and he dropped and screamed a lot. All the boches who were hit squealed like pigs. Then I shot the others.[7]

York went on to say that he killed all eight men before they could get near to him, a distance he said of around 20 yards. In his York diary, he stated that he killed this detachment systematically, shooting the rearmost soldier first and then working to the front. This description is not recorded in Pattullo's article.

There are some discrepancies here. In the York diary, he writes that a German officer and five men charged him. In his 1919 statement, it was a German officer and eight or ten men in the charge. The diary also states that the German who threw the grenade at him did so after the surrender of the Germans on the slope.

When the German machine gunners saw their lieutenant fall most of them stopped shooting and the battle faded. However, York kept shooting until approached by the German commander, Lieutenant Vollmer. York felt this officer had been firing his pistol at him during the fight. Examination of the pistol afterwards revealed it was empty (see Fig. 79). Vollmer put his hand on York's shoulder and said that if he didn't shoot anymore, he would make them surrender. York agreed, he stopped shooting and the German officer ordered his men to cease fire and stop shooting.

The Germans came down from the hill and joined the prisoners. They dropped their equipment on the slopes as they did so (many items of discarded equipment were discovered by the Nolan Group). York estimated the number of prisoners at this stage to be ninety.

Despite the fact they were being fired upon by Germans on the hills in their rear and they did not know how long it would be before other German forces might arrive, the Americans ushered the prisoners together. York told the wounded that they should follow in the rear; Sergeant Early, who was seriously wounded was brought in by Private Donohue. The wounded

Corporal Cutting and Private Muzzi could walk out unassisted. At this point, York gathered his thoughts on the correct direction out of the ravine. The German lieutenant volunteered his services, saying that they should follow the path to the south. York told him that they would not, and they would go north (see Map 22). As they went up the hill, York had an officer either side of him at the front of the column. Vollmer asked him how strong was his detachment, and York told him that he had plenty of men. They had gone 100 yards or so when they were challenged by another German machine gun nest. York thrust Vollmer in front of him and ordered them to surrender, which they did. They too abandoned their equipment and joined the long line of prisoners. Another machine gun nest was encountered. York pointed the spot out to Pattullo and said that he had to shoot a man there who was offering resistance. Someone was shooting at them as they progressed. They were probably the German machine gunners who Captain Danforth was to account for later that morning. It was near 1000 hours when York and the prisoners emerged at the battalion P.C..

At the beginning of the Pattullo newspaper article he says:

> He [York] is the crack shot of his battalion with the rifle, and in a contest with the automatic pistol against Major Tillman the corporal hit a penny match box every shot at forty paces.[8]

This is an important statement. The Nolan Group team found artefacts at the scene that bore many bullet holes. A small item such as a water canteen would not have so many bullets concentrated in one small area during one encounter (see Figs 2 & 3). It is felt that York gave a practical demonstration of his marksmanship, along with Major Tillman, in the shooting contest that Pattullo wrote about in his article.

Pattullo concludes his newspaper piece:

> There on the scene of the fight at the foot of York's Hill are six graves where our dead lie buried. Simple wooden crosses mark them, and at the head repose the helmets, rifles and belts of the soldiers of the soldiers who gave their lives. Close beside their last resting place purls a tiny stream, and over the wooded hills broods a cathedral hush.[9]

Some of these items of kit to which Pattullo refers would be recovered by the Nolan Group ninety years later.

Fig. 1: Grave of Corporal Murray Savage. KIA 8 October 1918. (U.S. Army, 1919)

Chapter 10

A Summary of the American Accounts

There are anomalies in the different accounts you have read, differences even in the same man's accounts. There are variations between the York diary in Skeyhill's book and those in the official statement.

- In York's 1919 statement, he said that on the first encounter with the Germans there were about seventy-five next to a little shack sitting together with their commanding officer and two other officers. He said that shots were exchanged and several Germans were hit. He said that one German continued to fire at him and York shot him.

- In the diary, York said there were only fifteen to twenty Germans sitting around a wooden shack. York says they fired a couple of shots just to impress them but does not mention any of them being hit nor does he say that he had to shoot one of them who continued to fire at him.

- Within the 1919 statement, York talks of during the fight on the slope, a German lieutenant and eight or ten soldiers rushed towards them. He says 'rushed towards us', indicating that the German assault was not necessarily directed at him, but the American group in general. He continues that one of the Germans threw a small grenade at him, but it missed and wounded one of their own men.

- In the diary, York says that a German officer and five men jumped out of a trench and charged him with fixed bayonets. They were 25 yards from him; he used both his rifle and pistol and began shooting the German assault from the rear-most to the front until they were all down. The grenade incident is not mentioned until all the Germans had surrendered and came down the slope to join the other prisoners.

- In the diary, it was a German officer and five soldiers that charged him. In his 1919 statement, York says it was a German officer and eight or ten men that charged him.

- In the 1919 statement, York states that as they were marching the prisoners back to the American lines, they came upon more machine gun posts. One German aimed a rifle at him. The German officer ordered the man to surrender and he did so.
- In his diary, York says as they marched back to the American lines, more machine guns were encountered and as they swung around to fire, the German officer blew his whistle for them to surrender. York says that all of them surrendered except one, the German officer told the man twice to surrender, but he did not so York shot him.
- In the 1919 statement, York says that when the machine guns opened fire from the slope, two of his men who were not hit by the initial bursts, got behind trees and fired about half a clip each, but in his war diary he says that when the fight with the machine guns was taking place, he did not have a chance to look around for the other boys, he didn't know what they were doing and did not know if they were still alive. He went on to say that in the thick of the fight, they did not fire a shot.

    It is known that other men in the patrol did fire their weapons as expended .30–.06 cartridges were found near the fight and not all were believed to be from York's rifle.
- In the diary, York states that on 9 October, the day after the fight, Captain Danforth gave him permission to return to the scene of the fight to see if there was anyone left behind wounded. He got to the scene and said the Salvage Corps had already been through and cleaned the place up. He continued that all the American dead had been buried and the Germans also had been buried or taken away. He emphasised that there were no bodies left around.

This cannot be possible. It is known that the American patrol members killed in the fight were not buried until 24 October by Chaplain O'Farrelly of the Graves Registration Services (GRS). Their departmental documents will corroborate this.

If York had indeed returned to the scene the following day, he would have seen the bodies of all the men and the enemy still lying on the ground where they fell, together with surrendered, discarded German equipment. Captain Danforth makes no mention of York's request to return, and York knew who the casualties were. It is extremely unlikely that a company commander would have allowed such a venture, particularly in view of the significant casualties his battalion had suffered and the fact that every man was needed for the upcoming assault upon Cornay.

York says the Americans had been buried upon his return on 9 October. In February 1919 York did return to the ravine as part of the U.S. Army investigation into his exploit. He would have seen that by this time, the American casualties had been buried with crosses marking the three burial sites.[1]

In his diary, York says that he saw a canteen with eighteen bullet holes in it, lying on the ground near where he stood. It is virtually impossible for a small object the size of a canteen to receive so many random bullet strikes in such a short fight. In the investigation section of this book, details of artefacts discovered at the scene will reveal exhibits that the Nolan Group believe were used as target practice. One such artefact is pictured, a German canteen found very close to the suspected burial site of Corporal Savage. The canteen had several .45 and 9mm bullet holes in it (see Figs 2 & 3). Whether this is the one York refers to or not, there are interesting similarities in what York describes and what was found in the archaeological investigation. It will be recalled that Pattullo hinted at possible target practice in his newspaper article.

Some members of the patrol give conflicting accounts of the two German Red Cross soldiers. Bernard Early said there was one. Some accounts say shots were fired at the German Red Cross men: Beardsley said that they fired at them, one stopped and gave himself up, another account says one was wounded and taken prisoner.

The Nolan Group believe that what York describes as taking place on 9 October 1918 was in fact the information he gave to the 1919 United States Army investigation.

The number of German machine guns that were purportedly involved in the fight is highly questionable. Anywhere between twenty and thirty machine guns appear in the count. To look at it from a German perspective, their accounts indicate that it would have been impossible for so many machine guns to have been anywhere in the entire area west of Châtel-Chéhéry that day. It is highly unlikely that the Germans would have had so many machine guns simply sitting in reserve, on the back side of the hill opposite to where a major

Fig. 2: Bullet–ridden German canteen. (Posey)

Fig. 3: It is possible the canteen was the subject of target shooting by York and the 1919 Investigative team.

American attack was taking place just a short distance away on the other side of the hill. Posey's report takes up the story:

> By all accounts, these twenty to thirty machine guns were twenty-five to thirty-five yards away from York. If they were all firing so heavily that the bushes were shot down around where York stood, as York claims, then why were dozens of Germans not killed since they were only a few feet away from York as he describes it? Even if God protected York, as he claims, there should have been scores of Germans killed from friendly fire at that range.

Posey has twenty years of experience firing machine guns with the U.S. Army on a regular basis, but even he cannot fathom a fight like this as is described in Skeyhill's book and the portions of York's War Diary.

Posey continues that in no way does he wish to diminish what York did on that October morning in 1918. He believes that York is wholly deserved of the Congressional Medal of Honor, which he was rightfully awarded for his actions on that day. There are, however, several discrepancies to be observed in the recorded history of this event. The purpose of the Nolan Group in highlighting these issues is not to belittle or demean York's actions. However it would be professionally remiss of them not to strive for the most accurate interpretation possible by using thorough historical research, which has been applied throughout by Doctor Nolan and his group. This same meticulous application to detail was employed in the search for the fight area, as will be seen later.

Posey continued:

> In my opinion, York did virtually single-handedly engage a large number of German riflemen supported by several machine guns firing from the slope thirty yards or so above him [a platoon of the 7th Bavarian Mineur Company]. He did virtually kill a number of these Germans until the German officer, Lieutenant Vollmer, amongst the initial group of German prisoners, saw that in order to save more German lives, he offered York a surrender proposal that resulted in the Bavarians on the slope cease firing and come down from the hill.

The archaeological evidence that follows will show that several hundred 7.92mm rounds and a dozen or so 9mm rounds were expended during this firefight, but there was a very limited use of machine guns. The Nolan Group believe that other members of the patrol did return fire, and it is possible that they hit targets.

Chapter 11

The German Accounts

After the Congressional Medal of Honor had been awarded to Alvin C. York, he returned to America, the hero of the Argonne. Before we examine the German statements and accounts from the period surrounding 8 October 1918, it is necessary to understand what instigated the 1929 enquiry in Germany into the York fight, and which resulted in the German rebuttal of the American claims as to the authenticity of the York firefight.

In early 1929, a German citizen living in Stockholm saw an article in a Swedish newspaper relating the Sergeant York story in the Argonne Forest. In a fit of national fervour and incensed by what he had read, he sent the article to the authorities in Germany and eventually, the Reichsarchiv, a government records office, took the lead. They recorded written statements from twenty-two soldiers who had been in the area to the west of Châtel-Chéhéry on 8 October.[1] They prepared a rebuttal of the American account. The result of the German enquiry is what follows. We will discuss in detail the flaws that came about.

The Nolan Group have studied the German rebuttal and the records contained in the archives in Germany. Brad Posey, fluent in the German language, spent many hours visiting different German archives and scouring the records. He compared the rebuttal statement with the contemporaneous records from the German war diaries of the time. Posey also discovered an important witness statement from Lieutenant Thoma in the Bavarian archives in Munich, never seen by any of the Sergeant York research groups. But before we proceed further, it is important that you should be reminded of the German names of the terrain features around the village of Châtel-Chéhéry (see Map 41).

Posey noted that there was a drastic switch in the way war diaries were recorded after the commencement of the Argonne Offensive on 26 September 1918. Compared with before this period, when the diaries had a plethora of maps, some of which were hand-drawn, with the meticulous Teutonic attention to finite detail, well written and annotated, toward the end of the war, there was almost an acceptance of the inevitable. Impending defeat loomed large on the horizon. As early as August 1918 senior officers in the German ranks were full of pessimism. Crown Prince Rupprecht of Bavaria wrote from Flanders to Prince Max of Baden on 15 August:

> Our military situation has deteriorated so rapidly that I no longer believe we can hold out over the winter; it is even possible that a catastrophe will come earlier … the Americans are multiplying in a way we never dreamed of, at the present time there are already thirty-one divisions in France.[2]

The very thought of thousands of American troops landing in France every week had a demoralising effect on the Germans, and by the time of the Argonne Offensive in September 1918 disillusionment was much apparent within their ranks.

In the German archives, Posey discovered that some of the unit war diaries did not exist, others were sketchy with abbreviated entries and the minimum of detail. Sometimes several days of action were contained within just a sentence or two, demonstrating an acceptance of the inevitable within the German rank and file.

The German rebuttal, written because of the investigation by the authorities into what took place on 8 October 1918, consisted of testimony from several officers: First Lieutenant Vollmer, commander 1st Battalion, 120th Landwehr Infantry (He was the officer York captured in the first instance); Lieutenant Glass, Battalion Adjutant, 1st Battalion, 120th Landwehr Infantry (captured); Lieutenant Endriss, commander 4th Company, 1st Battalion 120th Landwehr Infantry (he received a mortal abdominal wound after being shot by York during the 'charge'); Lieutenant Kubler, who commanded a platoon of 4th Company, 1st Battalion, 120th Landwehr Infantry (captured); Lieutenant Thoma, 7th Bavarian Sapper Company (captured); and Captain von Sick, commander, 120th Landwehr Infantry.

The focus of the German examination was on the 120th Landwehr Infantry Regiment (LIR) and Posey's in-depth research in the German archives reveals some interesting detail. The 3rd Battalion of the 120th LIR was commanded by Rittmeister von Sick, who by the morning of the 8 October had absorbed the 2nd Battalion and was effectively in command of the entire regiment in the field. In his report as well as his war diaries it was known to the Reichsarchiv that shortly after the American attack began on 8 October something occurred a little to the north of his position. Soldiers who had evaded capture reported to him that Lieutenant Vollmer had been captured and the 4th Company, 120th LIR, had gone. The 4th Company was part of the 1st Battalion under the command of Lieutenant Vollmer and in his statement he mentions not only the capture of himself and soldiers of the 4th Company, but those from what was left of the 210th Reserve Infantry Regiment (RIR) and the 7th Bavarian Mineur Company, which had both been placed under his command.

Posey discovered that care should be exercised when reading the statements from the officers and men from these units. The Reichsarchiv requested witness statements from those units mentioned above, but in addition, they also questioned men from the 125th LIR who had been on the adjacent Hill 167. None of these statements were ever used because the latter did not play any part in the York fight. Nevertheless, some modern researchers have misunderstood the list of soldiers that were questioned, as well as one of the statements from an officer in the 120th LIR who mentions seeing Lieutenant Lipp from the 125th LIR once they had been taken to the American C.P.. Lipp had been captured on Hill 167 and was with a group of prisoners who had been taken to the 2nd Battalion, 328th Infantry C.P., where York was with his 132 prisoners. We know that York was given additional prisoners to take back to Varennes. The Reichsarchiv decided that the following units were involved in the incident with York:

The Battalion headquarters and staff from the 120th LIR, 4th Company, 120th LIR, 2 platoons from the 7th Bavarian Mineur Company and a small group of men from the 210th RIR.

The operations officer of the 120th LIR was Major Spang, who made a statement to the Reichsarchiv. Although he was not present when this event took place, there are small pieces of information that are helpful:

Aided by the fog, the dense woods and numerous ravines, the enemy penetrated our lines at various points and some forces reached our local reserves which were located west of Hill 223. The 1st Battalion, 120th Landwehr Infantry, the 210th Reserve Infantry and the 7th Bavarian Sapper Company bore the brunt of this action.

We received one bad report after another in those days; some of them were exaggerated, others unfounded. Observers informed Division Headquarters that part of the 210th Reserve Infantry had removed their belts, dropped their rifles and surrendered, when some men shouted, 'The Americans are coming'.

It was impossible for the Division Staff to make a detailed investigation of each individual report. Captain Winzer, the Division Supply Officer, was sent to the Brigade and Regiments for the purpose of making an estimate of the situation. It is possible that these reports and the feat attributed to Corporal York have some connection. On the other hand, I heard nothing of certain elements having surrendered to one single man with only a few companions.[3]

Spang says that the event occurred where the local reserves were the 210th RIR and the 7th Bavarian Mineur Company.

The supply officer for the 120th LIR was Captain Winzer:

In the back area of the division, there prevailed a regular panic, 'The Americans have broken through!' In order to bring the stream of retreating men to a halt, the Division commander ordered a cavalry squadron, which he had at his disposal, to cut off the retreat in the rear. The Brigade commander had lost all contact with his regiments. I was surprised, therefore, to encounter a comparatively high morale in the frontline. Despite their heavy losses, the troops were still masters of the situation; there was not a sign of panic.[4]

The item of interest here is his comment regarding high morale. Other officers seriously disagree with him.

The Commander of the 3rd Battalion, 120th LIR was Rittmeister von Sick:[5]

Early in the morning, I heard lively rifle fire to the rear of my command post, that is, in the valley north of HOHENBORN HILL.

Shortly thereafter, several men of the 4th Company reached us with the message that strong hostile elements had broken through their lines and captured a number of their men, including First Lieutenant Vollmer. At first I did not believe this, as I thought that an enemy patrol might have penetrated our lines. Consequently, I dispatched a patrol to the north; after a while this patrol returned with the information that no trace of the 4th Company could be found, but strong hostile elements were pushing on through the valley in the direction of the observation tower on HUMSER HILL. It is probable that Sergeant York of the 328th American Infantry captured several prisoners in the course of this action. It is doubtful, on the other hand, that he single-handed, killed 25 German soldiers, not mention his capturing 132 Germans. The claim that he captured 35 machine guns is an outright lie. I cannot imagine where he could have found 35 machine guns in such a small area, even if he included the light machine guns. I do not believe that 35 machine guns were employed that day in the entire area between CHATEL and the NORTH_SOUTH ROAD.

The Nolan Group agree partly with von Sick. It is extremely unlikely that so many machine guns were placed in an area that was not in the front line. Von Sick states that the morale was high in the 2nd LDW division, and that it was 'boastful' of Sergeant York, probably counting other prisoners as those of his own. He continues:

> The 'Major' referred to in the American account must have been the Commander of the 1st Battalion, 120th LDW, First Lieutenant Vollmer, whom the Americans took prisoner at that time. I can contribute but little towards clarifying his case, inasmuch as the dense fog then prevailing shut out all view. Crown witness may be considered First Lieutenant Vollmer; to my knowledge, he was a postal official in Württemberg. Further I wish to name Captain Krimmel, now a factory director at Reutlingen.[6]

There now follows a most interesting report. That of Lieutenant Vollmer. It is necessary to explain a little about the background of this statement. He delayed submitting his report and Posey found that the Reichsarchiv displayed some frustration over the delay. When eventually Vollmer submitted it, he quickly retracted it until he had the opportunity to read the statements of the other officers involved. The report is hard to follow and it is confusing. Vollmer is much more interested in stating that it was impossible for him to surrender to such a small American force. These are excerpts from his report and here he describes his position on the night of 7 October:

> I noticed that the sector following the edge of the woods from south to north and opposite HILL 223 was occupied by very weak forces. Consequently, I ordered Lieutenant Endriss and his 4th Company to occupy the edge of the woods and establish contact with the adjoining sectors. I spent the night with the companies in reserve …
>
> In the morning of October 8, I called on Major v. Sick, 3rd Battalion, 120th Landwehr Infantry, and expressed to him my grave concern for the small force occupying the left flank. Major v. Sick requested me to assume command of the left half of the regimental sector, inasmuch as the entire sector was too large for him to control in addition to the 1st Battalion, 120th Landwehr Infantry. I thus assumed command over the 7th Bavarian Sapper Company and the remnants of the Prussian 210th Reserve Infantry; the latter I did not see, however, for the present …
>
> I went forward immediately to orient myself, crawled along the front from right to left and noted that the enemy apparently had moved up closer under the cover of darkness. Moving forward a short distance, I observed some German prisoners who were being removed from the hill south of CORNAY; these prisoners, I presumed, belonged to our neighbors, the 125th Landwehr Infantry.

This is an important statement as Vollmer has established that the 125th were neighbours and not a part of their forces defending the southern part of the valley between Hills 223 and 167.

Vollmer continues:

> Failing to notice anything that would point toward an impending enemy attack, I decided to visit the new elements that were placed

under my command. I was approximately 300–400 metres from the edge of the woods, when I heard loud shouting in the direction of Lieutenant Endriss's company. At the same time, I saw our men retreating eastward, pursued by American soldiers. Accompanied by my adjutant and a messenger, I hurried toward the point where I heard the noise and met some 30 or 40 men; all that remained of the 210th Reserve Infantry. These men were about to remove their belts and side arms; I had to force them at the point of my pistol to resume fighting. Without doubt, it was due to the flanking fire that the enemy turned south and southwest.

Vollmer's description of his positioning is a little confusing, but it does place him in the rear, 300 to 400m from where Lieutenant Endriss and his 4th Company were. It also places him with the 210th RIR who, as York stated, were getting ready to eat their breakfast.

Vollmer continues:

Suddenly, we heard some yelling in the rear. As I turned and looked across the valley, I saw a line of American troops, with about five paces between men, located half-way up the east slope of the NORTH–SOUTH ROAD. Possibly this was the same enemy who, I feared had penetrated the front of the 125th Landwehr Infantry and gained our rear; then again, the Americans might have pushed back that part of our front which had faced south. I ordered the few men who were still with me to open fire on these targets. My men had hardly begun to fire, when someone called from the valley, 'Don't' shoot, there are Germans here.' The situation was critical; I was commander without troops, moreover, reconnaissance was impossible on account of the dense undergrowth.

There is another German officer who will also describe firing on German prisoners by mistake. These prisoners are men from the 125th LDW who are being evacuated from Hill 167. Vollmer then writes:

There was little time to deliberate. Suddenly several American soldiers came toward me constantly firing their rifles, I returned the fire as well as I could under the circumstances, until I was surrounded and – alone. I had no choice but to surrender. One of the enemy, with his pistol aimed at me, directed me where to go; as to the others, I do not know where they went. Reaching the edge of the woods, we encountered the Bavarian Sappers with Lieutenant Thoma. I had no idea how strong they were; at any rate, I saw no more than four or five men. As a matter of fact, I did not know that the sappers had gone into position in my sector. Realising that it was hopeless to put up a fight, and in order to prevent further useless bloodshed, I called out to Lieutenant Thoma that the enemy had enveloped our right flank and gained our rear. After some hesitation, the Bavarian Lieutenant surrendered.

Lieutenant Thoma's statement, which will appear later, is most interesting. Not only does Posey have his statement from the Reichsarchiv, but another Thoma statement he found in the Munich Archives written in 1919 before anyone in Germany knew of the circumstances of Thoma's capture nor of the existence of the York patrol. Thoma thought he had been tasken by a larger force. It is believed that the Germans thought at the time they were being attacked in the rear by a major American breakthrough on Hill 244, when, in reality it was the seventeen-man American patrol and not the forward patrols of an advancing force.

Back to Vollmer's statement:

We moved on, crossed the position formerly held by Lieutenant Endriss's company and saw Endriss lying on the ground with a serious abdominal wound. Finally, I alone, guarded by the American soldier, reached the American advance guard company which was established immediately in front of the former position of the 4th Company. There I met a large number of other German prisoners, including several officers; additional prisoners continued to come. After the American Lieutenant tried to interrogate me, he motioned me and several other officers with his pistol to stand up under a tree. Through an American soldier who spoke German, I reminded the Lieutenant of the fact that we were prisoners and expected to be treated as such as prescribed by the International Law. I also asked the officer to take care of the seriously wounded Endriss. This was done. We officers were then removed to CHATEL. There I was separated from the other officers, led into a former German dugout and interrogated by an American Major.

Lieutenant Vollmer's claim that he was captured by a large American force is simply untrue; the claim is also contradicted by the other German statements. It is interesting to note that he established the location of the 4th Company as well as a machine gun position, which he says were directly in front of the American advance guard company. This is the 2nd Battalion, 328th Infantry C.P., which is plotted on the Buxton/Danforth map that will be introduced soon. It is also confirmed by the coordinates give for the C.P.[7] in 328th field messages written on that day.

Vollmer again:

If it was York who disarmed me and led me to the American advance guard company, it is very unlikely that he commanded those elements which gained our rear. The individual incidents followed each other so rapidly that he could not have made his way through the dense undergrowth and reach me in such a short time, as may be noted from my description, my entire staff consisted of three persons at the most. I was in no mood for drinking coffee. As to the remainder of York's description – provided it applies to me at all – it is true only in that York constantly kept his pistol in the small of my back. Everything else is pure imagination, probably a product of a typically American megalomania. As to the machine guns, I recall having seen only one gun of the 4th Company; in the morning of October 8, this gun was still in action, despite the fact that it was located only a few paces from the American advance guard company. I observed no minenwerfer; nor did I know where any were employed.[8]

Vollmer once again denies any coffee drinking, but he has confirmed where the 4th Company was and the machine gun that was firing into the left flank of G Company, 328th Infantry, that morning.

The next statement is that of Lieutenant Glass, the Adjutant, 1st Battalion, 120th LDW. He clearly gives a good description of where the fight took place in a wooded ravine:

> At daybreak, October 8, 1918, I received orders to report to the 1st Battalion, 120th Landwehr Infantry, and replace the Battalion Adjutant, Lieutenant Bayer, who was ill. The Battalion was commanded by First Lieutenant Vollmer. The Battalion was located in a wooded ravine. The 4th Company was placed at the exit of the ravine, near the edge of the woods as security element and first line; the Company was facing the CORNAY – CHATEL ROAD and partly the hill near CHATEL …
>
> … In the rear of the 4th Company, we met several groups of men who belonged to another regiment, probably the 210th Reserve Infantry. Their arms and belts laid aside, these men were eating breakfast. It may be that these men were the staff whom Sergeant York surprised during their morning meal. I do not recall whether there was an officer among these men. When we expressed our surprise over their carelessness, the men declared that they had hiked all night and, first of all, needed something to eat. We knew then these were the first arrivals of the support division which was promised to us.

This statement gives valuable clues. What Glass is describing is where the fight took place. It confirms what Sergeant York said about the Germans eating their breakfast and otherwise not fighting. This area had to be at least a short distance from the open valley where the main attack of E and G Company, 328th Infantry, was taking place, between Hills 167 and 223. A wooded ravine, as described by the others, would offer a certain amount of security. Lieutenant Glass then goes on to describe some Americans in the right front of the 4th Company that appeared and suddenly disappeared. Could this be the patrol as they left the American lines? Glass continues:

> … I then looked for the Battalion Commander and learned that he had gone to the rear, some seventy metres behind the line. I noticed him standing near me. I rushed up to him and had hardly started to make

my report when I was suddenly surrounded by a number of Americans. Not until then did I seen that Lieutenant Vollmer had been captured. I am not definite whether there were still more prisoners, nor how many Americans there were present. On the other hand, I still have in my mind a fairly clear picture of the American soldier in charge it was he who kept his pistol aimed at me. He was a large and strong man with red mustache, [sic] broad feature, and, I believe, freckle-faced.

From this description by Lieutenant Glass, we can surmise that the large, strong man with the red moustache was in fact Alvin C. York.

… These first prisoners possibly included the two corporals, Willig and Kirchner of the Light Machine Gun Company; these two non-commissioned officers had preceded their machine guns for the purpose of reconnoitring suitable gun emplacements. Outside of these two men and Lieutenant Kubler, whom I mentioned above, I knew none of the prisoners.

Willig and Kirchner come to light again later in the German war diaries. Lieutenant Glass:

The Americans drove us up the hill. Suddenly a German officer and several men with fixed bayonets jumped up on our left, that it, from the direction of our lines. Of all the shouting and yelling that ensued, I recall only the words exchanged between the officer and Lieutenant Vollmer. 'I will not surrender.' 'It is useless.' – 'I will do so on your responsibility.' The officer was Lieutenant Thoma of the Bavarian Sapper Company. It is possible that the American soldier ordered and threatened Lieutenant Vollmer. I did not see, however, that this American shot the companions of Lieutenant Thoma.

Here is another clue that agrees with the American accounts of what took place immediately after the fight when the Germans were driven up a hill where they ran into other Germans. Once again, Thoma is mentioned. We will discover more in the Thoma statement later.

Lieutenant Glass continues:

> Either in the course of this incident or a few steps farther on, we saw a trench before us. Approximately one meter deep, this trench was crowded with American troops standing not only man to man, but also in double rank. I noticed also several machine guns. I could see about 30 metres of this trench. About ten metres in front of this trench, a German officer was lying on the ground with an abdominal wound. The man was on his back; it looked as if he had been shot from the rear.
>
> Two Americans were taking care of him. While I failed to recognise the wounded man, Lieutenant Vollmer informed me later that he was Lieutenant Endriss, the Commanding Officer of the 4th Company. We crossed the trench and reached the meadow which I had observed while on reconnaissance. Here we saw a group of some 20 or 30 American soldiers. Additional prisoners were brought up; it is not impossible that Corporal York gradually rolled up the 4th Company from the flank and rear. Like myself, the Americans failed to recognise Lieutenant Kubler as an officer. I also recall an elderly officer, probably Lieutenant Link of the 125th Landwehr Infantry.

This part of the statement is of great interest because there is a good description of the march back after the fight. There were no trenches in the area that were dug by the Germans during the war; there are however, some medieval boundary ditches. One of them is on this hill just a short distance west of the 2nd Battalion, 328th C.P.. In Pattullo's 1919 *Saturday Evening Post* article, he describes spending three days with York and the investigating team from the 82nd Division at Châtel-Chéhéry. His article mentions an 'old trench' that the patrol used to gain access to the top of the hill and that the patrol passed back over this same trench on the way back to the battalion C.P.. Now, there is a German officer, Lieutenant Glass, who confirms this trench. It is still there now, on the northern slope of the hill, a short distance west of where the C.P. was located, running north to south over the hill. Glass also mentions seeing an officer from the 125th LDW and it is not clear in his statement but at this point they were at the American C.P. and the 125th officer was captured on Hill 167 by the main attack of E and G Companies.

Fig. 4: Photograph taken in 2016 of Hill 223 from the boundary ditch, the site of the German machine gun position York encountered on his return with his prisoners. (Author)

Fig. 5: The boundary ditch and the location of the German machine gun, facing Hill 223. (Author)

Lieutenant Glass statement concludes:

> … Another American cut off the shoulder straps on Lieutenant
> Vollmer's overcoat, opened his coat and took his Iron Cross 1st Class.
> To his protests and attempts to defend himself, Lieutenant Vollmer
> received as the only reply the words, 'hold still.'[9]

In his 1919 statement, Lieutenant Thoma will confirm what Glass says about
the Americans collecting souvenirs from the German prisoners.

This is the statement of Lieutenant Kubler, Platoon Commander,
4th Company, 120th LIR:

> At dusk of October 7, we took up a position west of HILL 223. I posted
> my men for the night and set out to make a final inspection of the
> company sector, when I saw that we had no contact on our right flank.
> Immediately I sent out patrols to establish this liaison. The patrols
> returned during the night with the information that the 2nd Machine
> Gun Company was located on our right. Personally, I regarded the
> situation as very dangerous, for the Americans could easily pass
> through the gaps in the sector of the 2nd Machine Gun Company and
> gain our rear. I called the attention of my company commander to my
> apprehensions, whereupon he dispatched a messenger to the Battalion
> Commander with a warning of our critical situation and a request that
> our company be permitted to occupy HILL 2.
>
> Unfortunately, my proposal was not approved. After several fruitless
> attempts on my part to contact the 2nd Machine Gun Company, I tried
> once more to effect a change in our position, by sending a messenger
> to the Battalion Commander. I informed the latter that, unless the gap
> was closed, I would, on my own responsibility, occupy HILL 2 with
> part of the 4th Company. I received the following reply; 'You will hold
> the position to which you have been assigned.'

From this account, Lieutenant Kubler had a good grasp of the desperate
situation his unit was about to encounter, with no contact to their right and Hill
2 being unoccupied by other German forces. It is also apparent that Lieutenant

Vollmer was not so well versed with the situation and was somewhere in the rear. Kubler mentions the 2nd Machine Gun Company that, once again, other modern day researchers have tried to link in with the York fight. This unit were to the right of the 1/120th LIR, but they were positioned at the junction of the North–South Road and the Decauville railway. The gap on Hill 2 is the subject here and the 2nd Machine Gun Company had nothing to do with that or the York fight as has been claimed by others.

There is further confirmation of the units involved in this incident when Kubler states that at daybreak they gained the support of one company of the 210th RIR and some Bavarian sappers.

He continues:

> At that hour, First Lieutenant Vollmer, the Battalion Commander, accompanied by the adjutant, Lieutenant Glass, called on us to inspect our position. Just at that moment a tremendous bedlam broke loose in the rear. The American artillery isolated us by delivering a heavy barrage on HILL 2. Showered with rifle grenades, our company lost a considerable number of dead and wounded, The Battalion Commander ordered me immediately to defend the edge of the woods with my shock troop; while he and my company commander intended to repulse the Americans with the other officers and men, that is, the remainder of the 4th Company, the 210th Reserve Infantry and the Bavarian sappers.

Kubler has established Lieutenant Vollmer's position in the rear with Endriss, the 210th RIR and the 7th Bavarian Mineur Company trying to organise them for a counter-attack.

Again, Kubler states:

> … things did not look right to me; placing Warrant Officer Haegle in charge of my shock troop, I left with two men to reconnoitre the situation. We were barely 100 metres away from my shock troop when, all of the sudden, we found ourselves surrounded by American soldiers with their fixed bayonets trained on us. The enemy challenged us to surrender. Realising that resistance was of no avail, I accepted the better fate.

From this point on, I wish to contradict the description given in the Swedish newspaper. Three Americans accompanied us three prisoners to the rear; while the enemy soldiers continued to advance against my shock troop. On a stretch 20 metres long, I passed at least 20 Americans. I noticed at least one squad of American soldiers at the exit of the woods, standing in a trench formerly occupied by a light machine gun of my company; further I saw Lieutenant Vollmer and the other officers surrounded by eight Americans who, flourishing their pistols, were describing a regular Indian dance round their prisoners.

Kubler goes on to describe the trench near the 2nd Battalion 329th C.P.:

I met Lieutenant Vollmer again at VARENNES and asked him how it happened that his men did not move up to support us. He replied that the 210th and the sappers were so demoralised that he had to threaten the men with his pistol before they would advance. Naturally, this confused also the men of the 4th Company.[10]

The next statement is from an unnamed soldier of the 4th Company, 120th LIR:

We were about to hurry back to our company, when about eight Americans came running down the hill in our rear.
    The enemy kept firing on us and killed several men of our party. In other words, they did not capture us, while we were drinking coffee; that is a lie. Shortly after we were captured, a company of sappers appeared on top of the hill, from which point they could see us and the American soldiers.
    The Sapper Company opened fire on us, but ceased firing when we called to them. Before long, the sappers too were driven towards us in the ravine; thus the number of prisoners became still greater.

It is extremely unfortunate that this soldier is not named. His statement presents a picture that matches the American accounts, that the incident took place in a ravine; the American patrol came running down the hill towards them and he says the Bavarians were on the ridge above them and were eventually forced down the hill, increasing the number of German prisoners.

And now we read what Lieutenant Thoma of the 7th Bavarian Mineur Company says:

I will gladly describe the details of my capture, so far as I remember them, although I can contribute but little toward explaining the article which appeared in the Swedish newspaper.

During the night of 7–8 October, two platoons of my company, including myself, were placed at the disposal of the 120th Wuerttemberg Landwehr Infantry and assigned to the command of First Lieutenant (Reserve) Vollmer. At about 8:00 A.M., October 8 Lieutenant Vollmer ordered me to fill a wide gap which existed in our firing line. I advanced with one platoon, while holding the other platoon in reserve behind a slope until I had reconnoitred the situation. We passed an infantry regiment with a high regimental number; I think it was the 210th Reserve Infantry. We were surprised at the indifference and lack of precaution exhibited by these troops; the men had taken off their belts and side arms and were eating breakfast.

The firing line was located on a slope covered with beech trees and undergrowth. On the left flank, I met a machine gun; its crew, I believe, consisted of only one man. This particular point afforded excellent observation. Instructing my platoon leader to send out a connecting patrol to the right and to place his men into position, I decided to remain with the machine gun. We had brought along several boxes of ammunition and, so far as I recall, one or two light machine guns.

I gave orders immediately to open fire on the Americans whom I saw walking about on an open slope to my left. It is possible that, at first, that I fired on American troops who were leading German prisoners to the rear. Naturally, I ceased firing on such targets as soon as I recognized them. I regulated my fire once more; as yet I had not received a message from my platoon leader, although I heard the sound of lively rifle fire from the direction of the platoon.

And so I decided further to reconnoitre the firing line and convince myself that the platoon had taken up the designated position. I had advanced by a few steps, when suddenly I hear shouting in the woods and the command, given in German, 'Take off your belts.' Quickly I gathered together a few of my men and hurried in that direction, all the while calling out loud, 'Don't remove your belts.'

We advanced with fixed bayonets. Suddenly we were face to face with some Americans and their German prisoners; I recognized only several men of my company and the Battalion Commander, Lieutenant Vollmer. I exchanged a few words with Lieutenant Vollmer, but cannot say exactly what these words were. In effect, I called out 'I won't let them capture me.' Vollmer replied something like this, 'It's useless, we are surrounded.' It was too late to withdraw, for several Americans appeared in my rear. And so I was lead off with the other prisoners. Unfortunately, I possess no notes regarding the activities of my company, nor did I keep a diary.[11]

There does not appear to be the cover-up in Thoma's statement that is found in the other senior leader statements. Thoma commanded two platoons of *mineurs*, or sappers, who were being used as replacements to fill the growing gap in the front line following the infantry casualties.

We next look at Lieutenant Thoma's statement that he made in 1919, just after his release from a prisoner of war camp. We can compare what he said then to what he said in the 1929 Reichsarchiv statement above. In the latter statement, Thoma notes that he placed his unit within proximity of the 210th RIR and the 210th soldiers were not in a state of readiness for battle. He goes on to say that he moved forward and left one platoon in reserve on a slope. The unnamed soldier's statement talks of the Bavarians being on a ridge. This agrees with the 82nd Division history in describing the soldiers on the 'western facing slope' that fired on the patrol as they were lining up the prisoners initially captured. Lieutenant Thoma agrees with Lieutenant Vollmer when they write about accidentally firing on German prisoners of war being evacuated from the hill on his left front, (the 125th LIR soldiers on Hill 167). Again, Thoma agrees with Vollmer regarding an exchange between the two that resulted in Thoma's surrender.

There were several German soldiers from the ranks who were interviewed. The soldiers who gave the statements are from the 7th Company, 125th LIR, who were on Hill 167 when the fight took place. A 125th LIR officer had been mentioned as being one of the other prisoners assembled at the 328th C.P.. It is apparent that the

Reichsarchiv left no stone unturned in attempting to find out all those who had been present during this event, yet there are no statements in the report from anyone in the 125th LIR or the 2nd Machine Gun Company. This is probably because the Reichsarchiv decided that the soldiers from the 125th LIR and the 2nd Machine Gun Company played no part in this specific incident. It is equally interesting that there are no statements from men of the 210th RIR or from the 1st Machine Gun Company, who are being documented as being captured or killed during this event. From what we know there were only a small number of men, perhaps twenty to twenty-five, from the 210th present and we have no way of knowing from surviving documents if an officer from that unit was present. The two non-commissioned officers captured from the 1st Machine Gun Company are documented in their unit's war diary and agree with the earlier statement placing Willig and Kirchner at the scene, yet there are no statements in the Reichsarchiv report.

It must be said, however, that the post-8 October fate of the German survivors and the ability of the Reichsarchiv to successfully contact these men, even if they survived the war, would have been an immense task. One gets the feeling that there appeared to be an officer corps attitude on behalf of the Reichsarchiv in the investigation of this incident.

These are the German soldiers interviewed by the Reichsarchiv, but their statements are not included in their report:

Medical Soldier Breitweg [21 February 1929]
Private Scheurmann, 4th Machine Gun Company [11 February 1929]
Private Hirsch, 2nd Machine Gun Company [12 February 1929]
Sergeant Beck, 7th Company [23 October 1928]
Private Fetzer, 7th Company [25 February 1929]

Lieutenant Thoma's 1919 statement follows:

> Lieutenant Thoma, 7th Bavarian Mineur Company, statement taken
> by the Bavarian Military in 1919.
> Landwehr – Lieutenant Thoma
> To: Bezirks-Kommando 3 Muenchen,
> Hauptmeldeamt.
> Subject: Capture
> Re. K.M.F. 100443 dated 25 August 1919

To a. During the night of 7/8 October 1918 two platoons of the Company in which I served were assigned to the Wuerttemberg Landwehr Infantry Regiment No. 122 [2 Wuerttemberg Landwehr Division], subordinate to the Battalion of First Lieutenant R. Vollmer. On 8 October at about 8:00 o'clock in the morning First Lieutenant Vollmer gave the order to occupy a large gap in the front line. I went forward with my platoon. I gave instructions to the second platoon to remain behind a slope and await further orders until the First Platoon was positioned. The front line lay on a slope covered in bushes and dense underbrush. On the left flank of the gap I encountered a heavy machine gun, with little ammunition, which was manned by infantry. From this ridge one had a good overview.

I ordered the platoon leader to send a liaison patrol to the right and to position his platoon as ordered. At first I stayed back with the heavy machine gun and saw that on the opposite hill, further to the left of us, German prisoners were already being led away. We had brought several cases of machine gun ammunition and I ordered them right away to fire at the advancing Americans to the left front of our position.

Suddenly a call rang from my right, 'Unbuckle everything' I immediately ran in that direction with my orderly; after about 100 metres I met some German prisoners, including my battalion commander. I called to First Lieutenant Vollmer, 'I will not let myself get captured.' He replied, 'It is useless, we are surrounded. I will take responsibility.' Since an escape to the rear was impossible, I let myself be captured.

To b. Answered with question a

To c. N/A

To d. During our march back we all noticed the immense amount of men and material – weapons of the Americans. The column of cars was kilometers long.

To e. Shortly after being taken prisoner I saw how officers' epaulets and Iron Cross First Class were being torn off by the American soldiers. The accommodations of the German enlisted soldiers, in part including those with high fever, in an American field hospital, the name of which I was never able to find out, were unfit for human habitation. The enlisted had to spend their nights on the stone floors of half constructed barracks, with no windows and only one or two blankets. I was in this field hospital from 13 to 28 October, 1918. I have no particular complaints about my treatment.

To f. I witnessed the behaviour of our people to be generally worthy.

To g. N/A

To h. No

To i. Home address: Forester Thoma, Gotzing, Post Thalham

To k. N/A

11 October, 1919

Thoma

(signed)

This is an official translation of the document. All the documents Posey obtained from the German archives have been translated by a German court-appointed translator and are therefore accurate in that they would be acceptable to a German court of law. The court-appointed translator seal can be found in the lower right corner. This is emphasised because the Nolan Group believe that previous attempts at locating the true location of the York fight have resulted in inaccurate and misleading translations.

It has been very necessary to present a full picture of the German accounts. It is important for the reader to understand what the Germans thought what was happening to them and how this detail was recorded into their unit histories. It can be ascertained that the German archival documents are not as accurate as some would have us believe.

The incorrect location of the present-day monument is the result of someone saying that the crucial key to the discovery of the York fight site are the German records. From what has been ascertained thus far, there is nothing in the 1929 German rebuttal or in the German unit diaries or personal statements that suggest the fight could not have taken place anywhere else other than where the American accounts agree it did, in the wooded ravine as discovered by the Nolan Group.

Landwehr-Lieutenant Thoma

To:
Bezirks-Kommando 3 Muenchen
Hauptmeldeamt

Subject:
Capture
re. K. M. F. 100443 dated 25 August 1919

19.

to a.   During the night of 7/8 October 1918 two platoons of the Company in which I served were assigned to the Wuerttemberg Landwehr Infantry Regiment No. 122 (2. Wuerttemberg Landwehr Division), subordinate to the Battalion of First Lieutenant R. Vollmer. On 8 October at about 8:00 o'clock in the morning First Lieutenant Vollmer gave the order to occupy a large gap in the front line. I went forward with my platoon. I gave instructions to the second Platoon to remain behind a slope and await further orders until the First Platoon was positioned. The front line lay on a slope covered in bushes and dense underbrush. On the left flank of the gap I encountered a heavy machine gun, with little ammunition, which was manned by infantry. From this ridge one had a good overview. I ordered the platoon leader to send a liaison patrol to the right and to position his platoon as ordered. At first I stayed back with the heavy machine gun and saw that on the opposite hill, further to the left of us, German prisoners were already being led away. We had brought several cases of machine gun ammunition and I ordered them right away to fire at the advancing Americans to the left front of our position. Lively rifle fire was heard to the right rear of our position. Suddenly a call rang from my right: "Unbuckle everything" I immediately ran in that direction with my orderly; after about 100 meters I met some German prisoners, including my battalion commander. I called to First Lieutenant Vollmer: "I will not let myself get captured" He replied: "It is useless, we are surrounded. I will take responsibility." Since an escape to the rear was impossible I let myself be captured.

to b.   Answered with question a

to c.   N/A

to d.   During our march back we all noticed the immense amount of men and materiel - weapons of the Americans. The column of cars was kilometers long.

to e.   Shortly after being taken prisoner I saw how officers' epaulets and Iron Cross First Class were being torn off by the American soldiers. The accommodations of the German enlisted soldiers, in part including those with high fever, in an American field

1

Fig. 6: Official translation of Lieutenant Thoma's statement.

hospital, the name of which I was never able to find out, were unfit for human habitation. The enlisted had to spend their nights on the stone floors of half constructed barracks, with no windows and only one or two blankets. I was in this field hospital from 13 to 28 October, 1918. I have no particular complaints about my treatment.

to f.   I witnessed the behavior of our people to be generally worthy.

to g.   N/A

to h.   No

to i.   Home address: Forester Thoma, Gotzing, Post Thalham

to k.   N/A

11 October. 1919

Thoma
(Signed)

Als in Bayern öffentlich bestellter und allgemein beeidigter Übersetzer für die englische Sprache bestätige ich: Vorstehende Übersetzung der mir als digitale Datei vorliegenden Abschrift in deutscher Sprache ist richtig und vollständig.
Langenzenn, den 31.03.2009

As a translator for the English language publicly appointed and sworn in the state of Bavaria, I herewith certify: The above translation, for which the digital files of the German transcript were presented to me, is correct and complete.
Langenzenn, Germany,
31 March 2009

Fig. 7: Page two of Thoma's statement.

There was an 'X' on the German map, but it is known to be incorrect (see Map 16). Other researchers have attached importance to the mark. It is not certain whether the Germans really had a clue as to where they were, or more likely, because of the discomfort caused by the Swedish newspaper article, they intentionally placed the fight *closer* to the main attack of 2nd Battalion, 328th Infantry, to illustrate that it was a larger force than the seventeen-man patrol that had caused them such embarrassment.

Our first archival document is the 120th LIR history. This was officially translated by a German-court appointed translator.

The following is an excerpt from the 120th LIR regimental history describing the night of 7 October:

Fig. 8: A Bavarian sapper. Their buttons were different to all other German units and were embossed with the Bavarian rampant lion. The only Bavarian unit in the 2nd Landwehr sector was BMK 7, Lieutenant Thoma's unit. A button was discovered on the slope at the Nolan Group site. (Posey)

…While these reserves were approaching, the 1st Battalion, 120th Landwehr was pulled forward from the Humserberg into the valley west of Chatel, and together with local reserves of the 125th Landwehr, and with the 210th Infantry Regiment (150 rifles), which had just arrived by motor truck, were to attack Schoene Aussicht. In heavy enemy artillery fire that was placed on the southern slope of the Humserberg the companies of the battalion led by Lieutenant Vollmer had lost cohesion, and it was only during the course of the night that they could re-establish contact with the Battalion Commander …

So at the end of the day the Hohenbornhoehe was held, but the Americans were in possession of Schoene Aussicht. And that was bad. The danger which threatened the rear could not be countered by reserves. Battalion Krimmel was engaged up to the last man, the 1st Battalion was scattered during the advance, and, based on what could be seen and heard, little could be expected of the few remaining men from the 210th Regiment lying in the meadows in the direction of Chatel.[12]

In summary: The 2nd LDW Division was pulling their reserves from the Humserberg and sending them in the direction of Chátel-Chéhéry, including Lieutenant Vollmer's 1st Battalion, 120th LIR. It would seem Vollmer had a bad night on the slope of the Humserberg. One also gets the impression that the few remaining men of the 210th RIR did not intend much involvement.

The history continues the morning of 8 October:

… The 4th Company from the 1st Battalion had finally arrived. They lay in the meadows in the direction of Chatel. First Lieutenant Vollmer went up to them; he had spent the night with Captain Krimmel. Suddenly, through the fog, Captain Krimmel heard the sound of loud infantry combat coming from the valley. Ricochets whistle through the air. That lasted some time then it became quiet.

The flank security element of the 6th Company reported an enemy surprise attack. Soon afterwards individual men from the 4th Company came up and reported that their company and men from the 210th Regiment had been attacked with surprise, that the company commander Lieutenant Endriss had been killed, and that the company had been reduced to stragglers or captured. Lieutenant Vollmer also fell into the hands of the Americans. Now the situation was worse than ever, bad news followed more bad news. From Chatel and from Schoene Aussicht heavy enemy columns penetrated, following the course of the Schiesstalmulde and Boulasson creek through the woods towards the North – South Road.

In the next document, there is an interesting message sent by pigeon on 7 October that contradicts some statements made by a modern researcher, who claims that Vollmer was preparing to retake Schlossberg (Hill 223) when the York fight took place. Reading the following extract from the 2nd LDW Division war diary, it looks more as though the attack on the hill was being cancelled.

4:50 P.M.

Just now a report came from my right flank that the enemy is pushing through there and has taken the greater part of 12th Company during hand to hand combat. Have sent the 7th Company to counter this, but its strength is just 1 platoon. Given the circumstances I have told 1st Lieutenant Vollmer (1/120) he should delay assault on Schlossberg, so that the enemy will not be able to break through at his rear. My 10th Company also completely wiped out. Enemy continues to attack repeatedly.[13]

v. Sick. 3rd Battalion, 120th Landwehr Infantry.

At 6.50 P.M., there is another message from von Sick and here he seems a little more sincere about his concerns for any attempt to retake Hill 223. He also gives a little insight into the condition of the German soldiers under his command:

6:50 P.M.

v. Sick, Rittmeister

Situation still threatening, 6th Company, which was to advance to its right flank at the North–South road to counterattack, is left hanging unsecured. Not currently possible to link up with 122nd. Therefore consider Vollmers' Battalion still to be urgently needed. From knowledge of local conditions I allow myself to urgently advise giving up the assault of Schlossberg in order to maintain secure hold on main line of resistance. Repeated enemy attacks, with forces far superior to the weak remnants of the committed companies, hence the need for reserves. The company commanders report their troops at the end of their strength; I must concur, nearly all leaders and non-commissioned officers are wounded. Average strength of companies is 12 – 15 men, thus very thin crews.

III/L120

There follow later messages by von Sick on the morning of 8 October. In this one he says that his right flank was probed; they would be elements of the 28th Division operating south-west of Châtel-Chéhéry. Von Sick indicates that the seventeen men from the 210th RIR went into position 400m north of him in the woods. That is in the wooded ravine:

8:40 A.M.

Carrier pigeon report

Night generally quiet. Towards morning the enemy probed the right flank with patrols. Still quiet at the North–South road before left and center. Battalion is holding its previous line with its own remnants and all companies of the 2nd Battalion.

6:10 in the morning, 2 officers and 15 men of the 210th Regiment arrived at this location and took up positions in the woods 400 metres north of here.

v. Sick 3rd Battalion, 120th Landwehr Infantry Regiment.

In the next message von Sick seems a little confused about the location of the Bavarians. By this time, the York fight had more than likely already happened, which would place the Bavarians no longer in reserve and in the ravine with the 210th RIR. The time, of course, may be the time that the message arrived at the 2nd LDW Division and it may actually have been sent much earlier.

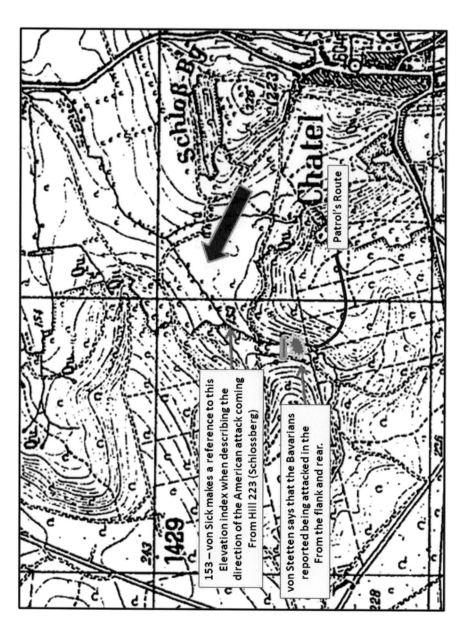

153 – von Sick makes a reference to this Elevation index when describing the direction of the American attack coming From Hill 223 (Schlossberg)

von Stetten says that the Bavarians reported being attacked in the From the flank and rear.

Patrol's Route

Map 25: Field message – Captains von Sick & von Stetten.

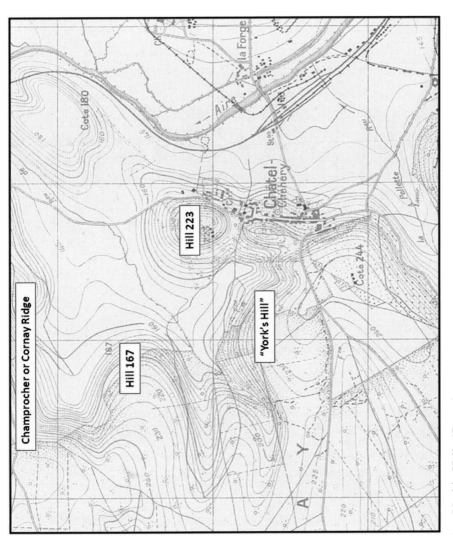

Map 26: Map showing York's Hill. (Posey)

10:15 A.M.

Carrier Pigeon Report

Schlossberg occupied by strong enemy forces, enemy now trying to push through the valley west of Lancon and in the direction of the wood line near '153'. Therefore the 4th Company, 120th Landwehr Infantry Regiment positioned to interdict; to the right, contact with left flank. Left with 7th Company, 125th Landwehr Infantry Regiment, behind it, 2 platoons of the Bavarian Mineur Company as reserves, so no fear of a breakthrough there.

v. Sick 3rd Battalion, 120th Landwehr Infantry Regiment.

Captain von Stetten sends the following report. These field messages along with a few war diary entries are the only real clues that the Germans can give about the fight as it occurred. What is very interesting is the location of the Bavarian Mineurs. He places them north-west of Hohenbornhoehe and says they were struck in the flank and rear. He is, however, misinformed in reporting that von Sick had been captured:

11:30 A.M.

From Captain v. Stetten

Three engineers from the Bavarian 7th Mineur Company returned from capture reported: 'Greater part of the Bavarian 7th Mineur Company captured along with parts of the 120th Landwehr Regiment.' Two officer patrols from the 120th Landwehr Infantry Regiment were sent forward. Rittmeister v. Sick appears to also have been captured. The Bavarian Mineur Company was positioned on the path northwest of Hohnbornhoehe and was struck in the flank and rear.

The German archives provided scans of the original documents and Posey had them officially translated by a German court-appointed translator. Transcribing the Suetterlin old German script into modern text was not an easy task. The list of the German documents may be found in the archives.[14]

In addition, Posey viewed the supplementary information folders for all the units listed as well as unit rosters (for those units that had them). He also viewed the personal folders of Captain von Sick, Lieutenant Vollmer and

Lieutenant Endriss, but, unfortunately, these three folders were missing a great deal of material and there was virtually nothing there that could link these three individuals to being captured, killed or otherwise involved in action at Châtel-Chéhéry other than a unit designation on one or two pieces of paperwork.

Interestingly, the archivist in the Munich archives said that the documents relating to Lieutenant Thoma and the 7th Bavarian Mineur Company had not been viewed for more than thirty years. Thoma's personal folder was intact and Posey located the military document Thoma signed in 1919 that gave details of his capture. The practice in Bavaria at least was that returning prisoner of war officers gave statements relating to their capture to determine if the officer had exhibited cowardice in the events leading to his capture and whether or not he had surrendered without a fight.

Posey has said all the documents he viewed within the archives for the years between 1914 and 1916 were extremely well detailed. However, in 1917 and 1918 this changed; the later documents are poorly written and are often summarised entries that discuss several days of action. Much of the 1918 material was altogether missing; the archivists said it is a common factor in late war German military records for them to be not present.

This is an excerpt from the war diary of the regimental staff of the 120th LDW:

> On 8 October at 9:45 in the morning the enemy attacked from the east in the direction of the Schiesstalmuide – Rezonvaunbachmuide after heavy artillery preparation, here the 4th Company, 120th Landwehr Infantry, 4 platoons of the 7th Bavarian Mineur Company and 210th Reserve Infantry Regiment were overrun and are largely missing since.[15]

The diary continues:

> Evening of 8 October 1918.
> … 4th Company was about 400 metres north [200 metres south of 153 in [square] 1429 Map 1:25,000], assigned to secure the edge of the woods opposite Schlossberg and Chatel in connection with Battalion v. Sick to the right and the 125th Landwehr Infantry to the

left. 1 platoon of the 1st Machine Gun Company is deployed at the crossroads Chatel-Lancon, the remainder to bolster the left flank. Lieutenant Bayer, the Battalion Adjutant, came down with fever due to the continued use of gas and is put into the military hospital. Acting Adjutant Lieutenant Glass.

This account specifically places the 4th Company where they should be, at the mouth of the ravine.

It continues:

8 October 1918

On the morning of 8 October, 1st Lieutenant Vollmer and Acting Adjutant Glass inspected the 4th Company's position. While he was there the enemy was apparently able to bypass and encircle the 34th Company. During the morning a large part of the company, including Lieutenant's Endriss and Kubler, 1st Lieutenant Vollmer and Lieutenant Glass were captured by the Americans. Soon after that a patrol arrived at the place and was only able to locate a number of dead from the 4th Company.

The 2nd Battalion, 120th LIR, war diary does not really provide much information about this since they were merged into the 3rd Battalion under von. Sick. They explain in some detail their losses over these two days and only mention that Vollmer from the 1st Battalion had been captured.[16]

This is an excerpt from the war diary of the 3rd Battalion, 120th LIR, under Lieutenant von Sick. The report is scant:

8 October 1918

The night was generally quiet. Toward morning the enemy probed with patrols against the right flank on the North – South road. The left flank and center are still quiet. The battalion is using its sentinels and all companies of the 2nd Battalion to hold its previous line.

6:10 in the morning the 210th Regiment arrives with a strength of 2 officers and 15 men, and takes up position in the woods 400 metres west of here.

9:45 in the morning. Heavy American attack from the east against the Schiesstalmuide where they succeed in overrunning the 7th Bavarian Mineur Company.

10:40 in the morning, west of the Boulancon creek in direction of the North – South Road, Americans in great numbers.

In view of the imminent danger of being cut off, the companies receive orders around 10:40 in the morning to immediately coordinate the pull out.

11:00 o'clock in the morning. Companies withdraw per orders. Withdrawal takes place without any interference from the enemy on the North – South Road. This road is occupied, with the front facing east, from fork in the road south of Chatel – Lancon along the North – South Road to the benzene-powered rail line 243 – 1329.

In the course of the afternoon, enemy patrols up to the road are repelled.[17]

One piece more of interest is to be found in the war diary of the 1st Machine Gun Company, 120th LIR:

8 October 1918
Nordsuedstrasse crossroads, Chatel Lancon... the enemy is firing on our position with light and medium calibers. Senior Sergeant Kirchner and Sergeant Willig were captured while looking for suitable machine gun positions.[18]

The two German non-commissioned officers, Willig and Kirchner were mentioned in the statements taken in 1929 by the Reichsarchiv. According to those statements, these two men were evidently looking for a suitable place for the weapons and were captured by York and the American patrol.

This is the end of the German accounts. It is necessary now having read the German testimony to return to the newspaper account by George Pattullo. It is a unique account. Pattullo was on the ground with York just a short time after the event and as such it is valuable. His description of the topography should be viewed closely and compared with German statements.

This is what Pattullo said in relation to this aspect when advancing on the outward section of the raid:

> About two-thirds of the way up the hill they came upon an old wide trench, probably built by the French earlier in the war. They entered this and followed it. The clamor of the fight on the other side of the hill now grew less ... the trench led over the crest. Going warily in single file ... the detachment penetrated upward through the dense woods and began to descend the other slope ...[19]

Lieutenant Glass, in his rebuttal statement of 1929, confirms the location of a 'trench' on the hill that they passed as they were being removed from the battlefield as prisoners. This is a comparison between Pattullo's article and the account of Lieutenant Glass:

> Lieutenant Glass, Adjutant, 1st Battalion 120th LDW
> ... Either in the course of this incident or a few steps farther on, we saw a trench before us. Approximately one meter deep, this trench was crowded with American troops standing not only man to man, but also in double rank ...
> ... We crossed the trench and reached the meadow which I had observed while on reconnaissance. Here we saw a group of some 20 or 30 American soldiers. Additional prisoners were brought up; it is not impossible that Corporal York gradually rolled up the 4th Company from the flank and rear ...

And the capture of Lieutenant Thoma, which is this incident as described in the following excerpt from the Pattullo article:

> It was impossible to see where they were going, on account of the thick brush, but York knew that the direction was right to bring them out on the side of the hill where the Americans ought to have established a post of command by this time. A hundred yards or more, and they were challenged. They had stumbled upon another boche machinegun nest. York thrust the major in front of him, covered the crew with his

Fig. 9: Photograph of the landscape from Hill 223 and York's description of the 'little rise'. The boundary ditch in which the German machine gun was firing from is in the area below the red arrow. (Posey)

pistol and ordered them to surrender. They abandoned their weapons and equipment and joined the prisoners.

During the journey back they flushed several more nests. In one the crew offered resistance. 'I had to shoot a man there,' remarked York regretfully.

The Pattullo article concludes thus:

There on the scene of the fight at the foot of York's Hill are six graves where our dead lie buried. Simple wooden crosses mark them, and at the head repose the helmets, rifles and belts of the soldiers of the soldiers who gave their lives. Close beside their last resting place purls a tiny stream, and over the wooded hills broods a cathedral hush.

Fig. 10: Grave of Corporal Murray Savage, Killed in action 8 October 1918. (Private 1st Class F.C. Phillips, U.S. Army Signals, 1919)

Fig. 11: Graves of Privates Swanson, Wareing, Weiler & Dymowski. (Phillips, 1919)

PART II

The Discovery of the York Fight Location

'Facts do not cease to exist because they are ignored.'

Aldous Huxley.

Chapter 12

The Beattie/Bowman Field Study

Lieutenant-Colonel Taylor V. Beattie was a regular Army special forces officer with an impressive service record, serving in Bosnia, Liberia, Panama, Germany, Turkey and Italy. His colleague, Major Ronald Bowman, was an Army reserve special forces officer working as a resource management officer for Special Operations Command in Korea. It was Major Bowman who introduced Lieutenant-Colonel Beattie to the battlefields of the First World War whilst serving in Stuttgart, Germany.[1]

Beattie wrote an article for *Army History*, which is the shop window magazine for Army military matters in the United States:

> Since the Spring of 1994 we have made frequent visits to the ravine, tracing and attempting to reconstruct the events of the day. Through the course of these visits to the area, we believe we have identified the key positions from which the German machine guns once controlled the valley. Given these positions relative to the terrain, archaeological evidence, and the tactical situation as presented though military records, we have been able to postulate where, why and how certain events unfolded on that foggy morning of 8 October 1918.[2]

The Beattie/Bowman investigation was a professional attempt to locate York's firing position. They did locate the German fighting positions on top of Hill 223, finding many German Mauser shell casings. This would have been the position the Germans held above the village of Châtel-Chéhéry on 7 October 1918 when the American attack took place on the village.

The two officers admitted they were not trained historians but soldiers. They applied the tactical concepts of METT-T and OCOKA [Mission, Enemy, Terrain and weather, Troops and Time available and Observation and Fields of fire, Cover and concealment, Obstacles, Key terrain and Avenues of approach.] These same principles were used several years later by Lieutenant-Colonel Mastriano and the SYDE.

Beattie and Bowman asked themselves the question, 'How did York do it?' They entered 'the ravine' applying the doctrines as explained above:

> ... understanding of the 'military use of terrain' and the subtle significance in the location of archaeological evidence relative to the tactics, techniques, and procedures of the day. In our analysis of the situation, we pieced all these and other factors together to develop a picture of how events could have unfolded on a foggy fall morning in 1918. The archaeological evidence included actual prepared fighting positions, rolls of barbed wire, discarded ammunition cans, shell casings, a German ration spoon, and even some discarded rails from the Decauville field railroad.[3]

It is known the area where they were searching was very close to the same area where the SYDE later claimed that they, with 100 per cent certainty, had located York's firing position. The presence of the shell casings found by Beattie and Bowman served to corroborate the findings of the Nolan Group and the German .77mm gun positions, discovered close to their site. It is not likely that York and the seventeen-man patrol would have infiltrated anywhere close to those positions in the full face of the American 2nd Battalion attack.

At no stage in his 2000 *Army History* article does Beattie make any claims to have found the York firing site. He wrote another article for the magazine in the winter of 2008. This was after the Nolan Group's discovery of the unit collar disk and after the SYDE claim to have discovered the site. In this article Beattie states that he and Bowman did not use metal detectors as they realised that there were strict regulations in force for such unauthorised activities on the French battlefields that would result in impoundment of vehicles and equipment. This, most sensibly, was a risk they were not prepared to take. In his later article, Beattie refers to the investigation by the SYDE and their team of military officers, veterans and battlefield archaeologists. He wrote of the excavation of four .45 calibre slugs, and twenty-one .45 calibre shell casings that was believed to come from the Colt pistol used by York.

Lieutenant-Colonel Beattie's article is well constructed and he makes mention of the SYDE claims in that they:

> uncovered exhaustive documentation of the disposition of the German forces in the ravine on the morning of 8 October 1918.[4]

It appears to be regrettable that Beattie chose to dismiss the Danforth/Buxton 1929 map, stating the location as annotated and 'was not supportable from a military standpoint', whatever that may mean; possibly that it didn't fit in with the rigid military doctrine that both he, and later, the SYDE placed so much importance in. It follows that Beattie is of the view that the SYDE claims to have discovered the fight location are correct because it agrees with the position that he and Bowman had selected in 2000. In fairness, this article appeared in print the year before the Nolan Group made the compelling discovery of the temporary graves and the other G Company 328th artefacts.

In his summation of the two team findings, Beattie is honest, admitting to being clearly biased in the debate because:

> Mastriano's SYDE report is backstopped by superb German archival research and is in keeping with the military situation of the day. In other words, it is supportable from a military standpoint. The conclusions of the report mesh with documented military history. German unit dispositions, tactical analysis, terrain analysis and battlefield archeology to pinpoint key locations associated with York's actions in the ravine. It is a compelling and well documented argument. In fairness to both sides, I have read Mastriano's report in its entirety. The Nolan Group issued a comprehensive report in 2007. It reflects a tremendous amount of disciplined research, analysis and purposeful direction.[5]

It would seem that too much emphasis has been placed on the METT-T, OCOKA principles by the military teams. It may have been an aide to senior officers in planning operations, but not to a seventeen-man patrol in 1918 who had to act quickly to destroy enemy machine guns. There is no evidence either that those who detailed the patrol insertion ever considered the principles.

Brigadier Ray McNab states:

> ... a big difference between a deliberate application process [that may
> use such refinements as tools] and quick attack, as I suspect actually
> happened. And I wonder if Corporal York would have been trained in
> such techniques, let alone use them.[6]

Beattie concludes in his 2008 article that he felt the ravine might still hold
at least one uncovered indicator that could provide a persuasive edge to
the argument over location. He writes that the temporary burial site of
Murray Savage may have left a man-sized scar in the ground. Perhaps,
Beattie states:

> the sweep of an authorised metal detector could reveal a metal button,
> collar disk, rank or identification tag, or some other piece of personal
> gear that would provide convincing evidence about the origins of that
> hole. Such an artefact could link the scar in the ravine to the temporary
> grave of Corporal Savage, who apparently was buried within feet of
> where he had been shot.[7]

The Nolan Group did find personal items of kit and much more in 2009 during
Phase III, which provided critical evidence that the York fight took place in the
ravine where they said it happened.

Stephan van Meulebrouck is a freelance journalist and historian from the
Netherlands who had visited the site where the Nolan Group were working
in 2009. He decided to write an article on York and his paper was to become
an intriguing piece of investigative journalism. He approached many people
and interviewed them, one such individual being Taylor Beattie. During the
interview, Beattie told van Meulebrouck that he appreciated Nolan's academic
approach but he could not support the theory. In his view, the Danforth/
Buxton map did not match the terrain since there were many battles there
afterwards. Beattie was not able to provide any explanation for the six graves
and the conclusions of the Nolan Group (The discovery of the graves came
after Beattie's article in *Unknown Soldiers*). He believes there was more than
one patrol, so the finds could indicate another unit of the 2nd Battalion.

However, he goes on to criticise the SYDE approach, saying that Mastriano's report lacked proper annotation:

> This is actually one of the things I warned Mastriano about. Somebody should be able to retrace what he did.[8]

It seems Beattie believes considerable additional research should have been carried out before any memorial was placed. This seemingly did not take place. The SYDE levelled the site with a bulldozer, ostensibly to make room for the memorial, at the same time, rendering any further archaeological investigation impossible. In Taylor Beattie's view the site should have been preserved. No one ever said to Mastriano, Beattie continued, 'Wait a minute, there's another side to it. He just bulldozed through.' After the interview, Beattie stated:

> One of the things why I think nobody ever questions what Mastriano is doing is that he brings in Christianity and religion, that he says he contributed everything he did to God.[9]

Lieutenant-Colonel Taylor Beattie continues to support the SYDE claim for their location. Beattie told van Meulebrouck that he had been Mastriano's instructor at the Joint Forces Staff College in Virginia. During this time Beattie showed Mastriano the location where he thought the York fight took place and that location was depicted in the SYDE report two years later, but with no special mention of Beattie. Only after mentioning this to Mastriano did Mastriano include Beattie as a reference. That SYDE report was taken down from their website and can no longer be viewed.

Chapter 13

The Nolan Group Objectives

The area the Nolan Group was to search around Châtel-Chéhéry was subjected to fighting during one day, 8 October 1918, which was the day of the York patrol encounter with the Germans. This meant that all battlefield artefacts discovered came from the fighting on that day and, unlike other Great War battlefield sites, they cannot be confused with detritus from countless earlier engagements. Additionally, the area identified by the Nolan Group as being the site where York fought was not on the route of the main assault. There was no fighting in that ravine at any time later that day or, contrary to the comments of other observers, at any time afterwards.

There have been other attempts to locate the site where York's fight took place. The first was the Bowman/Beattie search in 2001. They made their evaluation by adopting the METT-T application. These doctrines, however, proved unhelpful and failed to locate York's fight site, or indeed the location of the Germans involved in the York confrontation.

Around the same time that the Nolan Group was undertaking research Lieutenant-Colonel Mastriano of the U.S. Army was searching for the York site. As already explained, he is a disciple of Bowman/Beattie's same principles of METT-T. His commitment to that methodology may well have contributed, in part, to him placing York in the wrong area. His team proclaimed that they had discovered the site of York's battle, yet the American official histories place Mastriano's site in the full face of the 2nd Battalion attack. The memorial that was subsequently erected on the site leaves the visitor with the impression that the York fight took place there.

What follows will describe the meticulous application to detail that was adopted at the outset by the Nolan Group. It will demonstrate that amongst the many hundreds of artefacts discovered, there is extremely sound evidence, supported by historical documentation, which has been available for all to examine and which proves beyond reasonable doubt that York fought his fight several hundred metres from the site declared by SYDE. There has been a distortion in history and this book will serve to correct it, allowing the reader to make his own judgement. One may ask the question, as indeed some senior U.S. Army observers have asked, 'What is the historical significance of the different interpretations regarding the location of the York action?' 'How would they change our understanding of the entire action?'[1] This question will be answered later, but the Nolan Group believe that if the SYDE and other research group interpretations of the location of the York site are accepted as correct then the official histories describing the 2nd Battalion battle at Châtel-Chéhéry would have to be rewritten.

The idea of searching for the Sergeant York fight site was born whilst drinking a beer. Two good friends from America and England sat in the twilight of a summer's evening in Lincolnshire, England, discussing their favourite subject, the Great War. The exploits of Alvin C. York arose. They discussed the findings of the Beattie/Bowman article that had appeared in an edition of *Army History* magazine in 2000, and there and then they decided that they would form a team and search for the site where Sergeant Alvin York fought in France in 1918. This meeting between Tom Nolan and Michael Kelly took place in 2004, and it led to the eventual formation of a professional team of highly experienced and motivated academics and individuals who would give of their time freely in an investigation that would last for six years.

A preliminary visit to France to set the whole operation in motion was carried out. Permission had to be sought from many different landowners around Châtel-Chéhéry. This was undertaken by Michael Kelly and Frédéric Castier, who at the time was the operations officer for the McCormick Tribune Foundation and who now is a counsellor for the national chairman of Le Souvenir Français, the French war memorials association.

A permit was also required from the Champagne Regional Archaeology Department to conduct any archaeological procedures in France. French laws are strict and metal detecting activity where permission has not been given can attract arrest and seizure of equipment. Alain Jacques, the regional archaeologist for Arras, and Yves Desfossés, the Champagne–Ardenne regional archaeologist, in whose area the York site was located, helped the Nolan Group to gain this permission and Desfossés was the archaeologist assigned to the team from the second phase onwards. He proved to be an asset to the team, willing to loan mechanical equipment and archaeologists who worked closely with James Legg, the Nolan Group archaeologist.

Doctor Tom Nolan's discipline is geography. Before his retirement, he was the Director of the Laboratory for Spatial Technology in the Department of Geo-Sciences at Middle Tennessee State University. He decided the purpose of the study, which was to locate Alvin York's firing position during his Medal of Honor action. In his own words:

> Geographic Information Science (GIS) technology will be used to integrate historic maps, reports and other documents in a spatial database that will model the landscape as it was in October 1918. Global Positioning Systems (GPS) technology will be used to navigate to York's most probable position based on historical spatial data. A metal detector will be used to locate artefacts related to the fight. The artefacts will be mapped using GPS and added to the spatial database. GIS will be used to analyse the spatial data to determine the most probable location of Alvin York's firing position.[2]

Doctor Michael Birdwell is professor of history at Tennessee Tech. He is the curator of the Sergeant York papers on behalf of the Sergeant York Foundation, and he is a lifetime follower of Alvin York, his legacy and culture. This vast collection of documents, held by the Foundation, consists of details of the more intimate and unknown segments of York's history and life, much of which has never been published. Birdwell has collated information about Alvin C. York for use within the project and was with the team on both phase one and two field investigations.

Chapter 14

Phase I of Field Study, 3–9 March 2006

There were three periods of on-site investigation between 2006 and 2009. During these phases, more than 2,600 artefacts were discovered, the majority from the 2009 expedition. The first phase commenced on 3 March 2006. The team consisted of Doctor Tom Nolan, Doctor Michael Birdwell, David Currey, a historian and film-maker from Tennessee, Michael Kelly and Fred Castiér. They started searching along the stream running north–south, corresponding with Alvin York's description of the contact point. The conditions were hardly perfect, about 4in of snow lay on the ground and daytime temperatures hardly ever rose above freezing. The team had gained permission from the Champagne-Ardenne regional archaeologist, Yves Desfossés, to conduct a surface metal detector study in a specific area, as can be seen on this map.

Interest was shown from the current mayor of the village, Roland Destenay and the then mayor of Fléville, Damien Georges, who is now the project manager at the Studies Agency Bourgogne, Champagne Ardenne Region, in the Office National des Forêts. Damien assisted in explaining some topographical features in the forest; one feature was a ditch that ran up the side of a hill. The team had mistaken this for an old trench but Mons. Georges explained it was an ancient ditch that had been constructed pre-First World War to mark the boundary between communal forest land and private property. These features were used tactically during the war by both sides as they were ready-made trenches.

Little was found on the first day, but on the second it was decided to continue exploration in this area as it did link up with the detail on the Danforth map from 1929.

The boundary ditch referred to faced Hill 223, the direction from where the American attack came on 8 October (see Fig. 5). It was not long before a German machine gun point was detected in the boundary ditch. There were 161 7.92mm expended cartridges, several unfired cartridges, a muzzle

Study Area For Alvin York Project

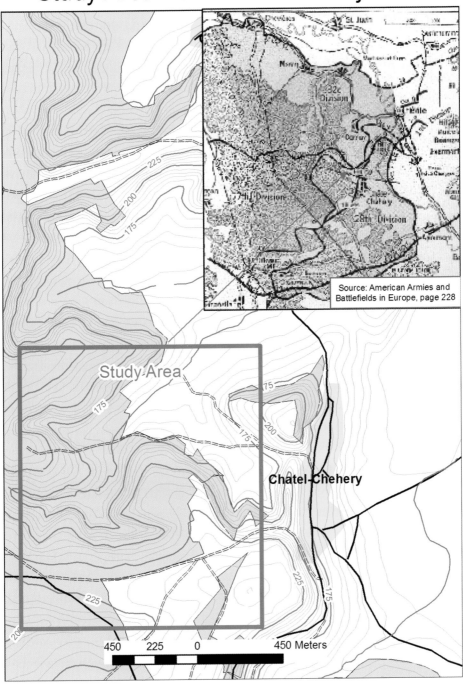

Source: American Armies and Battlefields in Europe, page 228

Study Area

Chatel-Chehery

450   225   0   450 Meters

Map 27: Study area for Alvin York Project. (Doctor Nolan)

protector for a Gewehr 98 rifle, and a German mess tin. This was clearly one of the German machine gun posts that had wreaked havoc on the attacking Americans and which gave the Germans an excellent field of fire on Hill 223. At the time of the discovery of this machine gun post there were many trees that obscured the field of fire, but on a visit to the site by the author in 2016 many of those trees had been felled, giving an excellent view of Hill 223, as indeed it would have looked in October 1918 (see Fig. 4).

As in all the teams finds, on each occasion, the artefacts were mapped in situ, using during the first phase a Trimble Pathfinder Pro XRS GPS receiver with a TD-2 data collector. The following day, 4 March, the team moved down the slope toward the stream and two full clips of .30-.06 and some fired .30-.06 cases and an empty American brass stripper clip were found. This was an indication that an American soldier had been in action, firing and reloading his weapon. Further finds were made but no .45 cartridges. This was not the York site, albeit, as would be discovered later, it was closer to the scene than was the site of the SYDE claim. The dreary, cold weather continued and there were no more discoveries save for a few items, further .30-.06 cases, and a collection of French Viven Bessiére [VB] rifle grenades.

This field visit served to apprise the team of the topography of the ground and to appreciate the problems that affected the 2nd Battalion on that day. It became much clearer as they stood on the western slope of Hill 223 in driving snow and the extreme conditions as to how the patrol infiltrated the enemy lines and worked behind them. The U.S Army official histories were instrumental in this most important orientation. Criticism has been levelled at the Nolan Group for failing to research the German archives. This was fair comment and at this stage, and leading into to Phase I and Phase II, it was indeed correct. To obtain a full picture of what took place historical accounts from all sides should be explored. The Nolan Group was, however, not based in Europe, and their time on site was taken up purely in site excavation, based upon close examination of the excellent American histories. The SYDE claimed that the German archives sources provided the definitive answer, that their site was the true York fight site. It was as a direct result of this that Brad Posey, fluent in German and living in Germany, two years later accessed the German archives. The results of Posey's visits to the German archives were revealing; this evidence will be produced later.

Chapter 15

Phase II of Field Study, 14–24 November 2006

The second phase was carried out in November 2006. This time, there were some new team members and one was Birger Stichelbaut, a Belgian archaeologist from the University of Ghent. His area of expertise is First World War battlefield interpretation using GIS together with aerial photography. Birger was undertaking his PhD at this time, and his knowledge of First World War aerial photography and his ability to translate those to both modern day and historical mapping was invaluable.

Michael Birdwell again travelled from Tennessee accompanied by Jim Deppen, a tall genial man, a lecturer and historian from Tennessee. Two Englishmen, Eddie Browne and Ian Cobb, joined the team. Ian is ex-military having served with the 1st Battalion, Wessex Regiment, of the British Army. Both men are battlefield explorers seasoned in the use of metal detectors and have a wealth of experience in amateur battlefield archaeology. Michael Kelly was present and Fred Castier, the interpreter, joined the team later. The field work commenced on 15 November 2006. Yves Desfossés brought a backhoe and specialist French archaeologists to excavate an area around the north–south road, where it was felt the action took place close by. However, news had leaked out of the team's presence and a French news film crew were present, so rather than give away any ideas about where team thought was the area where York fought, which would attract the unwanted attentions of trophy seekers, the team started to work on another part of their plan. This was to locate the position of four German 77mm field guns that had been captured on 8 October by the 2nd Battalion. Tom Nolan had received a document from Jimmie Hallis, who worked at the archives of the 82nd Airborne Division Museum at Fort Bragg, North Carolina. This was a transcript of a question and answer held between Major-General Edward Buxton and Major Tillman, commander of the 2nd Battalion 328th Infantry, It reflected the battalion attack on 8 October 1918. Tillman could describe the position of the guns in his account of the attack:

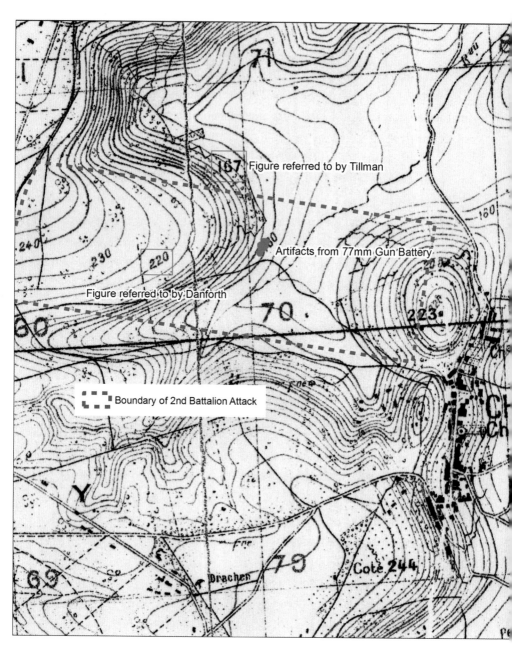

Map 28: Captain Tillman's map for the positions of the German 77mm guns. Map references given by Buxton and Tillman. (Posey)

The fog was clearing up then and up to the point of that Hill, just west of 223-167 – we found there a battery of 77s, 4 guns and about 25 yards to the rear was a signal outfit and trench mortar outfit. 100 yards up the hill was a nest of 25 machine guns causing casualties in the left flank. The right flank got in behind them and cut them off from the rear and they were all captured – 43 men, we took that day between 250 and 275 prisoners. About ten in the morning we got messages that the front line was held up by snipers and machine gun fire from the left flank. One platoon was sent around to protect the left flank and another platoon from Support Company brought up to replace it. This platoon went out and an hour and a half later they brought back 132 prisoners. The platoon was under the command of Sergeant Parsons. Corporal York however is the man who took these prisoners with his one squad. He had only to shoot one officer of the three captured before he took these men. We took 124 machine guns that day. The four 77s were here [pointing to the map] I think caused Col. Blalock that trouble the day before and also cut up the advance Battalion of the 328th in the counter attack. These 132 men were gotten right here [pointing to map].[1]

Discovering the site of the gun position was essential to locate the right flank of the 2nd Battalion attack and it would also confirm the reliability of the 82nd Division records.

Almost immediately upon commencement of the search, three live 77mm projectiles were discovered. The copper driving bands had been chiselled off, almost certainly by post-war salvagers; copper was a valuable commodity to the poor local populace. After further searching, twelve expended 77mm cartridges and seven protective shipping covers for 77mm shell fuses were located. This confirmed the reliability of the source information and fixed the right flank of the battalion attack. This was indeed the position of the four 77mm captured by the 2nd Battalion, and referred to by Major Tillman. This action took place at about the same time the York patrol was fighting on the left flank. Brad Posey was present in 2008 when Mastriano found a 77mm gun position only 25m from the clearing where the SYDE monument is located. There is no mention of any 77mm German gun positions in any SYDE presentations.

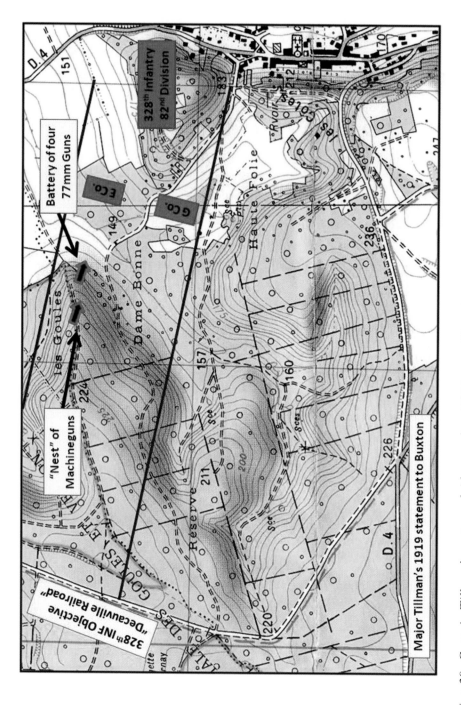

Map 29: Captain Tillman's map overlaid on modern IGN map. (Posey)

Fig. 12: German 77mm site in the foreground. Note the York monument through the trees. (Author, 2016)

Fig. 13: Doctor Nolan at the same 77mm site. (Author)

Fig. 14: Finds (ammunition spacers) from the 77mm German gun site. (Author)

Unlike previous investigative attempts to locate York's position, more importance was placed by the Nolan Group on the historical material that was available. One important document was the Danforth/Buxton map, annotated by the officers independently of each other in 1929 for the re-enactment.

Using this map, the Nolan Group began searching in the area indicated by it. Working on the premise that the American official records indicated that York's fight took place on a *western facing* slope, it wasn't long before the team, thanks to the skill of Eddie Browne and Ian Cobb, started to locate artefacts. Along the creek, the remains of an American cartridge belt with eight full clips of .30-.06 ammunition, loose unfired cartridges, stripper clips, part of a brass cover for a field dressing container, and a pocket knife were discovered. It was thought that this was the position of an American casualty. Artefacts started to be unearthed quickly; a button to an American tunic and some mess utensils were uncovered and soon a backlog of items accrued, all waiting to be mapped on the GIS equipment by Tom Nolan. It proved difficult to map the artefacts

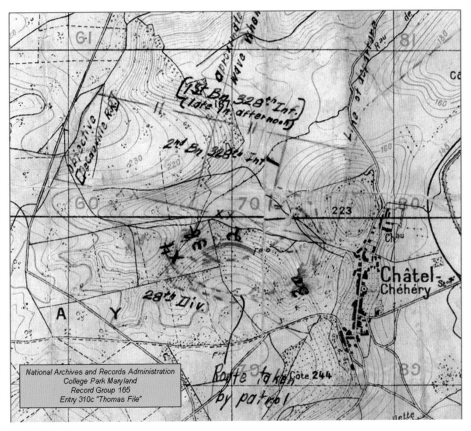

Map 30: Danforth/Buxton 1929 map.

quickly; it didn't help that trees were in full leaf and cover was minimal. Sketchy satellite availability meant that it often took twenty minutes to log a find.

Despite the difficulties, the artefacts kept surfacing; each position was marked by a metal flag or flagging tape, each given an identification number that was resultantly entered in the GPS rover file comment field. The artefact would then be bagged with ID numbers on both the inside and outside of the bag. These artefacts would be identified where possible and at the end of each day photographed and catalogued. At this time, a large amount of expended and unexpended German 7.92mm cartridge cases were discovered at the top of the hill above the ravine. Close by were expended .30-.06 and .45 calibre cartridges along with some 9mm cartridges. It was thought at the time it may have been the site of York's encounter with the German machine gun.

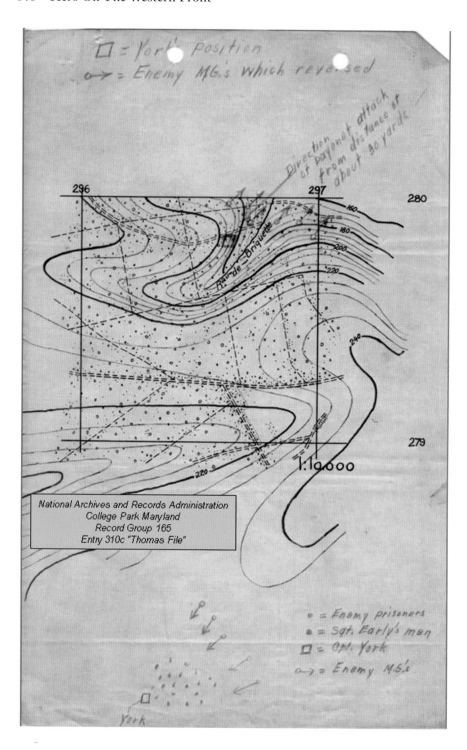

Map 31: Part of Danforth/Buxton map showing York's prisoners scene of capture.

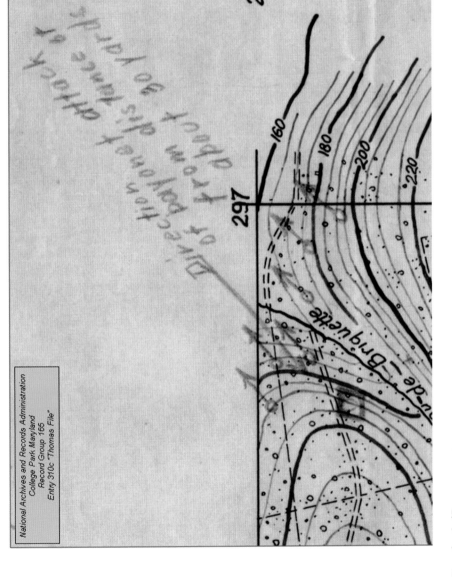

Map 32: Danforth/Buxton map.

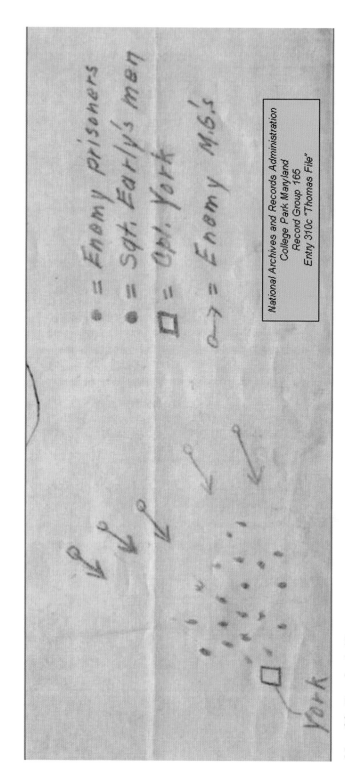

The map legend reads:
- = Enemy prisoners
- = Sgt. Early's men
□ = Cpt. York
o—→ = Enemy M.G.'s

York

National Archives and Records Administration
College Park Maryland
Record Group 165
Entry 310c "Thomas File"

Map 33: Danforth/Buxton map.

It was during this period a bronze American unit collar disc, inscribed with the number '328' crossed rifles and the letter 'G', was found close to the stream, at the bottom of the slope where the German machine gun was located. This was an excellent find, indicating the presence of York's unit, G Company 328th Infantry, at this position. However, the marrying of the two artefact locations, albeit encouraging, was not conclusive; further evidence and corroboration was needed and that would come during the 2009 phase when other parts of the puzzle would fall into place. It must be emphasised once again that, contrary to other field reports, this area saw action on one day only, 8 October 1918. The 2009 phase III would confirm that and reveal much more besides.

Fig. 15: U.S. collar disk, 328th Company G. Found near the creek at the site of the York fight in 2006. (Castier)

Chapter 16

The Brad Posey Story

During 2008, Brad Posey became interested in the SYDE claim to have found the Sergeant York fight site. He visited the site and walked the 'York Trail' as described by the SYDE After returning to his home in Germany, Posey was contacted out of the blue by Lieutenant-Colonel Mastriano by email, who was interested in several First World War U.S. uniforms that Posey was selling. It was established that Mastriano was the person behind the Sergeant York discovery site. Posey returned the email, telling him that he felt his work was of great importance, but there were a few things in his report and conclusions that gave him some doubt. Posey asked if it were possible for him to go to the site and assist with the metal detector search. He told Mastriano that his own experience in metal detecting extended over a period of thirty years in the United States and in Europe, with the last eighteen years exclusively on European battlefields, ranging from the medieval period through to the Second World War. Posey suggested that it was important to search for negative evidence by broadening the search area, with a lack of evidence supporting his claim and giving a clearer picture of the events that took place on that ridge.

On Monday, 7 July 2008, Mastriano telephoned Posey and said he would like to visit to look at the uniforms. They then had a long conversation on the telephone regarding the discovery.

These are the bullet points of that conversation as remembered by Posey:

- Posey asked Mastriano why he did not search a broader area and told him that he thought there should be more German machine gun positions on that ridge. Mastriano replied they had found a lot of evidence of German machine guns, but would usually stop digging after they found enough cartridges to confirm it was a machine gun position. He said that through their research in the archives they had narrowed down the location of the 'York spot' to a specific area and concentrated their efforts there and were not able to broaden their research area.

- Posey asked Mastriano if they had found any .45 magazines and added that he thought there would be at least one or two, since it would have been doubtful York would have had time to put the empty magazines back into his magazine pouch in such a fight. Mastriano told him that they had searched on discriminate [a setting on a metal detector] to avoid ferrous targets such as shovels, shrapnel and other iron or steel artefacts that were not of interest. He added that since this was such an important event, salvage companies probably would have cleared up anything left lying around, including magazines, which would be easy to see.

- Posey asked him about the German and Prussian buttons, belt clasps and emblems that he said he had found. Mastriano told him that no Prussian or Wuerttemberg *gefreite* or sergeant buttons were found; all the buttons they had uncovered had a crown on them, which was issue to all German units. He also said no complete buckles with German state emblems had been found. The only emblem was the crown, which was displayed on the SYDE website.

- Posey asked if Mastriano thought it was possible to return and conduct more metal detector searches and he said that the French authorities were satisfied with his findings. He said that with the upcoming monument dedication, scheduled for 4 October 2008, the French authorities would not authorise any more searches. Brad asked that if he was granted permission, he would really like to go along.

On 10 July 2008 Mastriano visited Posey and looked at his uniforms and equipment. He said he would like to photograph them as this would assist in the identification of artefacts that they had found. He bought a Model 1917 American tunic, which Mastriano said would be donated to a museum in the United States to represent Sergeant York. Again, Posey asked if he could metal detect the area, stating that Mastriano could have anything he found. Four days later, Posey received an email from Mastriano telling him that he had received permission to finish his work in the Argonne, that he would like to invite Brad and his girlfriend, Birgit Anderson, the coming weekend and that he would like to keep this to people he trusted. The final passage stated that it was his final opportunity to secure this part of history before treasure hunters cleared the area.

The following weekend, on 18 July 2008, a group gathered at the site of the newly installed monument near the village of Châtel-Chéhéry. A briefing was carried out by Mastriano in which he gave a brief account of the events of 8 October 1918. Afterwards he stipulated the objectives of the search. These were:

1. To ensure the safety of the Boy Scouts who were conducting work on the trail.
2. To locate as many artefacts as possible that would be sent to a museum in the United States.
3. They wanted to if possible locate Lieutenant Endriss's dog tag since he was said to have been killed there by York whilst leading the bayonet charge.

Mastriano continued that he wanted to break down the teams to cover the following areas:

1. The alleged York spot itself, to which Posey and his partner, Birgit, volunteered.
2. Search around Lieutenant Vollmer's suspected headquarters building, which had been a concrete structure in the meadow, just below the York spot.
3. Search the trench [a boundary ditch], used by the Germans and from where Lieutenant Endress led the bayonet charge.
4. Search the sunken road just above the York spot. Mastriano believed it to have been used as a German trench.
5. Search the machine gun position the SYDE had identified in their report.

Posey noted that the group consisted of the following: A U.S. Army or Air Force officer using a very cheap-looking metal detector with no experience in metal detecting, and a Danish Army officer, a friend of Mastriano's who had served with him in Afghanistan a short time before. He had a very cheap looking metal detector and had no experience in metal detecting. There was also a U.S. Civil Service employee using a very cheap-looking metal detector. He had no experience in metal detecting and he left the site after only a little while. Posey noted that Mastriano was using a White's Spectrum metal detector he had borrowed; normally, he told Posey, he used a Titan 3000XD. Posey and Anderson were using a Fisher CZ-5 metal detector, searching on all metal mode with no discrimination. (This setting allows the operator to receive signals from all metals.)

Before the search was started, everyone was issued with plastic bags and told that any artefacts found at the various locations should be placed in separate bags so they could be labelled later.

Mastriano took Posey and Anderson to the York spot, which was just below the monument. Starting his search, he almost immediately found the three brass pieces to an early war issue [pre-1916] German 'Pickelhaube' helmet chin strap and many unfired German 7.92mm cartridges. Anderson found an expended .45 cartridge right next to a stump that could be seen on the SYDE website with yellow flags in the ground around it. About 10 metres up the slope she recovered a fired .45 calibre projectile in the same area indicated by Mastriano as where the other projectiles were found. In the immediate area around the York spot there were countless iron or ferrous signals, most of which Posey elected not to dig. The few he did were pieces of shrapnel and one fired German 7.92 bullet. He discovered that the German 7.92 projectiles were coated in a layer of tin or some other ferrous metal layer, explaining why there were none recovered by the SYDE or indeed by the Nolan Group except for the single projectile. It had to be assumed that many thousands lay undiscovered since they register as a very small ferrous signal on metal detectors such as the Fisher make Posey was using, or undetectable with machines using a high level of discrimination as the SYDE used. Posey only dug a few of the small ferrous signals since they were in such great abundance throughout the battlefield, and it would have taken many hours to cover small areas to conduct such a thorough grid search. This was evidence that the area was in the midst of a full-scale attack and defensive battle.

When the day ended, Posey and Anderson returned to the monument and gave the artefacts to Mastriano, who put them in a bag and labelled it 'B&B' for Brad and Birgit and 'York Spot'. Mastriano told them he had found a Sergeant York cartridge and bullet. Posey enquired about the twenty-one cartridges that were on the SYDE website and said that with the one they had found, it made twenty-two. Mastriano replied that the division history stated that York had fired at least twenty-one rounds and more than likely had another magazine from which he also fired rounds. This would account for the extras.

Posey asked Mastriano why the hill above the York spot had not been searched; he responded that they were looking for a needle in the haystack and did not have time to look elsewhere. However, he told Posey that they had found a U.S. officer's crossed rifle collar insignia with no regimental number somewhere in the direction of the top of the ridge.

Posey then started up the ridge directly above the York spot. He noticed a significant decrease in non-ferrous signals. He found several fired French 8mm Chauchat projectiles, a few small pieces of brass, copper or zinc artillery fuse/rotating band and a U.S. National Army collar insignia with the nut still attached. Countless other ferrous signals were discounted. This was due to the limited amount of time that was available. It was more desirable to locate additional German machine gun positions on the ridge, thereby obtaining a better understanding of the amount and distribution of other both expended and unfired small arms cartridges and projectiles.

Posey returned to the monument and gave the collar disk to Mastriano, who was very excited when he saw it. He immediately put it away, giving Posey no time to photograph it. Other members returned to the monument having found another double handful of German cartridges and a few American .30-.06 cartridges near the German machine gun position. Brad never saw any artefacts that Mastriano may have discovered.

The artefacts were collected and the date, the finder's name and the general location of the find were written on the bag. On Posey's bag containing the collar disk, the 8mm bullets and the fuse parts, Mastriano wrote 'Humserburg above York Spot'.

The following day, Saturday, 19 July 2008, work commenced at 0900 hours. Posey and Anderson immediately went into the woods on the north-eastern point of Hill 167, where the fence for the cow pasture ends and the dirt road goes into the woods, a couple of hundred metres north of the York spot. Working their way to the crest and just inside the tree line, they found two fired .45 calibre projectiles, a five-round stripper clip of American .30-.06 cartridges as well as a few fired .30-.06 cartridges. In a flat area, just before the dramatic elevation increase of the ridge itself, they found the following items of interest:

- Seven expended .45 cartridges
- One fired .45 projectile
- Several expended and unfired French 8mm cartridges
- Several fired French 8mm projectiles
- Two U.S. mess kit forks
- A U.S. metal pocket mirror
- A German cartridge extractor for MG08 or MG08/15 machine gun

- An unfired German 9mm Parabellum pistol cartridge
- Several expended German C96 pistol cartridges [7.63 × 25]
- Several iron bands and latches from ammunition boxes
- Two German uniform buttons with crown on them and one plain German uniform button.

They reached the eastern crest of the road bed; here Posey found three complete American five-round clips of .30-.06 ammunition. He started searching the road beds and on the edges. Everywhere there were large quantities of German 7.92 expended and unfired cartridges. There were so many signals that he only dug enough to confirm there must have been between ten and twenty German machine guns located in the 100m section of ridge. Mixed in with it all were many unfired French 8mm cartridges and another group of five American five-round stripper clips of .30-06 ammunition.

Posey noticed that there was a point in the centre of the machine gun positions where distinct pits could be seen. He thought there were at least five of them, one after another, in a row right next to each other. German cartridges were found in and around the pits. The following day, the Danish Army officer found a brass coupling with a portion of metal tube attached to it. This piece was used to couple a water hose to the machine gun barrel cooling assemble. In addition, a German bayonet scabbard was discovered at this location.

As Posey moved south-west along the crest of the ridge, the side of the sunken road became shallower, eventually becoming a normal path. The only artefacts recovered here were several unfired German 7.92mm cartridges and one German uniform button, located in the proximity of the brass parts to a complete U.S. ammunition belt, U.S. pack and one U.S. coat button.

As one moves further south-west, the ridge broadens out quite dramatically, the elevation continuing as you move further along. Several artefacts were found in the wide area in the centre of the ridge. Concentrations of U.S. artefacts were found almost in a line, scattered along the northern edge of the ridge, and they continued for the entire distance of the search. These finds included:

- Several unfired American .30-.06 cartridges and several complete five-round clips.
- Several unfired French 8mm cartridges

- A French VB rifle grenade
- A British No. 37 Mk 1 White Phosphorous grenade
- Numerous snaps from U.S. ammunition belts
- Several adjustment buckles from American ammunition belts
- Three sections of a brass cleaning rod along with one brass attachment. These were found co-located with several unfired French 8mm cartridges and American .30-.06 cartridges
- One fired American .45 projectile
- Scattered fired 8mm projectiles
- A part of a wristwatch, believed to be related to the 1918 action.

In the centre of the ridge where Posey had found the collar brass the evening before he discovered a concentration of empty U.S. five round .30-.06 stripper clips. There were a few unfired .30-.06 cartridges and several complete five-round clips, not enough to account for the number of empty clips that were found, which numbered more than forty. They were scattered in a 50 × 50m area. Within this area, two U.S. coat buttons were discovered, parts of a pack, parts of an American ammunition belt, a cleaning rod attachment, several snaps from ammunition belts and several .30-.06 cartridges and projectiles that had been taken apart. One had the bullet put back in the cartridge upside down. There was no propellant (powder) in that cartridge.

Several artillery fuses were uncovered, including a complete German 77mm Minenwerfer (mortar) time fuse, a complete French (long type) percussion or instantaneous fuse, parts to another French percussion fuse, parts of a French time fuse and an occasional fired French 8mm projectile.

By this time, Posey and Anderson had quite a collection of artefacts, almost as much as they could carry. They returned to the monument with the artefacts to find Mastriano digging a large hole in the ditch next to the dirt road at the monument site. He had found a huge pile of German 77mm protective cages for the projectiles and fuses.

They gave him the artefacts they had found and Mastriano seemed amazed. He told them that they had found more in two days than his team had found in forty days of searching. He added that they had found the best quality U.S. artefacts, apart from the York cartridges and bullets. Everything was put in one bag and written down that they were found on the Humserburg. Posey asked him why he was so interested in artefacts that had obviously nothing to do with the York fight. Mastriano's response was that they were going to be representative relics for the museum in the United States.

Other team members returned with more German 7.92 cartridges and a couple of pieces from a U.S. ammunition belt that they found near the first German machine gun position. Posey showed him a map he had found in the five-volume history of the 28th Division. He asked Mastriano if he had read any of the 28th Division history since they were the adjacent unit that day. He said that he hadn't. The map was drawn on 7 October 1918 by the United States Army intelligence troops assigned to the 28th Division.

It showed the regimental boundary of the 120th and 125th Württemberg Landwehr Infantry Regiments on 7 October in the German line that ran further to the east of their location, across Hill 223. The regimental boundary between these regiments was located just to the north of Hill 223. There were lines drawn back in the same direction as the planned axis of advance by the U.S. Army. Mastriano did not see it in the same way; his idea was that the lines represented the regimental boundary in depth. The boundary line on the map crossed the northern edge of the ridge where they had been detecting, several hundred metres north of the regimental boundary that Mastriano had indicated on his report. Posey explained that when the regiments fell back they may not have proceeded along the U.S. axis of advance, but had fallen back to the west, which would place this regimental boundary in another area, farther south than where Mastriano believed the boundary to be.

Mastriano did not share Posey's opinion, stating that it was U.S. intelligence and therefore it had to be somewhat accurate. (The SYDE chose to discount other U.S. records because they felt that they were inaccurate.) Posey told him that where the lines appear to look like the regimental boundary on the northern end of the ridge was the same location he had found an additional ten to twenty German machine gun positions that he was unaware had been there, together with several American .45 cartridges and projectiles.

At the end of the day, Posey asked Mastriano again what he thought about the German machine gun positions on top of the ridge that he had found. There was no reply. Posey continued, asking about the collar brass that the group from Tennessee found from G Company, 328th Infantry. Mastriano agreed that the guys from Tennessee had found such brass but in the wrong valley, pointing in the direction of where the Tennessee group had been searching. (The Tennessee group is the Nolan Group.) Posey asked him how he explained why that brass was over there and he replied that guys from the 328th Regiment were deployed on all sides of the valley. Posey said, 'But, Company G?' Mastriano made no reply.

The following morning, Posey and Anderson arrived one hour before Mastriano. They started searching the same ridge and found more of the same type of artefacts they had found on the previous day. At noon, they had to prepare to return to Germany, so they went back to the base of the ridge where they had found the seven .45 cartridges the day before. They found Mastriano still searching there. He didn't seem to be as excited as he had been on the previous two days. He said he had found several more of the German 77mm ammunition cage protectors near where Posey had discovered the ammunition box straps the day before, just at the base of the ridge. Mastriano told Brad that the artefacts were going to be sent to the U.S. Army Center of Military History, from where he thought they would be distributed to museums such as the 82nd Airborne Division museum at Fort Bragg, North Carolina and other museums. Mastriano continued that he was requesting the Air Force give him a C-17 cargo plane to transport the artefacts to the United States.

Having returned to Germany, the following day, Posey sent an email to Mastriano thanking him for the invitation to detect and asking if anything else had been uncovered in his absence. That same day, Mastriano responded stating they had found another big pile of the German 77mm ammunition cage protectors, and one of the others had found a U.S. canteen and two U.S. entrenching tools. He said that the window for searching was now closed.

In the days following, Posey read again the 82nd Division History and Sergeant York's account and he became convinced that the action could not have possibly occurred where Mastriano had said it had. In Posey's opinion, the action occurred on the hill directly to the south-west from Hill 223, as indicated in the official report of the incident conducted by the 82nd Division after the war.

Posey searched the internet and found a link that led him to Doctor Nolan's dissertation on the subject. Through studying Nolan's paper, Posey formed the opinion that this team (the Nolan Group) had missed out on a legitimate claim of the discovery of the real site of the York fight.

And, as they say, the rest is history. Posey became a member of the Nolan Group.

Chapter 17

Phase III of Field Study, 6–18 April 2009

For this phase the team was joined by Brad Posey, who, as explained in the previous chapter, had previously been working with the SYDE but had become disillusioned by their methods and believed they were searching in the wrong location. With him was his partner, Birgit Anderson, and her daughter, Jessica, both of whom were experienced in battlefield metal detecting and exploration.

The team was pleased to welcome Jim Legg, an experienced archaeologist from the South Carolina Institute of Archaeology and Anthropology at the University of South Carolina. A good friend of Posey, the two had worked together on other battlefield projects. Both men were to prove invaluable, both for the identification of artefacts and the evaluation of historical events. Again, Ian Cobb, Eddie Browne, Michael Kelly and Fred Castiér were present, together with Tom Nolan and Yves Desfossé. A new member was welcomed to the team in the form of Gordon Cummings, an Englishman, a friend of Michael Kelly. He was full of enthusiasm and energy and he proved to be a key member of the team, not just in fieldwork but in the very important role of supplier of victuals and assisting Margie Nolan, Doctor Nolan's wife, in cooking duties. It was not an easy task, feeding such a large team after the day's toils, but there were some delicious recipes concocted and cooked by this duo. Barbeques played a big role and on one occasion the local dignitaries were invited along. The team enjoyed some spacious accommodation in a large gîte in Fléville, owned by the village mayor, Damien Georges.

As mentioned earlier, Posey's first involvement in the Sergeant York exploration had come during the summer of 2008 when he was invited by Lieutenant-Colonel Mastriano to assist him in a project in the Argonne. He claimed to Posey that he had found the exact spot where York fought, and that he had even unearthed all twenty-one .45 cartridges York was supposed to have fired.

The Army officer wanted to remove as many artefacts as possible before relic hunters moved in. By this time Mastriano had pleaded his case with the French authorities and the Sergeant York monument had been put in place at the site. (where the .45 cartridges had been found.) Posey started to search with his partner and very quickly unearthed another .45 cartridge and .45 bullet in addition to many other artefacts that the SYDE had missed. We have read how Brad and his partner were there for four days, during which time many artefacts were recovered from all over the ridge of the SYDE site. Many of these appear in the SYDE report and are described as items found at the York spot.

Over the four days, Posey became massively disillusioned with the methods employed by the SYDE; there was no system or methodology in place to record the location or provenance of any of the artefacts discovered.

Upon his return to Germany, Posey did some research and found the Nolan Group. He was impressed by their professional approach and the fact that they had asked for, and been given, permission to conduct their exploration; permission the SYDE had not sought. In addition, the area of the Nolan Group search fitted with all the historical accounts. It further served to convince Posey that they were a professional outfit, and that where they were searching was the right place. His further investigation into the U.S. official histories confirmed the area where the SYDE were operating had borne the full force on the right flank of the 2nd Battalion attack on 8 October 1918.

GIS technology was used extensively during all periods of investigation. Historic maps, reports and other documents could be put into a spatial database that recreated the landscape as it was in October 1918. Tom Nolan says:

> Mapping grade GPS receivers were used to collect multiple points for each artefact location. The points collected at each location were differentially corrected and averaged to provide the maximum accuracy. This produced an average horizontal precision for all points of 1.23 metres.

The team used surface metal detectors to locate artefacts, and when found they were marked by tape or flag. Doctor Nolan continued:

The artefact was mapped as a point feature and given an identification number based on the date and a sequential number for that date. The identification number was entered as an attribute of the GPS point feature and the artefact was put in a bag with the identification number on the outside and a label inside the bag. Artefacts too large to put in bags had a tag with the identification number tied to them. At the end of each work day, the artefacts were identified, photographed and catalogued.

The tasks undertaken here meant that Nolan could produce extensive maps that show the relevance of the artefacts discovered assisted by the historic documentation:

Information concerning the modern landscape was obtained from the French Institut Geographique National 1:25,000 paper topographic quadrangle sheet titled Varennes-en-Argonne. The paper map was scanned in 24bit colour at 600dpi and saved as a TIFF image. The TIFF image was imported into ArcGIS and georeferenced to UTM zone 31 North WGS 84 datum, using control points from the UTM grid printed on the map.

Many of these maps will be shown in the pages that follow, but before the Nolan Group explorations and finds are explained it is necessary to give further details of the historical background.

Chapter 18

The 1929 Re-enactment

In 1929 there was a re-enactment of the York fight arranged by the U.S. Army War College as part of a military carnival for the benefit of the Army Relief Society. Patrol veterans were invited to take part and Captain Henry Swindler was tasked with writing an account of the action so he could guide the re-enactment. From the resources available to him, Swindler was not able to get the information he required. He wrote to Colonel G. Edward Buxton on 17 July 1929 to ask for his assistance in the recollection of detail. Buxton was an obvious source of information, not only had he been York's battalion commander, but he had written the history of the 82nd Division in the First World War. Also, both he and Captain Danforth had been present at the 1919 visit to the York site.

Swindler enclosed in the letter a copy of the French 1:20,000 Forêt d'Argonne map sheet. From this he asked Buxton to sketch on the map the location of G Company when the attack stalled, the path taken by the patrol, the location of the German machine guns and York's position, that also of the German prisoners and the other patrol members in the fight. Buxton responded on 23 July 1929 with a detailed letter, and the map he had annotated showing the details that were asked for.

This is Buxton's letter:

Captain Henry O. Swindler   July 23rd 1929
The Army War College,
Office of the Commandant,
Washington, D.C.

Dear Captain Swindler:

G Company, Second Battalion, 328th Infantry was the left flank of the battalion attack early morning October 8th launched from the crest of hill 223. The objective was the Narrow Gage railroad about a kilometre and a half a little north of west from hill 223. The advance of the battalion was stopped not only by heavy fire from the front which was expected, but chiefly by continuous bursts of machine gun fire from the nose southwest from hill 223 about where I have written the figure '2'; Lieutenant Kirby Stewart had just been killed leading the left flank. Sergeant Parsons, a New York vaudeville actor, directed Acting – Sergeant Early, an Irish born American from New Haven, to take 3 squads to stop the fire from that nose on the left. One of the 3 squads was commanded by Corporal York. Early led a skilful reconnaissance in which the 3 squads crawled back under cover of the brush on hill 223 and circled southwest on the route shown as '3-A' gaining the crest of the hill due-west from the hostile fire. Early could hear voices from West and straight down the wooded hill in the direction of '4'. He decided to attack – though all told, his force numbered 17 men, including him. They ran down the hill in a skirmish line, pushed through the brush, crossed a little creek and came into a small clearing at the foot of the hill where they found about 60 of the enemy gathered around their Major and, apparently, receiving instructions as to a counter attack to be made shortly. The Americans fired two or three shots into this mass at close range. The others threatened the enemy with their bayonets. The Germans believed they were surprised by a large force of which this was only the advance party, they surrendered and started throwing down arms and ammunition belts.

A command in German came from the steep hillside over their heads immediately east and northeast. The prisoners threw themselves on their faces. York and the others standing immediately behind the prisoners did the same thing. A burst of fire from the hillside overhead struck the Americans in the outer ring – killing six and wounding three, one of them was Early, who received three machine gun bullets in his side. York was the only non-commissioned officer left and lying on the ground beside the prisoners carried on the fire fight against the forces scattered 50 to 60 yards above him. He emptied 3 clips from his rifle and 3 from his pistol. It is evident that he missed few targets (he does not think he missed any). Only two of the other seven survivors testified that they fired any shots during this fight. One soldier said he killed 2 or 3 men – Sergeant York told me that he saw him kill one. As you will see by the affidavits which I took, and which are published in Sergeant York's book, most of the survivors were busy covering the mass of prisoners huddled in front of them. Lieutenant Cox of F Company, 2nd Battalion came down this hill about an hour later with his platoon. He estimated that there were 20 to 25 dead Germans on the scene of the fight and the bodies of the 6 dead Americans.

I could never satisfy myself that the German bayonet attack amounted to anything more than the isolated actions of groups – a squad or less – whose leaders made unrelated efforts to rush York since they could not hit him without firing into the prisoners who protected him by their close proximity. The machine gunners picked up on the return route, about due East to the Valley (shown as 3 B) must have been survivors of the fight on the hillside and those still further to the West who had been flanking the battalion and whose position is shown as '2'.

I presume you have nearly all the details you need to fill in this statement. If not, ask me any specific questions you like. If a further check seems desirable I suggest that you submit my replies to Major E.C.B. Danforth, Jr., Southern Finance Building, Augusta, Georgia, who was Captain of G Company on that morning and led his company forward to its objective on the railroad during a day of stiff fighting. Major Danforth has very carefully checked this fight with Sergeant York and went over the terrain with him personally as I did myself.[1]

Sincerely yours,

Signed: G. Edward Buxton

On 29 July 1929, Swindler wrote to Major Danforth enclosing Buxton's letter and the 1:20,000 map with Buxton's annotations. At the same time, he sent a 1:10,000 map of the same area. He then asked Danforth to draw the details on the maps. Major Danforth was quick to respond. On 25 August 1929 he replied,

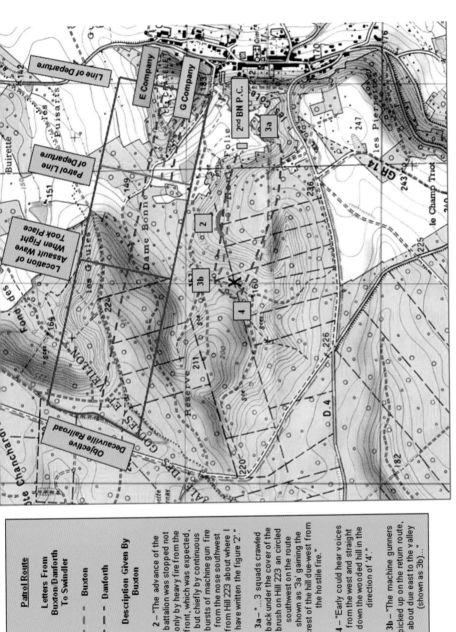

Map 34: Danforth/Buxton map with details thereon from letters sent from Buxton and Danforth to Captain Swindler giving details of the route of the patrol. (Posey)

answering specific questions that had been asked by Buxton. He said the route of the battalion advance 'passed over and slightly south of the slope 150 metres south of the figure 220 in square 60'. He was referring to the 1:20,000 map. (See Maps 30, 31, 32, & 33)

This is a copy of Danforth's letter to Captain Swindler:

I am enclosing two maps of the York area of the exploit which I have marked with the information requested in your favour of July 29th. My knowledge of the general situation is first hand and, I believe accurate. The particulars of the actual fight of Sergeant York is, of course not based on my own observation but has been gained by investigations which I made on the ground shortly after the armistice and from a subsequent study in which I have been interested in making during the past year or two. I am afraid that no one, not even York himself, can give you a very accurate lay-out of the fight but my sketch contains what I believe to have been the situation.

Answering your questions specifically, please note the following:

1.   The route of advance of the battalion passed over and slightly to the south of the slope 150 metres south of the figure 220 in square 60. This may have encroached upon the territory of the 28th Division but that division attacked from Cote 244 and my company had no contact with them until later in the afternoon. The position of the Battalion P.C. as given in the message of Lt. Wood is correct. (See Fig. 16)

2.   I am at a loss to account for the message that Company G reported their arrival at 9:30 A.M. at the point 96.4-79.9. I am sure that no elements of my Company reached this point unless it were some members of York's Patrol. Point 97.5-81.0 which was reported as the right of the 328th Infantry was, as you believe, a point reached by Patrols of Company E. It is well to note that the direction of the attack of the 328th and 327th Infantry was not the same because the original direction – ten degrees north of west – was changed prior to zero hour and this change

was not received by the 328th Infantry. This resulted in a considerable part of our front being left uncovered as indicated on the 1:20,000 map.

3. The position of the Battalion at the time of the York fight I have indicated on the map to the best of my knowledge and belief.

4. The location of the York fight as given by the officer of the 1st Battalion is incorrect.

I am very much interested in the plan to re-enact this fight. Please ask me any further questions you may wish. I will be delighted to give you any possible assistance. Can you tell me when the re-enactment is to take place and if it would be possible for me to witness it? I should also like very much to have you send me a copy of your account of the exploit when it is completed.

Sincerely yours,

Signed: E.C.B. Danforth

P.S. The bayonet attack, as Major Buxton says, was not a concerted action by the whole of the enemy force but merely a rush by some five or six Germans that had succeeded in getting to within thirty or forty yards of York.[2]

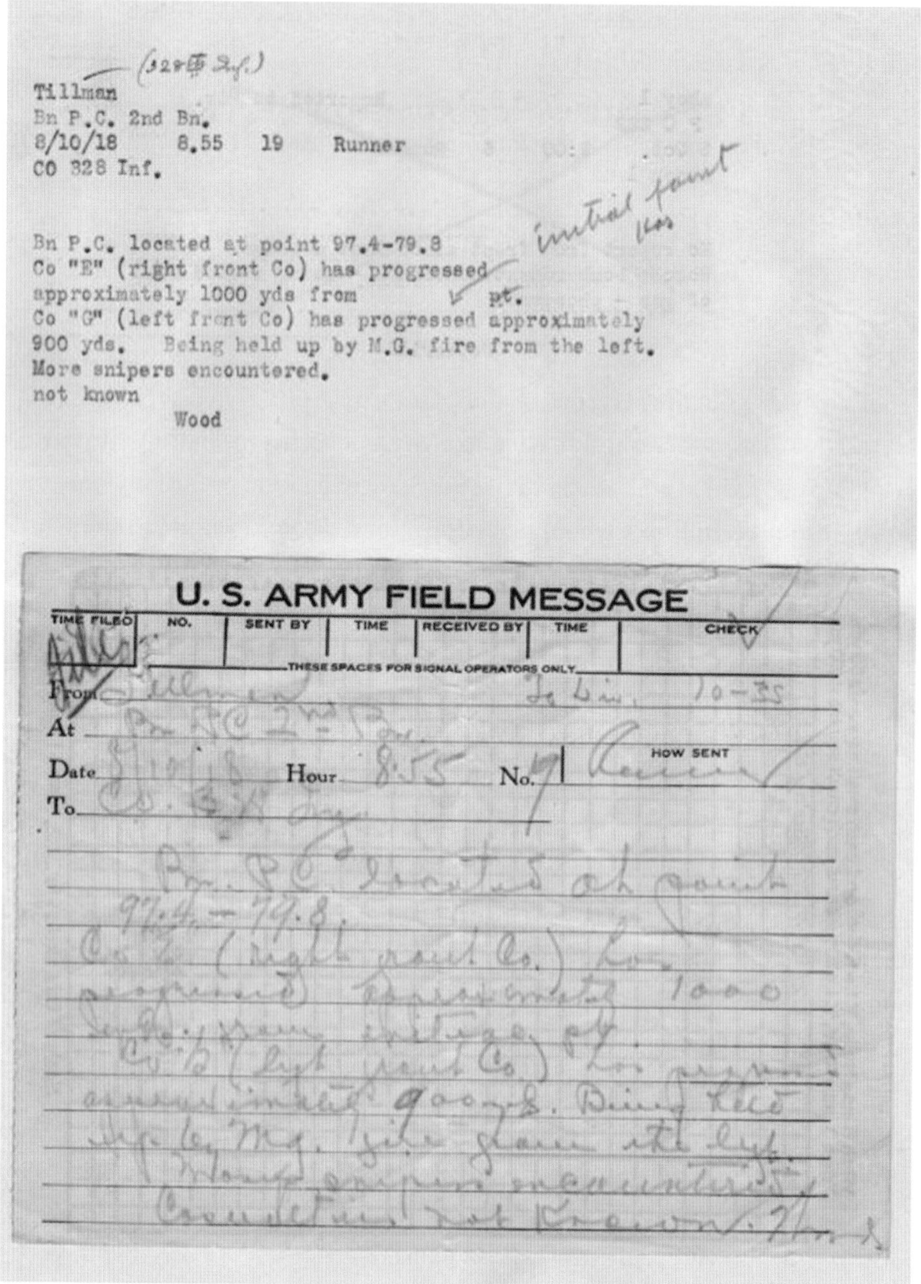

Tillman   — (328⊞ 2y.)
Bn P.C. 2nd Bn.
8/10/18   8.55   19   Runner
CO 328 Inf.

Bn P.C. located at point 97.4-79.8
Co "E" (right front Co) has progressed
approximately 1000 yds from   pt.
Co "G" (left front Co) has progressed approximately
900 yds.   Being held up by M.G. fire from the left.
More snipers encountered.
not known
        Wood

Fig. 16: Message from Lieutenant Wood giving location of Battalion P.C..

Chapter 19

The Graves Registration Service

The six members of the patrol who were killed on 8 October 1918 were buried by Chaplain John O'Farrelly of the 303rd Engineer Regiment, part of the 78th Division, on 24 October 1918. Alvin York said he revisited the scene on the following day, 9 October, to find all the American dead been had buried. This cannot be the case.

The burial records provide spatial information about the location of the York fight. Conjoined with the testimony of the survivors and the official histories, one can get very close to where the action happened. There was an anomaly with the burial records and the record completed by the Graves Registration Service (GRS). The initial burial of the dead was carried out by the combat organisations, with a chaplain officiating. The grave was marked with a peg and one of the two identification tags of the casualty. The other identification tag was left on the body. Often items of his equipment would be left on the grave (see Fig. 29).

Officers reporting the burials had to keep a record of each burial. Map references were also kept of the grave location and the edition, name and number of the map had to be given. Details of how the grave was marked also had to be recorded.

The Grave Location Blank completed by Chaplain O'Farrelly for all burials, except Corporal Savage, indicated that four men, Privates Wareing, Dymowski, Weiler, and Private Swanson, were buried in the order listed, side by side in a linear grouping.

There is no Grave Location Blank in Savage's file, but a letter written by the G Company commanding officer states that he was buried by a chaplain of the 78th Division, undoubtedly, Chaplain O'Farrelly. The letter gives the grave location as 97.4-80.5 on the Forêt d'Argonne map. The chaplain recorded the location of the other five burials as 297.4-280.2, and presumably would have recorded the same coordinates for Savage. The temporary grave of

Location of American Burials From Grave Location Blanks and Graves Registration Service

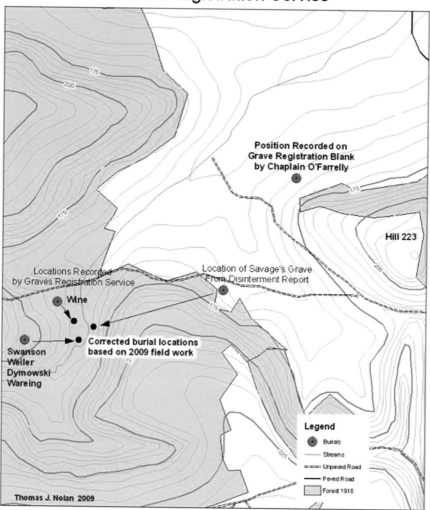

Map 35: Locations of burials of U.S. casualties from the Grave Registration Service records. (Doctor Nolan)

Wareing   Dymowski   Swanson   Weiler

GRAVES OF 4 MEN, 327TH. REGT.
Inf., 82nd.Division who were
killed while aiding Sgt.Alvin
C.York and 13 other men ,327th.
Regt. Inf., in capturing 132
Germans. Argonne Forest, near
Cornay, Ardennes, France.

Fig. 17: The four graves. The infantry regiment should read 328th.

Private Wine was not located by the Nolan Group until Phase III in 2009. He was separate and a little distance away from the other burials, some 20 yards from the four-man burial, but nevertheless O'Farrelly had pulled him in with the same coordinates on his burial record. Doctor Nolan believes that the discrepancy between the easting in the letter and the easting on the other five Grave Location Blanks is probably a typographic error in the letter. The explanation in the anomaly of O'Farrelly's use of the three-digit grid coordinates and the letter's use of two-digit coordinates, used on the same Forêt d'Argonne map sheet is that the 1,000m Lambert Coordinate System grid is used on the French maps. Grid lines on the 1:20,000 series maps like the Forêt d'Argonne quadrangle use a two-digit numbering system. The 1:10,000 series map use the same grid numbering system but with the number '2' added as a prefix to the two-digit coordinate. These two grid systems could be and were used interchangeably. It will be seen from the table below that Chaplain O'Farrelly used the same map coordinates, 280.2 north, and 297.4 east, for all six graves. Compare that with the coordinates as given by the GRS (see Map 35).

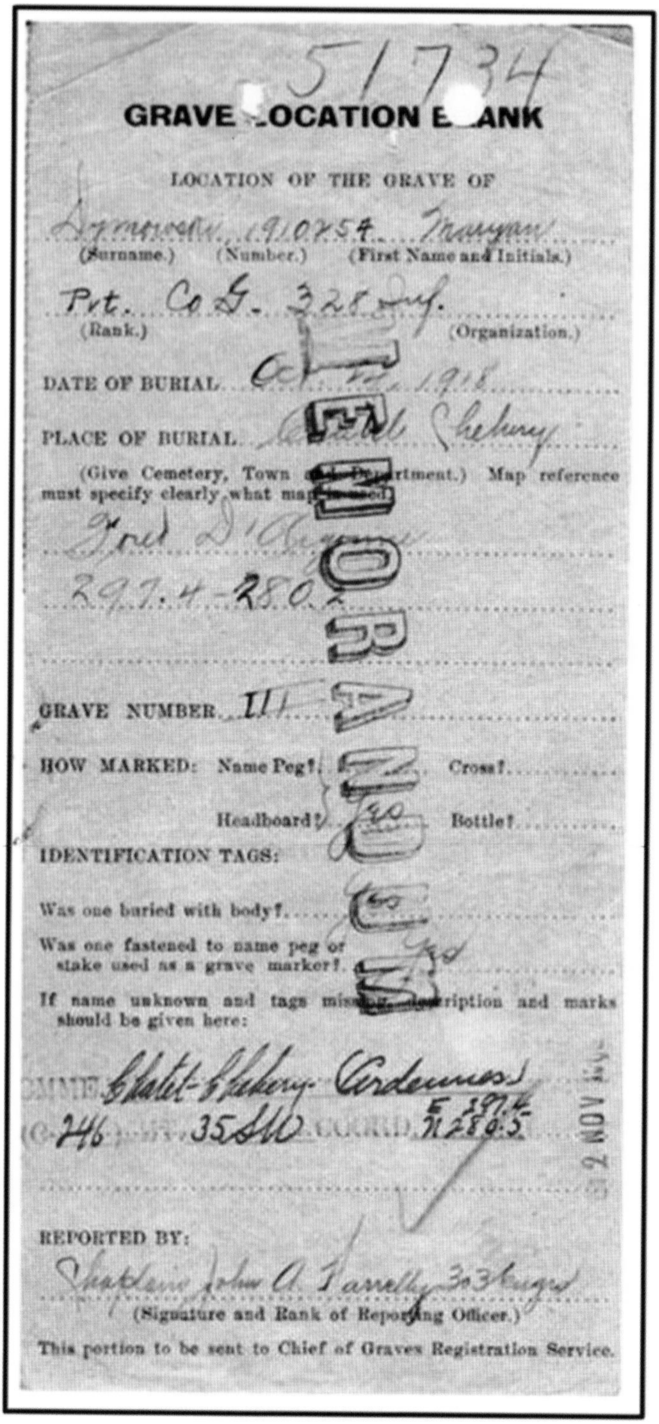

Fig. 18: The Grave Registration blank of Private Maryan Dymowski.

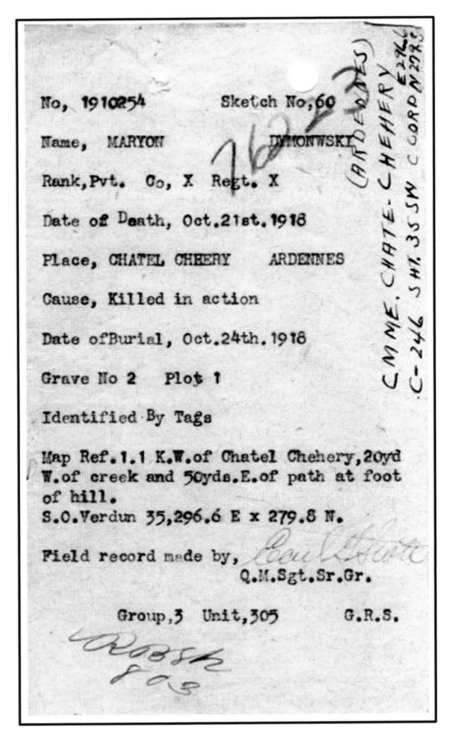

Fig. 19: Maryan Dymowski's grave Location.

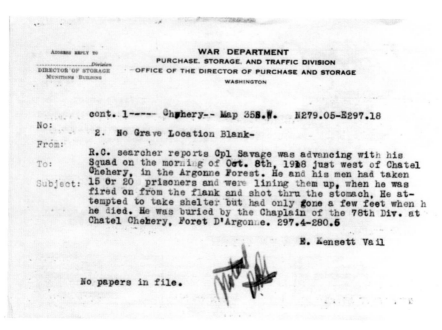

ADDRESS REPLY TO
..............Division
DIRECTOR OF STORAGE
MUNITIONS BUILDING

WAR DEPARTMENT
PURCHASE, STORAGE, AND TRAFFIC DIVISION
OFFICE OF THE DIRECTOR OF PURCHASE AND STORAGE
WASHINGTON

cont. 1----- Chehery-- Map 35B.W.   N279.05-E297.18

No:

2. No Grave Location Blank-

From:

R.C. searcher reports Cpl Savage was advancing with his
To: Squad on the morning of Oct. 8th, 1918 just west of Chatel
          Chehery, in the Argonne Forest. He and his men had taken
Subject: 15 or 20 prisoners and were lining them up, when he was
          fired on from the flank and shot thru the stomach, He at-
          tempted to take shelter but had only gone a few feet when h
          he died. He was buried by the Chaplain of the 78th Div. at
          Chatel Chehery, Foret D'Argonne. 297.4-280.5

E. Kensett Vail

No papers in file.

Fig. 20: Letter describing Corporal Savage being fired on from the flank.

NAME OF SOLDIER	CHAPLAIN O'FARRELLY	GRS
Private Wareing	Grave Number 1	Grave 1, Plot 1
	280.2 N – 297.4 E	279.8 N – 296.6. E
Private Dymowski	Grave Number III	Grave 2, plot 1
	280.2 N – 297.4 E	279.8 N – 296.6 E
Private Swanson	Grave Number IV	Grave 3, plot 1
	280.2 N – 297.4 E	279.8 N – 296.6 E
Private Weiler	Grave Number V	Grave 4, plot 1
	280.2 N – 297.4 E	279.8 N – 296.6 E
Corporal Savage	Form Missing	Form Missing
	280.2 N – 297.4 E	279.05 N – 297.18 E
Private Wine	Grave Number II	Isolated Grave
	280.2 N – 297.4 E	279.9 N – 296.7 E

As can be seen in the Army photograph (see Fig. 17), the four soldiers: Wareing, Dymowski, Swanson and Weiler were all buried together. The GRS records indicate that the four soldiers were buried 20 yards west of the creek and 50 yards east of the path at the foot of the hill, the GRS record records Private

2. Disinterred (date):   From (give complete location):

May 25, 1921.   Isolated grave, Bois de Chatel, Chatel- Chabery,
                             Map 35SW N279.05 E297.18.
     By : Group J. F. Richards.   Unit Area #1.

3. Reburied (date):   In (give complete location):

May 25, 1921.   Grave #189, section 113, plot 4,
                             Argonne American Cemetery #1232.
     By : Group G. T. Parker,   Unit Cem.1232, Area #1. Nature of reburial Regulation.

4. Report as to nature of original burial and condition of body upon disinterment : Body was buried in
uniform, shoes about size #6. Body badly decomposed. Temporary grave marker marked
grave and had an identification tag attached.

5. (a) Identification tags : Buried with body ?   Yes (1). On grave marker ? Yes (1).

   (b) Other means of identification found upon disinterment, and general remarks : The identification
tag found on temporary grave marker read MURRAY L. SAVAGE PVT USA other side 1910275.
The identification plaque found on wrist read M. L. SAVAGE USA 1910275.

6. What does examination of body show as regards the following identifying items ?

   (a) Height (actual measurement) Impossible to determine.

   (b) Weight (estimated) Impossible to determine.

   (c) Hair—Color None.

       Quantity None.

       Characteristics None.

   (d) Hair on face—Color None.

       Location None.

       Quantity None.

   (e) Permanent marks on body (old scars, peculiarities, or

   missing parts) None.

   (f) Wounds or missing parts (received at time of casualty) None.

Body examined by Major H. C. Bierbower, M. C.

7. Disinterment   J. F. RICHARDS,
   supervised by Civ. Empl., AGES, QMC., in E.   Approved : L. O. MATHEWS,
                                                                          Major, Q.M.C.
                        H. C. BIERBOWER,   (Title) L. O. MATHEWS,
8. Reburial   Major, M. C.   Major, Q.M.C.
   supervised by   Approved :

                                                     (Title)

Fig. 21: Murray Savage, disinterment and burial record. GRS

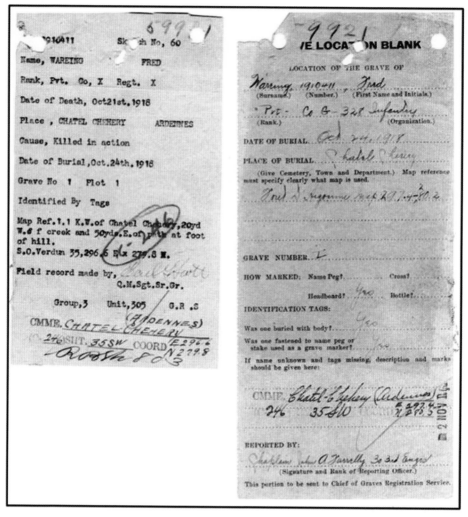

Fig. 22: Private Wareing's Grave Registration blank and location. GRS

Wine's grave as being 30 yards west of the creek and 20 yards east of the path at the foot of the hill.

The bodies of Swanson, Weiler, Dymowski and Wareing were exhumed on 2 September 1919 and reburied in the Meuse–Argonne American cemetery on the same day.[1] The disinterment records indicate the bodies were buried in their uniforms 2½ft deep and were badly decomposed. Wareing was recorded as having a fractured skull at the time of casualty. Murray Savage was disinterred

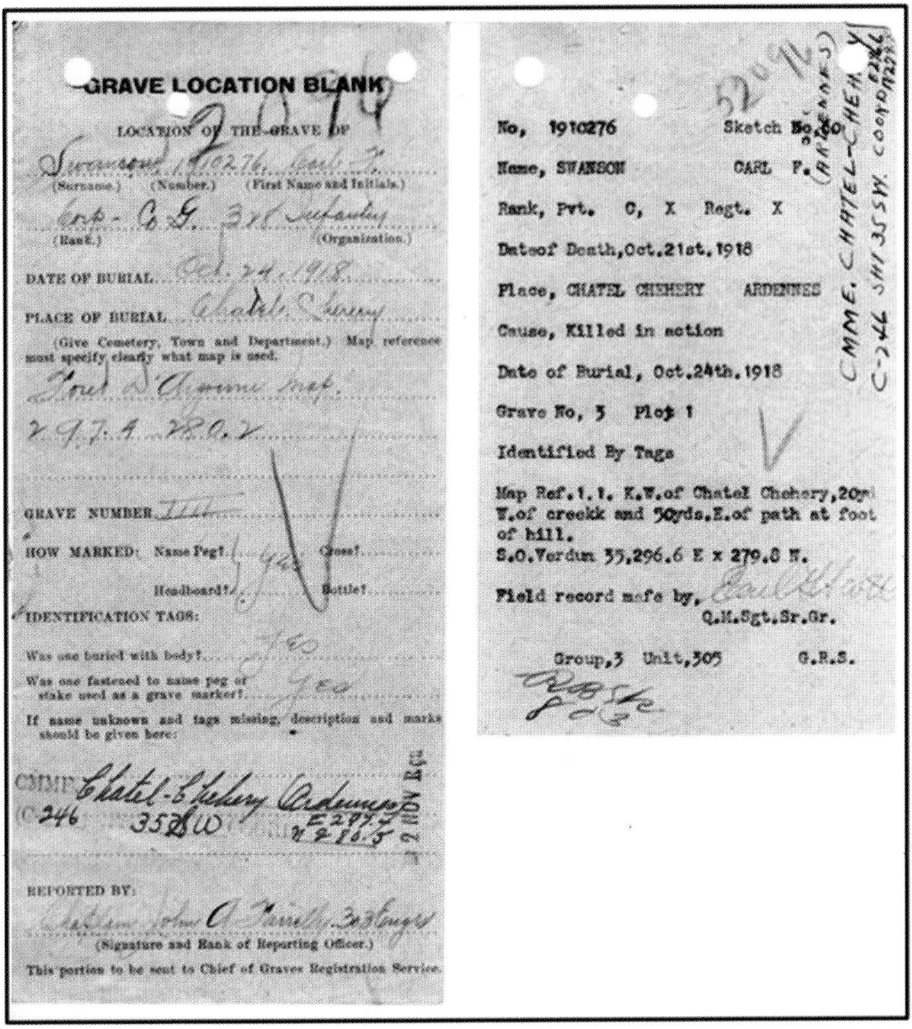

Fig. 23: Private Swanson. Grave Registration blank and location. GRS

on 25 May 1921. He was buried in his uniform and his body was badly decomposed. Private Wine was disinterred on 2 November 1921 from a grave 1ft in depth; he was in his uniform and had a fractured left scapula at the time of casualty. The GRS cards for everyone but Savage give map coordinates close to the location of the fight, according to Buxton and Danforth. The absence of the records in Savage's burial folder, and map coordinates with two decimal places instead of the usual one decimal place on his disinterment records,

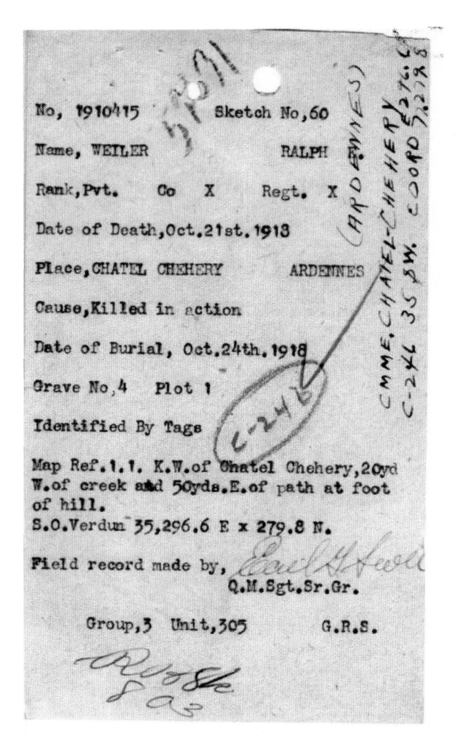

No, 1910415   Sketch No,60

Name, WEILER   RALPH

Rank,Pvt.   Co   X   Regt.   X

Date of Death,Oct.21st.1918

Place,CHATEL CHEHERY   ARDENNES

Cause,Killed in action

Date of Burial, Oct.24th.1918

Grave No,4   Plot 1

Identified By Tags

Map Ref.1.1. K.W.of Chatel Chehery,20yd
W.of creek and 50yds.E.of path at foot
of hill.
S.O.Verdun 35,296.6 E x 279.8 N.

Field record made by,

          Q.M.Sgt.Sr.Gr.

     Group,3 Unit,305   G.R.S.

Fig. 24: Private Weiler, disinterment and burial record. GRS

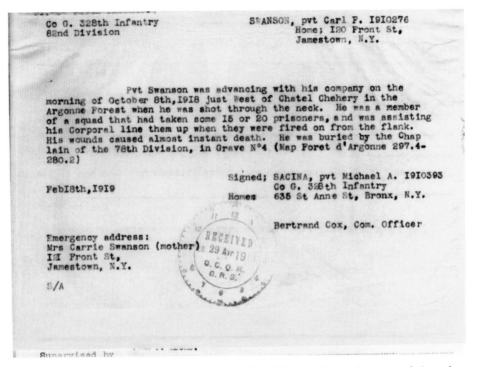

Co G. 328th Infantry
82nd Division

SWANSON, pvt Carl F. I9I0276
Home; I20 Front St,
Jamestown, N.Y.

     Pvt Swanson was advancing with his company on the
morning of October 8th,I9I8 just West of Chatel Chehery in the
Argonne Forest when he was shot through the neck. He was a member
of a squad that had taken some I5 or 20 prisoners, and was assisting
his Corporal line them up when they were fired on from the flank.
His wounds caused almost instant death. He was buried by the Chap
lain of the 78th Division, in Grave N°4 (Map Foret d'Argonne 297.4-
280.2)

                     Signed; SACINA, pvt Michael A. I9I0393
                           Co G. 328th Infantry
Feb18th,I9I9   Home: 635 St Anne St, Bronx, N.Y.

                         Bertrand Cox, Com. Officer

Emergency address:
Mrs Carrie Swanson (mother)
I2 Front St,
Jamestown, N.Y.

RECEIVED
29 Avr 19
Q.C.Q.M.
G.R.S.

S/A

Fig. 25: *Statement from Private Sacina describing Private Swanson being shot through the neck from the flank.*

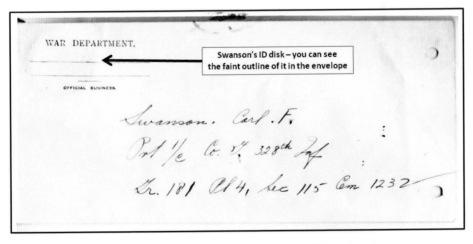

WAR DEPARTMENT.

OFFICIAL BUSINESS.

Swanson's ID disk – you can see
the faint outline of it in the envelope

Swanson, Carl. F.
Prt ½ Co. G. 328th Inf
Gr. 181 Pl 4, Sec 115 Cem 1232

Fig. 26: *Army document regarding Private Swanson. There is a faint mark on the top left of the envelope where Swanson's I.D. disc would have been.*

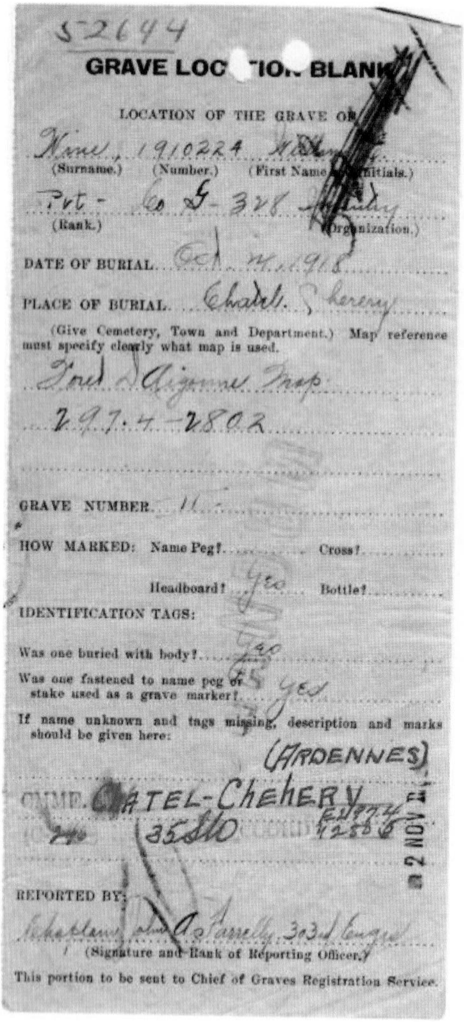

52644

GRAVE LOCATION BLANK

LOCATION OF THE GRAVE OF

Wine, 1910224 W.E.

(Surname.) (Number.) (First Name and Initials.)

Pvt - Co G - 328 Infantry

(Rank.) (Organization.)

DATE OF BURIAL Oct 24 1918

PLACE OF BURIAL Chatel Chehery

(Give Cemetery, Town and Department.) Map reference must specify clearly what map is used.

Foret d'Argonne Map

297.4-280.2

GRAVE NUMBER 11

HOW MARKED: Name Peg? Cross?

Headboard? Yes Bottle?

IDENTIFICATION TAGS:

Was one buried with body? Yes

Was one fastened to name peg or stake used as a grave marker? Yes

If name unknown and tags missing, description and marks should be given here:

(ARDENNES)

CMNE. CHATEL-CHEHERY

246 35 S10 COORD. E 297.4 N 280.2

2 NOV 21

REPORTED BY:

Chaplain A. Farrelly 303rd Engrs

(Signature and Rank of Reporting Officer.)

This portion to be sent to Chief of Graves Registration Service.

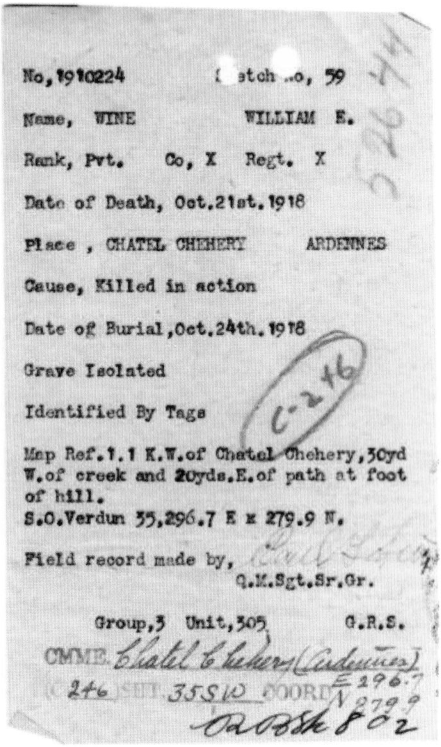

No, 1910224 Sketch No, 59

Name, WINE WILLIAM E.

Rank, Pvt. Co, X Regt. X

Date of Death, Oct.21st.1918

Place , CHATEL CHEHERY ARDENNES

Cause, Killed in action

Date of Burial,Oct.24th.1918

Grave Isolated

Identified By Tags

C-246

Map Ref.1.1 K.W.of Chatel Chehery,30yd W.of creek and 20yds.E.of path at foot of hill.

S.O.Verdun 35,296.7 E x 279.9 N.

Field record made by,

Q.M.Sgt.Sr.Gr.

Group,3 Unit,305 G.R.S.

CMNE. Chatel Chehery (Ardennes)

246 SET. 35 S10 COORD. E 296.7 N 279.9

802

5264

Fig. 27: Private Wine GRS blank and location report. GRS

shows that there was some confusion by the GRS regarding his initial burial location. Savage was exhumed in May 1921 but Wine was not disinterred until November 1921. The time lapse between the exhumation of the four graves on the same day in 1919 and the recovery of Savage and Wine on separate occasions more than two years later suggest there was a problem in locating the last two graves.

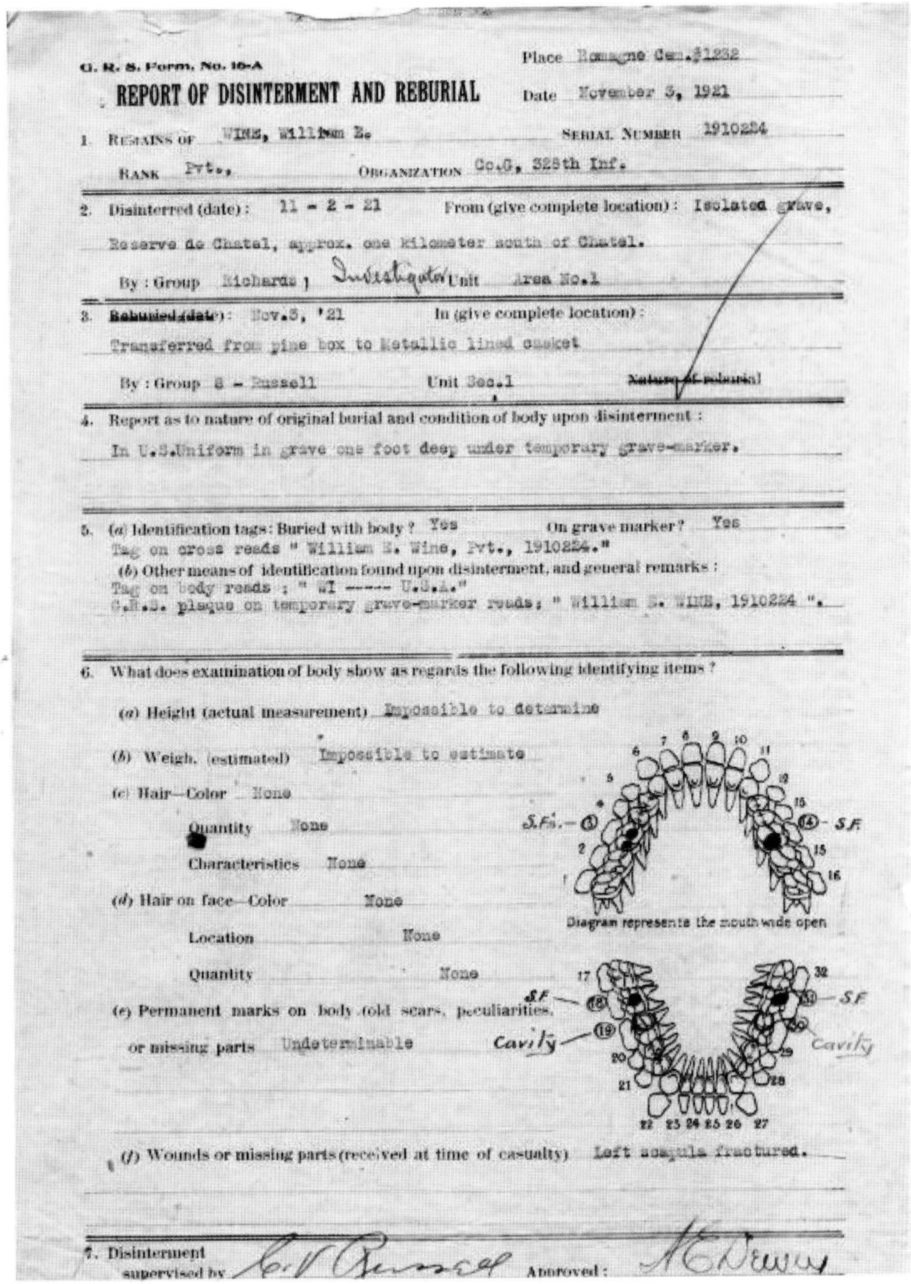

G. R. S. Form. No. 16-A

REPORT OF DISINTERMENT AND REBURIAL

Place Romagne Cem. #1232
Date November 3, 1921

1. REMAINS OF   WINE, William E.   SERIAL NUMBER 1910224

RANK Pvt.,   ORGANIZATION Co.G, 328th Inf.

2. Disinterred (date):   11 - 2 - 21   From (give complete location): Isolated grave,

Reserve de Chatel, approx. one kilometer south of Chatel.

By : Group Richards , Investigator Unit Area No.1

3. Reburied (date): Nov.3, '21   In (give complete location):

Transferred from pine box to Metallic lined casket

By : Group 8 - Russell   Unit Sec.1   Nature of reburial

4. Report as to nature of original burial and condition of body upon disinterment :

In U.S.Uniform in grave one foot deep under temporary grave-marker.

5. (a) Identification tags: Buried with body ? Yes   On grave marker? Yes
Tag on cross reads " William E. Wine, Pvt., 1910224."
   (b) Other means of identification found upon disinterment, and general remarks :
Tag on body reads : " WI ----- U.S.A."
G.R.S. plaque on temporary grave-marker reads; " William E. WINE, 1910224 ".

6. What does examination of body show as regards the following identifying items ?

(a) Height (actual measurement) Impossible to determine

(b) Weigh. (estimated) Impossible to estimate

(c) Hair—Color None

Quantity None

Characteristics None

(d) Hair on face—Color None

Location None

Quantity None

S.F.—

S.F.

Diagram represents the mouth wide open

(e) Permanent marks on body, old scars, peculiarities.

or missing parts Undeterminable   Cavity—   Cavity

(f) Wounds or missing parts (received at time of casualty) Left scapula fractured.

7. Disinterment
supervised by C. V. Russell   Approved: M. E. Drury

Fig. 28: Private Wine disinterment record. GRS

```
Co G. 328th Infantry              WINE William E. Pvt. I9I0224
    82nd Division                  Home : I922 Harrison St. Philadelphia
                                                            Pa.


        " Pvt. Wine was a dvancing with his Company on the morning
of Octoner 8th under very heavy Machine Gun fire , just West of Chatel
Chehery , in the Argonne Forest , when he was killed . The point where
his Company was advancing was densely  wooded and no member of this
Company saw Pvt. Wine , but he was buried at Chatel Chehery by Chaplain
of the 78th Division , in Grave No 2. Forêt d'Argonne , 297.4-280.2 . "


                Informant : Not given .


                        Signed  : Bertrand Cox ,
                                  Comdg. Officer .
                                  February I3th I9I9
Emergency Address :-
Mrs. Agnes Wine (Mother)
I922 Harrison St. Philadelphia , Pa.


C.F.
```

Fig. 29: Report from Captain Cox on Private Wine.

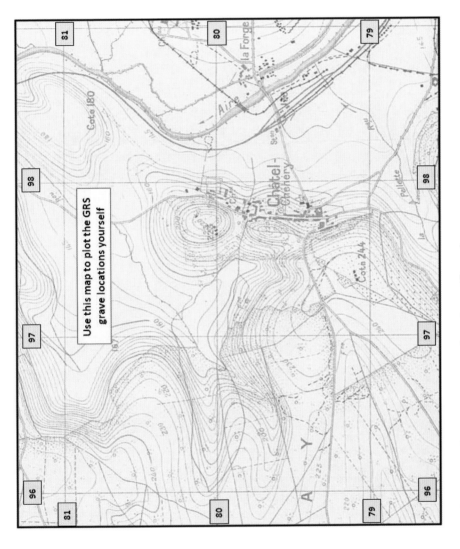

Use this map to plot the GRS grave locations yourself

Map 36: Your opportunity to record your own grave locations. (Posey)

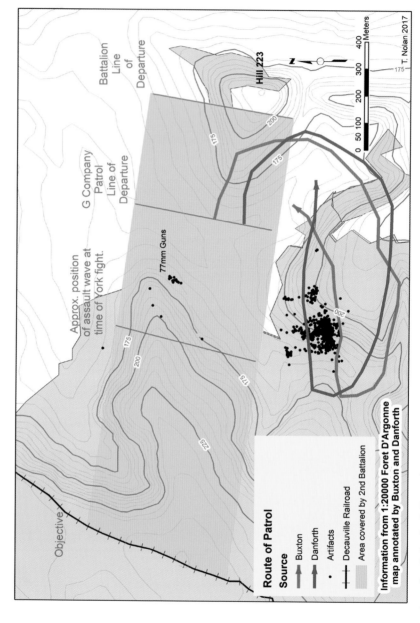

Map 36a: Attack of the 2nd Battalion and route as depicted by Danforth & Buxton. (Doctor Nolan)

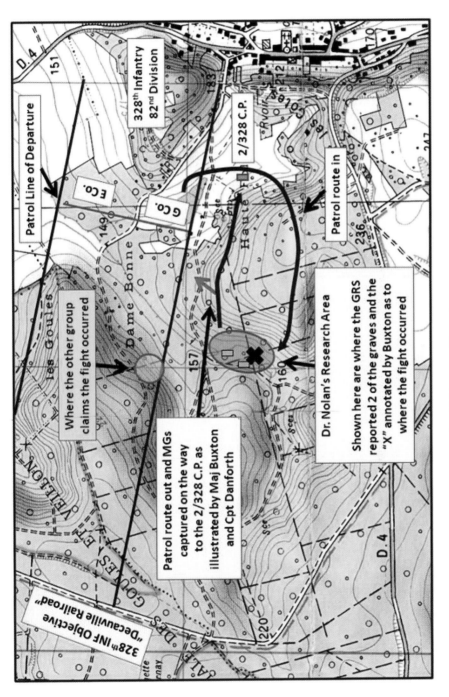

Map 37: Site of the 'X' as recorded by Buxton on his 1929 map. (Posey)

Chapter 20

The Artefacts from the Third Phase

It had been three years since the Nolan Group had last conducted investigations on site, but time in the interlude had been well spent. Working as always with the source documents and official histories in mind, Tom Nolan had scoured the archives in Washington D.C. and had uncovered the GRS documents used for the initial burials and later exhumation of the six killed in York's patrol. This was one of the two primary objectives in the third phase exploration; to locate the temporary graves of the six men killed in the fight, and to undertake a systematic metal detector survey of the engagement area to establish the engagement boundary. It had not been possible to do this on previous field visits owing to time constraints, but it was most necessary to ensure that all artefacts related to the site were recovered.

The weather during this visit was good, little rain fell and the team were not hampered by the ticks that had plagued them on the second phase investigation. It was decided to excavate a 1 × 2m unit to a depth of 25cm at the place where it was thought Murray Savage had been buried. The coordinates as provided by the GRS were at the location where parts of an American cartridge belt had been discovered in 2006. On this occasion, the hobnailed sole of an American boot and rubber spacers from an American helmet were discovered. The archaeologist James Legg found an 'American Railroad' pocket watch close to this scene.

It had been a mild autumn and the tree canopy was still intact. This proved to be a stalling point for the mapping of artefacts. A state-of-the-art Trimble GeoExplorer, GeoXH receiver and data collector had been brought in from the States, but the GPS satellite reception was hampered by the tree canopy and the fact that the ravine was steep. It often took up to an hour to map one single artefact so a new system of mapping was devised. A series of survey stakes were installed across the study area, and GPS positions were recorded for each stake. Then azimuths and distances to artefacts located nearby each stake were recorded for each artefact. Gordon Cummings became highly proficient in

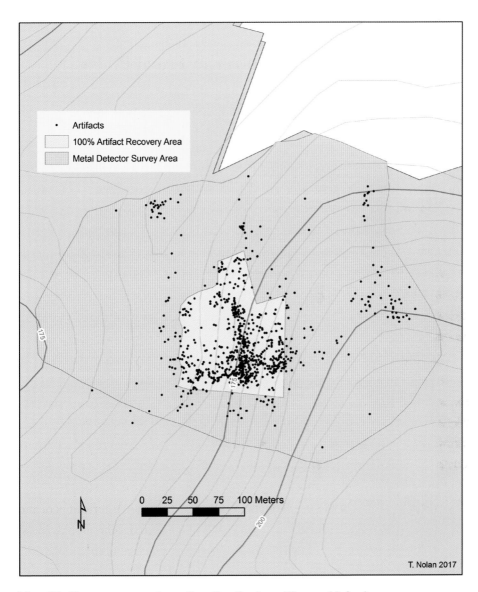

Map 38: Survey area and artefact distribution. (Doctor Nolan)

this work, using distance and direction tools in the form of measuring tapes and compass. Many artefacts were found, cleaned, identified and catalogued. Nolan explains:

> Before analysis can begin, it is important to consider what the recovered artefacts represent and what kind of spatial relationships

An archaeologist working in a 1x1 meter unit where the brass belt parts were found. Here he is working around the sole of a boot or shoe with hob-nails.

Fig. 30: James Legg, archaeologist working in Savage's temporary grave. (Posey)

In addition to the shoe sole a German tooth brush and several American Cartridge Belt parts were found in the 1x1 meter unit the

Fig. 31: The discovery of a boot, believed to be that of Corporal Savage. (Posey)

When the metal detectors could find no more artifacts the French regional archaeologist Brought in a backhoe and began to scrap layer of soil away which would be checked Again with a metal detector.

Fig. 32: The backhoe working and James Legg in the trench where the boot was found. (Posey)

Fig. 33: Work continues.

Fig. 34: A Railroad watch unearthed close to where the boot was found. (Posey)

Fig. 35: Corporal Savage grave, the topography is very similar. (Army Photographer 1919 – inserts by B. Posey)

Fig. 36: Corporal Savage grave, with items of kit, some of which was found in 2006 and 2009. (Army Photographer 1919 – inserts by B. Posey)

Fig. 37: Murray Savage burial on the slope. (Inserts by B. Posey)

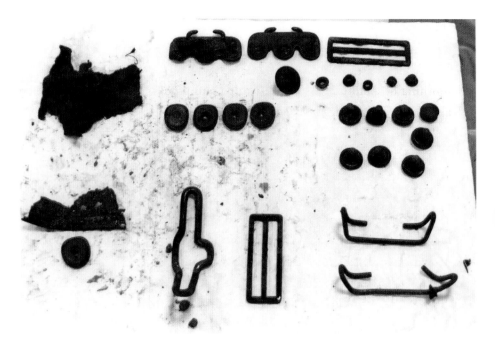

Fig. 38: Artefacts recovered from the area believed to be the site of Corporal Savage's temporary grave. (Posey)

Fig. 39: The watch after cleaning. Inscribed 'Railroad Watch. Swiss Made' possibly belonging to Corporal Savage. (J. Legg)

their location symbolise. The artefacts recovered are the material remains of an engagement between a patrol from G Company, Second Battalion, 328th Infantry and elements of several German units on the morning of October 8 1918. Discarded equipment, broken weapons, and dead soldiers mapped the course of the events.

The area in the ravine has never seen a plough, not in any recent history. There is a Medieval dam that was possibly a fish pond for a monastery located close by. Trees grow in profusion and there is a soft carpet of leaf on the ground. After the fight, salvage teams moved in to recover items of equipment that would eventually be recycled. The burial parties would go about their business, and time and weather would conceal the remaining equipment. Objects that remained, waiting to be discovered nearly 100 years later, were those that were overlooked by salvage teams as being not worthy of salvage, or perhaps too bloody to collect. As time passed by, the location where the fight took place was lost, even to the local French populace. More than 2,600 artefacts were recovered from the area of study. Nolan gives an explanation of the scientific possibilities:

> The artefacts were classified by category to facilitate analysis. The classification code and quantity for each artefact were entered into the spatial database attribute table. It was anticipated that several spatial patterns would be revealed by the arrangement, quantity, and class of artefacts. American uniform and equipment items would indicate the location of death or the burial of Americans killed in action. A concentration of artefacts in the area described by the documentary evidence would confirm the site of the engagement. Individual firing positions, weapons, and the intensity of combat would be revealed by the quantity and location of expended ordnance. The location, quantity, and type of German equipment and weapons would indicate the surrender of German personnel.

The details regarding the burial of the six American dead have been explained but to summarise, all six men were buried on 24 October 1918 by Chaplain John O'Farrelly of the 303rd Engineers. He recorded the locations of the burials on the Grave Location Blank for five of the men as being 297.4 East and 280.2 North on the Forêt d'Argonne map sheet. The Murray Savage file did not contain a Grave Location Blank. This location was due west of Hill 223 and contradicted much of the other spatial records. An examination of the burial records for other members of the battalion buried the same day showed the same coordinates listed for the six members of the patrol. In short, O'Farrelly did not practice accuracy in any of the burials he carried out that day.

Prior to the GRS exhuming the bodies, they surveyed all the burials and recorded the map locations. They recorded Wareing, Swanson, Dymowski, and Weiler as buried at 296.6 East and 279.8 North. Private Wine was a little further away at 296.7 East and 279.9 North.

There were no GRS records for Murray Savage, only a report on his disinterment and subsequent burial at the U.S. Meuse-Argonne cemetery.

It can be seen that the American artefacts were in three groups. The first, on the west side of the stream, consisted of forty unexpended .30-06 rounds in stripper clips and two loose rounds, part of the brass cover for a first aid

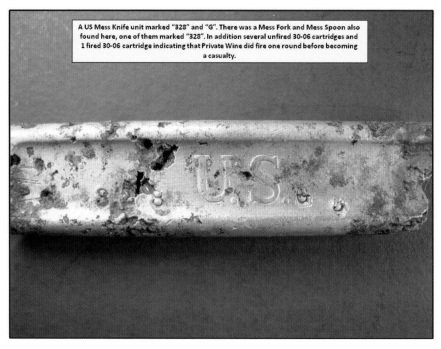

A US Mess Knife unit marked "328" and "G". There was a Mess Fork and Mess Spoon also found here, one of them marked "328". In addition several unfired 30-06 cartridges and 1 fired 30-06 cartridge indicating that Private Wine did fire one round before becoming a casualty.

Fig. 40: A mess knife marked '328 g' believed to belong to Private Wine. (Posey)

Fig. 41: James Legg's notes, written contemporaneously. (Posey)

Fig. 42: A U.S. helmet, believed to have belonged to Corporal Murray Savage. (Author)

dressing, a pocket knife, fragments of a U.S. helmet, tunic button, knife and fork, and collar insignia inscribed with '328', crossed rifles, and the letter 'G.' A point plotted at the centroid of this artefact scatter measured 14.8 yards from the stream. This corresponds closely to the location recorded by the GRS for the burials of Wareing, Swanson, Dymowski, and Weiler.

Near a small clump of trees further artefacts were discovered that were entered into the coordinates. They were a leather sweat band for a U.S.

Fig. 43: The remains of a first aid dressing kit. (Posey)

Fig. 44: U.S. tunic button.

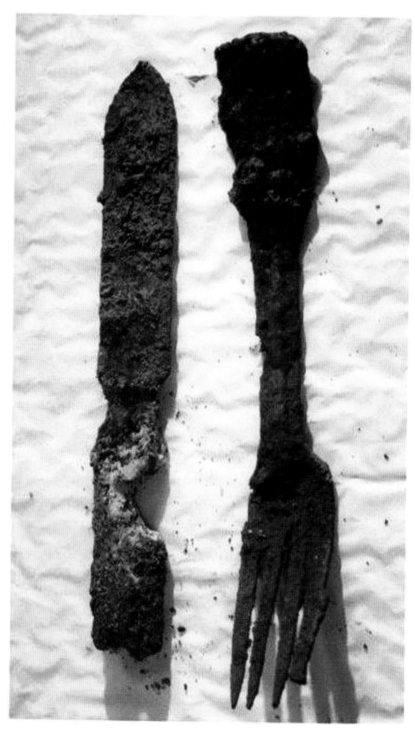

Fig. 45: U.S. knife and fork.

Fig. 46: Excavating at the burial site of Private Wine. (Posey)

Fig. 47: The remains of a helmet liner, believed to have belonged to Private Wine. (Posey)

Fig. 48: Metal detecting at Private Wine's burial site. (Author)

Fig. 49: 30.06 rounds in stripper clip, believed to have been Private Wine's.
(Author)

Fig. 50: Private Wine's spoon. (Author)

Fig. 51: Part of a tent pole found at Private Wine's burial site. (Author)

Fig. 52: Parts of a belt, possibly belonging to Corporal Savage. (Author)

Fig. 53: U.S. pouch, possibly belonging to Corporal Savage. (Author)

Model 1917 helmet and a five-round clip of .30-06. There was also an expended .30-.06 cartridge, a brass tent pole, a U.S. fork, a spoon marked '328' on the back, and a knife marked '328 G'.

A point plotted at the centroid of this artefact scatter measured 33.7 yards east of the stream and, again, corresponds closely to the recorded location by the GRS for Private Wine's burial. It is believed that Wine was able to discharge at least one round before becoming a casualty.

The evidence to support the project belief that this indeed was the site of the York fight, was steadily mounting. Their confidence that the historical records, if followed, would yield the evidence was bearing fruit.

These items that were recovered were artefacts that lay on the top of graves or that became easily detached from clothing during disinterment. When the evidence from the GRS records was coupled with the unit collar disk from G Company, 328th Infantry, the tunic button and other artefacts, there was a strong indication that this was the original burial site for Wareing, Swanson, Dymowski, Weiler and Wine.

On the east side of the stream, a third group of artefacts were recovered. They were the remains of a 1910 model cartridge belt manufactured by the Mills Company, the remains of a first aid pouch and dressing, the remains of a canteen cover, and eighty-eight unexpended .30-06 cartridges, many still in stripper clips. The crown of an American helmet and an 'American Railroad' pocket watch were just a few metres away. In subsequent excavations, additional parts of the cartridge belt, part of an American boot sole with hobnails, and rubber spacers for a U.S. helmet liner were discovered. The hilt of a U.S. model 1917 bayonet was found close by. When the team looked at the photograph taken by the Army photographer in 1919, close examination revealed the same items of equipment on top of the grave of Murray Savage. Clearly visible are a cartridge belt with full pouches, canteen cover, helmet, and a rifle with bayonet. This confirmed the location of Savage's burial and corroborated the GRS record detail.

The archaeologist James Legg concluded that the failure during backhoe trenching to discover the grave shafts was attributable to the character of the soil and the shallow burial depth. The burial records indicated that the bodies were buried from 1 to 2½ft deep.

Chapter 21

The Site of Engagement

The 82nd Division history states that the attack on 8 October was stopped by 'machine gun fire from a hill directly south-west across the valley from Hill 223'.[1]

It was these machine guns that were the objective of the patrol from G Company, who were on the left flank of the 2nd Battalion attack. The metal detector search was focused on the hill south-west of Hill 223. A large concentration of artefacts was found on the south slope of this hill. It was described by both Buxton and Danforth in their accounts and annotated maps and is illustrated on showing the attack on the 2nd Battalion on 8 October.

The artefact concentration is south of the wood line in the vicinity of hill '2', described by Lieutenant Karl Kubler as the site where he surrendered. You will recall Lieutenant Karl Glass, 1st Battalion, 120th LIR, when he described the location of Kubler's 4th Company, 120th LIR, as at the exit of a wooded ravine at the edge of the woods. Glass states that to the rear of the 4th Company he saw several groups of soldiers eating breakfast with their equipment and weapons put aside.[2] Doctor Nolan says that this is consistent with the pattern of expended cartridges at the wood line and the concentration of German equipment on the steep slope to the rear (see Maps 38 & 38b).

Nolan Group member Brad Posey made an important discovery when visiting the German archives in Munich. We have read the contents of his report previously, but it is now necessary to make further reference to it as it describes succinctly Lieutenant Thoma's position on the battlefield. Max Thoma began his military service in 1899 aged eighteen, rising from private to a non-commissioned officer in the Bavarian Reserve Infanterie Regiment 17. In 1915 Thoma was commissioned as a lieutenant, and in June 1916 he was assigned to the 7th Bavarian Mineur Company.

Thoma is an extremely valuable source of information because in addition to the statement he made to the Reichsarchiv statement in 1929, he made an

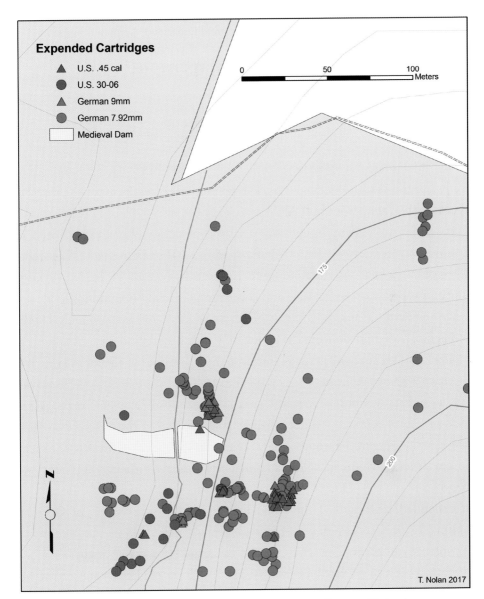

Map 38a: Type of expended small arms ammunition. (Doctor Nolan)

earlier statement on 10 October 1919. This is the one found by Posey and it represents the *first* German eyewitness account of the York firefight (see Figs 6 & 7, 65 & 66).

Thoma said that at 8 am Vollmer ordered him to occupy the gap between Vollmer's battalion and von Sick's battalion. He moved forward with one

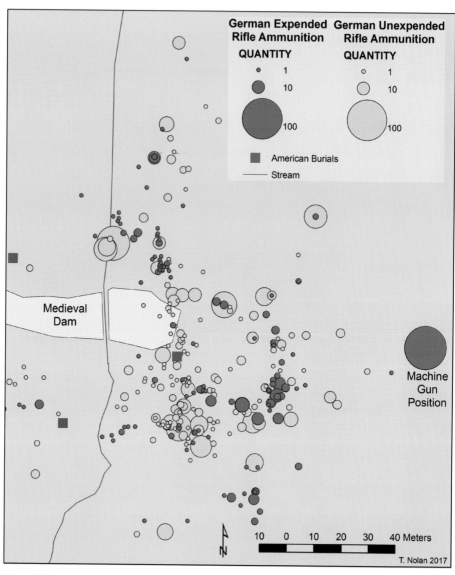

Map 38b: German expended and unexpended rifle ammunition. (Doctor Nolan)

platoon, leaving the other on the slope. Along the way, he passed a machine gun manned by infantry (without doubt, an MG08 heavy machine gun from 4th Company, LIR 120.) From his new position on the forward slope of the hill Thoma noted that he had a 'good overview' and that he 'ordered the platoon leader to send a liaison patrol to the right and to position his platoon as ordered'.

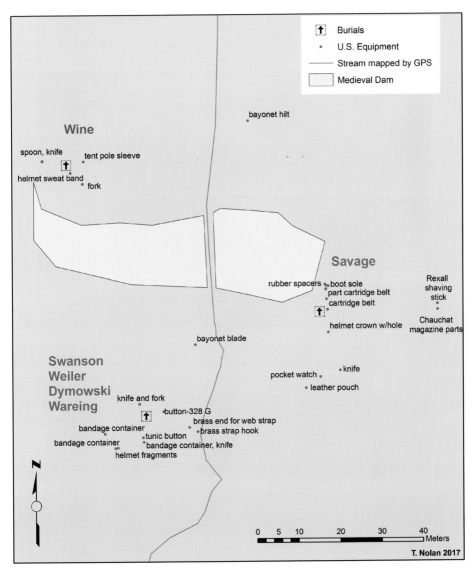

Map 38c: American Equipment Artefacts & Probable Burial Sites. (Doctor Nolan)

[Thoma is referring to the platoon left on the slope; he wanted to extend them to the right in the direction of von Sick on the Hohenbornhöhe.]

It is necessary to remind the reader of Thoma's report; it bears important information as to where he was as he surveyed the situation and ordered fire upon American forces around Hill 167:

49191. Sergt. Alvin C. York, 328th Regiment Infantry, 82nd Division, who with aid of 17 men, captured 132 German prisoners; showing hill on which raid took place in background. Argonne Forest, near Cornay, Ardennes, France. Feb. 7, 1919.

(Raid took place Oct. 8, 1918)

Fig. 54: York in February 1919, standing at the scene of the fight. Note the high rise of the ground behind him and George Pattullo to his left rear (see also Figs 58, 60 and 64). (Army photographer. 1919.)

Savage Burial

This is a sunken path

1919 photo was probably taken at this angle

Fig. 55: A 2009 photograph taken at the same spot where York stood in 1919. (Nolan Group)

Fig. 56: A photograph at the spot in 2016. (Author)

Lively rifle fire was heard to the *right rear of our position.* [Italics by author] Suddenly a call rang from my right. 'Unbuckle everything'. I immediately ran in that direction with my orderly; after about 100 metres I met some German prisoners, including my battalion commander. I called to First Lieutenant Vollmer, 'I will not let myself get captured.' He replied, 'It is useless, we are surrounded. I will take responsibility.' Since an escape to the rear was impossible I let myself be captured.[3]

Lieutenant Thoma had heard gun fire and also the order to drop equipment from the area where the firefight with York was taking place. The liaison platoon delivering his orders was too late; the platoon had already been captured. The events that follow indicate strongly to Posey that Vollmer's act of offering York the surrender of Thoma's men, who were resisting capture, punctuates what little remained of the German soldier's fortitude. The men of LIR 120 and the rest of the 2nd Landwehr division were gradually whittled away as the war progressed, and the division itself existed only on paper. By October 1918, its remaining members were divided among other units. An officer summarised the German will to fight in his statement to the Reichsarchiv:

Anyone who knows the morale of our troops as it existed in those days must admit that it was comparatively easy for the Americans to perform heroic acts. I must confirm that the fighting value of the men in the trenches had sunk very low. A few days prior to this incident, we were unable to carry out a counterattack because our men simply would no longer go over the top. Racing through the enemy barrage at the head of my company, I found myself in the frontline with only one sergeant and four privates; the remainder of my company was 'unaccounted for'. When I ran back to the rear, I saw my men, together with other companies and even their commanding officers lying at the edge of the woods.[4]

The German artefact distribution found in the ravine bottom and on the western facing slope indicates that a German surrender occurred there. Numerous gas mask parts, mess equipment, weapon system parts and accessories, and many unfired cartridges were found.

Fig. 57: A photograph of the fight area from the German perspective, taken in 2009. (Posey)

George Pattullo (with Pipe) and Major
Buxton after Writing the Sergeant
York Story for the Saturday Post

Fig. 58: Officers and George Pattullo. (See also Fig. 54 Pattullo in the background).
(History of 805th Infantry, P. Bliss)

Fig. 59: The 'charge' of Lieutenant Endriss. (Posey)

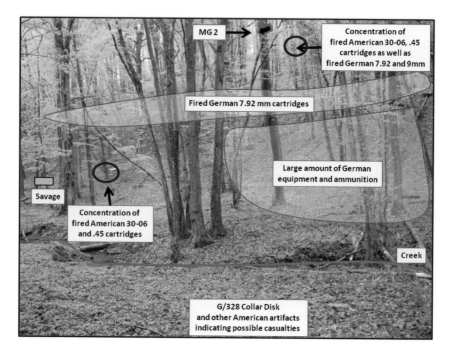

Fig. 60: Sequence of events in the ravine. (Posey)

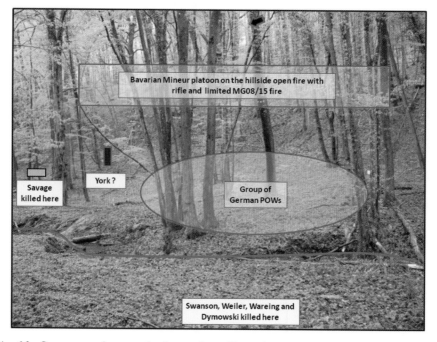

Fig. 61: Sequence of events in the ravine. (Posey)

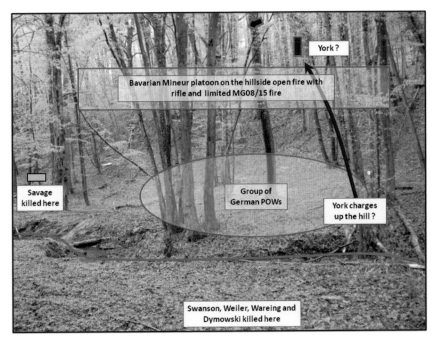

Fig. 62: Sequence of events in the ravine. It is highly unlikely that York charged up this very steep hill. (Posey)

Fig. 63: Sequence of events in the ravine. (Posey)

Fig. 64: York's fight site. See the topographical comparison with Fig.60. (Army photographer 1919)

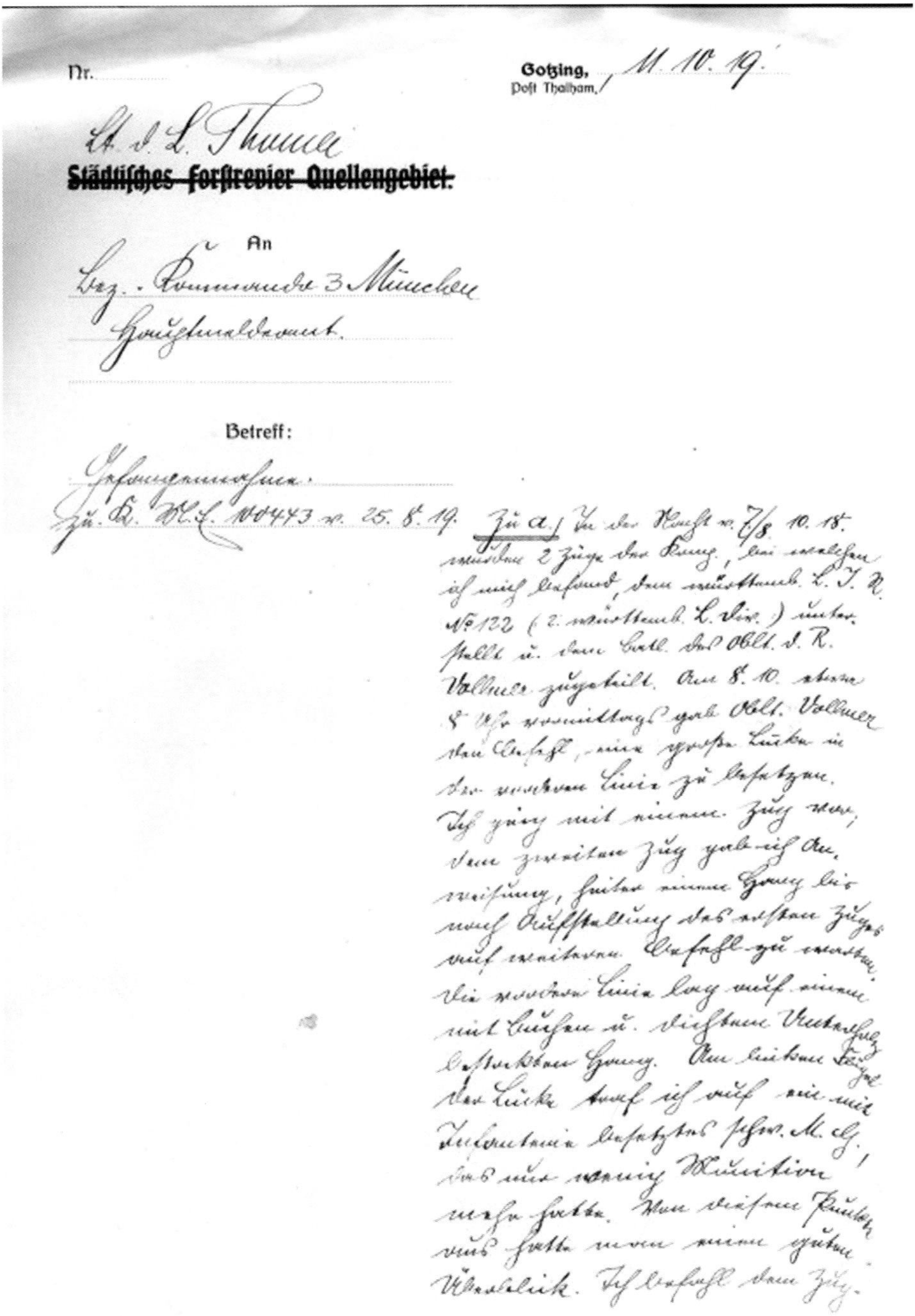

Nr.

Gotzing, Post Thalham, 11. 10. 19.

Lt. d. L. Thoma
~~Städtisches Forstrevier Quellengebiet.~~

An
Bez.-Kommando 3 München
Hauptmeldeamt.

Betreff:
Gefangennahme.
Zu B. W. L. No 4473 v. 25. 8. 19.

Zu a./ In der Nacht v. 7/8. 10. 18. wurden 2 Züge der Komp., bei welchen ich mich befand, dem württemb. L. I. R. No 122 (2. württemb. L. Div.) unterstellt u. dem Batl. des Oblt. d. R. Vollmer zugeteilt. Am 8. 10. etwa 8 Uhr vormittags gab Oblt. Vollmer den Befehl, eine große Lücke in der vorderen Linie zu besetzen. Ich ging mit einem Zug vor, dem zweiten Zug gab ich Anweisung, hinter einem Hang bis nach Aufstellung des ersten Zuges auf weiteren Befehl zu warten. Die vordere Linie lag auf einem mit Büschen u. dichtem Unterholz bedeckten Hang. Am linken Flügel der Lücke traf ich auf ein mit Infanterie besetztes schw. M. G., das nur wenig Munition mehr hatte. Von diesem Punkte aus hatte man einen guten Überblick. Ich befahl dem Zug-

Fig. 65: Lieutenant Thoma's statement, page one. written on 25 August 1919.

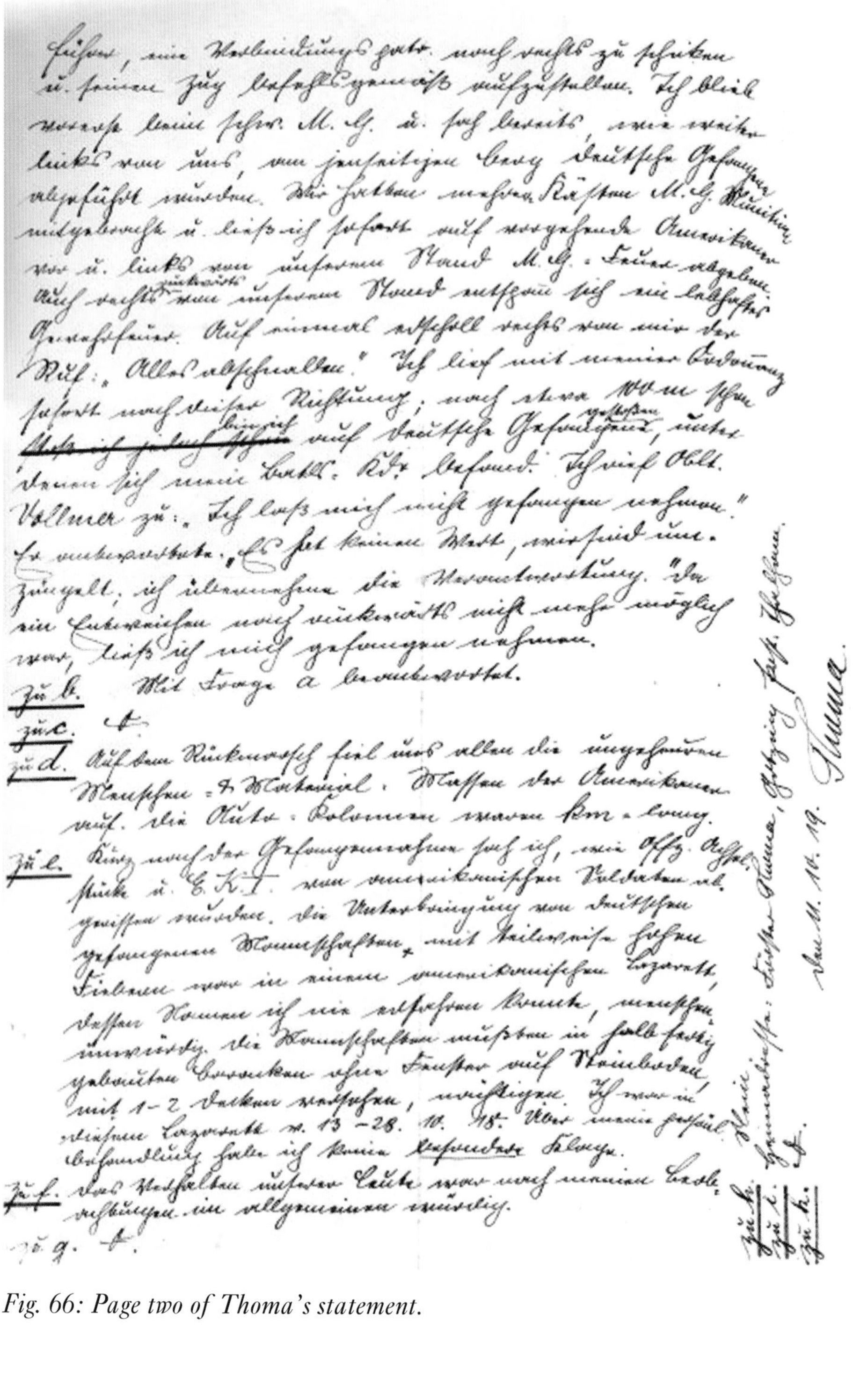

Fig. 66: Page two of Thoma's statement.

Fig. 67: Parts of a German machine gun. (Posey)

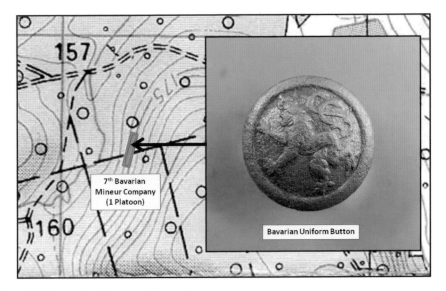

Fig. 68: Bavarian button. (Posey)

Fig. 69: Table of artefacts, 2009. (Author)

Fig. 69a: More 2009 artefacts. (Author)

Fig. 70: Boot polish. (Posey)

Fig. 71: German ink well. (Posey)

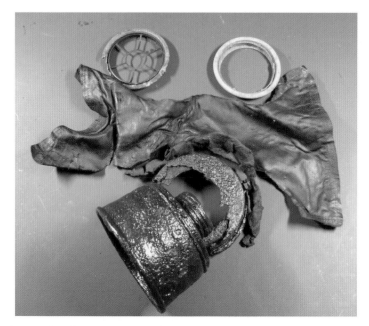

Fig. 72: Parts of a German gas mask.

Fig. 73: German canteen.

Fig. 74: German pan with a .45 cal bullet hole. (Posey)

Fig. 75: German toothpaste. (Posey)

Fig. 76: Toothbrush. (Posey)

Fig. 77: Tin of weapon grease, with the fingerprint of the last user. (Posey)

Contrary to a statement made by Colonel Mastriano in his book[5] to the effect that the Nolan Group had never found evidence of a German machine gun(s); several German machine gun drag sling hooks, used to carry the German heavy MG-08 sled-mounted machine gun, were discovered on the slope. In addition, a Bavarian uniform button was unearthed. The Bavarian Army wore different buttons from other German units, their buttons were embossed with the

Fig. 78: German chewing gum tin. (Posey)

distinctive Bavarian rampant lion. The only Bavarian unit operating in the 2nd Landwehr [LDW] Division's sector was the 7th Bavarian Mining Company. This find provides physical evidence that Thoma's Bavarian sappers were on this slope firing at the American patrol (see Figs 8 & 68). Further evidence was uncovered when a large concentration of expended German 7.92 mm cartridges was found. This indicated the position of a German machine gun. The slope was littered with German cartridges, gas mask and personal equipment parts, and a Schanzzeug 96; a large German spade used by pioneer or sapper units such as the 7th Bavarian Mineur Company.

Chapter 22

Individual Firing Positions

I ndividual firing positions are indicated by location and quantity of expended small arms ammunition. Expended cartridges from the bolt action rifles used by both sides are ejected to the right and rear of the shooter. The point of impact of each ejected cartridge creates a pattern pointing to the shooter's position. In this case, the pattern of the ejected cartridges has been modified by the steep, 40 per cent slopes at the engagement site. The ejected cartridges recovered in the metal detector survey have been displaced down a slope from their point of initial impact by the momentum of their ejection from the weapon and subsequently by overland precipitation flow, freezing and thawing, and logging operations. Consequently, the patterns created by recovered expended small arms ammunition can only provide a general location of the firing position of individual combatants.[1]

The pattern and quantity of German expended and unexpended rifle ammunition (see Map 38b) clearly shows German infantrymen engaging targets to their rear and subsequently dropping their cartridge belts on the ground. Most of the unexpended ammunition was in stripper clips. Few cartridge belts were recovered, indicating salvage crews emptied the cartridge belts prior to removal from the battlefield. There are also indications of German rifle fire from the 4th Company, 120th LIR, along the road at the edge of the woods directed against the U.S. 2nd Battalion, 328th attack to their front. The distribution of expended German rifle ammunition on the middle and upper western slope of the hill is consistent with statements from American survivors that they were fired on by Germans halfway up the hill when they crossed the stream from the west.

Two German machine gun positions were indicated by a large quantity of expended 7.92 mm cartridges concentrated in one spot. The machine gun position of most interest was in the ravine within sight of the stream that the patrol had crossed. The artefacts recovered here consisted of ninety-one expended 7.92 mm cartridges and 110 unfired 7.92 mm cartridges in twenty-two stripper clips, with evidence of cloth bandoliers between the clips. Some additional artefacts were indicated by the metal detector but owing to tree roots these could not be recovered.

The distribution of .30-.06 cartridge cases (see Map 38c) is consistent with the American accounts that members of the patrol fired several rounds when they first encountered the Germans on the side of the hill, before Sergeant Early issued the command to cease fire. It appears that York's squad moved partway up the hill to gather prisoners when the German machine guns opened fire. Private Beardsley of York's squad stated that he took cover behind a tree about fifteen paces to the rear of York, with Private Dymowski on one side and Private Wareing on the other. Dymowski and Wareing were killed by German machine gun fire. Beardsley told George Pattullo that machine gun fire on both sides of the tree from ground level to 4ft high prevented him from using his 8mm Chauchat Automatic Rifle.

Buxton stated York fired twenty-one rounds from his pistol and fifteen rounds from his rifle (three clips of each).[2] It is difficult to identify York's firing position from the scattered pattern. However, when the symbols representing cartridge cases are made proportional to the number of cartridge cases recovered at that location, an entirely different picture emerges.

The small area contains fifty-two expended .45 calibre cartridges and nine expended 9mm cases. The large number of .45 calibre cartridges may be explained by an occurrence referred to by journalist George Pattullo in his newspaper article of 1919. Pattullo describes a marksmanship contest between Major Tillman and York in which York hit a penny matchbox with every shot at 40 yards.[3] Other items were discovered with multiple bullet holes: a German entrenching tool with a large and small calibre bullet hole and numerous items of German equipment, including mess kits and canteens with multiple bullet holes that provide further evidence of post-engagement target practice. The bullet-struck artefacts were all found at the scene of the fight on the western facing slope, and most of the bullet holes were made by a weapon of at least .45 calibre with a few smaller calibre holes from .30 calibre or 8mm rifle. The canteen (see Figs 2 & 3) has multiple impacts from .45 calibre and a smaller hole from a 9mm weapon. It is virtually impossible for these many objects to have been struck so many times by several weapon types during the firefight, and this kind of artefact is to be found nowhere else on the battlefield.

These are the bullet–struck artefacts:

ARTEFACT NUMBER	ITEM DESCRIPTION	CALIBRE TYPE
061	German model 1896 large pioneer spade	Three .45 cal bullet holes
160.04	German model 1898 rifle lower receiver	.30 cal or 8mm bullet strike through magazine well
218.02	German model 1898 spade variant	Three .45 cal projectile impact and exit holes
1164	German model 1915 water bottle complete	Multiple .45 cal and 9mm projectile impact entry and exit holes. Some blue enamel intact
1367	German model 1908 or 1908/15 machine gun water can with pewter cap.	Multiple .45 cal projectile impact entry and exit holes.
1396	German model 1915 mess kit steel lid and handle with black enamel	One .45 cal projectile impact at angle
From machine gun pos. two	German model 1898 spade variant	One .30 cal bullet impact/exit hole and .45 cal impact at angle
1117070	German model 1915 mess kit	Several steel fragments, one large fragment with two .45 cal projectile impact entry holes and two exit holes.
1117086.01	German model 1915 water bottle	Two large fragments and one small fragment, large fragment with two .45 cal projectile impact entry holes.

During the 2006 investigation a large amount of German 7.92mm expended and unexpended cartridge cases were discovered at the top of the slope. At the time, it was felt that this may be the site where York fought, especially as there were a number of expended .30–.06 cartridge cases and some 9mm cartridge cases.

These finds and those of the artefacts on the lower slope in 2009 as referred to within the preceding pages introduced new channels of thought amongst the

Nolan Group. If the York fight had taken place at the top of the slope, it would have meant him running up a steep hill under fire for 60 yards, followed closely by Lieutenant Vollmer firing his pistol at him. This was not thought likely, by so doing York would have removed himself from the cover of the prisoners on the lower slope. He would have been a target with the chances of his survival drastically reduced. An explanation for the presence of the .30–.06 and 9mm cartridge cases at the top of the slope might have been a result of the 1919 target practice. These two scenarios have been and still are subject of debate within the group. The fact remains, Doctor Nolan explains, that the evidence uncovered on *both* the upper and lower slopes tell a story and *that* evidence is incontrovertible.

Why was the German machine gun at the top of this slope? It was not operating from a tactical position whereby it could fire upon the main assault of the attacking Americans. It was out of line of sight of Hill 223 and in a forested area. It may possibly have been 'in transit' at the time, being moved from the rear to a frontal position, and when the surrender on the lower slope commenced with the initial shots being fired, it was brought to bear and commenced firing. We may never know the answer to the puzzle. Doctor Nolan has proved in his depiction of 'fields of fire' that the position of the upper placed machine gun would have enabled the Germans' line of sight of the lower slope and the creek.

Having presented the facts, it has to be said the most likely site of the action is located on the lower slope close to where the 'American Railroad' watch was discovered and adjacent to what is believed to have been the grave of Murray Savage. The numbers of .30–.06 and .45 calibre cartridge cases found in that area are most likely to have been York's from the 8 October 1918 fight. It was from this position that he may have repelled the bayonet charge. York had estimated the distance to the German machine gun during the fight as 30 yards.[4]

This large concentration of expended .45 cal. cases is York's probable firing position when he engaged the machine gun and the German bayonet charge. A total of eight 9mm cartridges were recovered from York's firing position. In his account, York stated that a German officer amongst the prisoners fired a pistol at him but missed.[5] When Lieutenant Vollmer later surrendered his pistol to York, the ammunition clip was empty. The 9mm cartridges provide confirmation that Vollmer fired his pistol at York before he surrendered, and Vollmer's approximate position. It was also close enough that York could hear Vollmer's request to surrender.

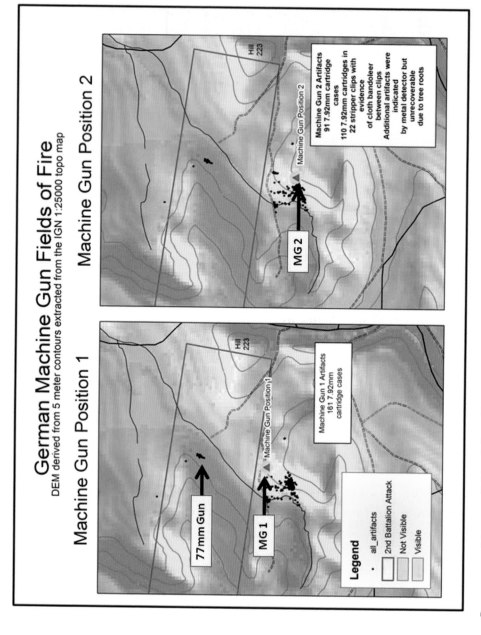

Fig. 78a : German machine gun fields of fire. (Doctor Nolan)

Fig. 79: German P/08 Parabellum pistol, the weapon type used by Lieutenant Vollmer. (Courtesy of Ed. Church)

In G. Edward Buxton's letter to Captain Henry Swindler, dated 23 July 1929, it will be recalled he stated:

> York was the only non-commissioned officer left and lying on the ground beside the prisoners, carried on the firefight against forces scattered fifty to sixty yards above him. He emptied three clips from his rifle and three from his pistol.[6]

A total of eight expended .30-.06 cartridges and two empty .30-.06 stripper clips were recovered from the flat area beside the stream. It confirms the fact that a few surviving members of the patrol besides York engaged the German machine gunners.

Chapter 23

German Equipment Items

The transition of a soldier from combatant status to that of prisoner is not without risk. During the critical moment when a soldier stops resisting, it is imperative for him to demonstrate clearly and slowly his intention to surrender. During the First World War he affirmed his intention to surrender by putting down his weapon and removing his belt and equipment. A soldier might also remove the bolt from his rifle to render it inoperable. Several of the German and American accounts of the engagement refer to soldiers removing their belts to indicate surrender.

The field equipment of a German soldier consisted of three cartridge pouches worn on each side of the front of the belt, containing a total of ninety cartridges. A bayonet and scabbard, entrenching or other tool, canteen, mess tin and eating utensils were also suspended from the belt or carried in a knapsack. Another item of equipment carried by the German soldier was a small can of weapon lubricating grease. In addition to his personal weapon, the German soldier was frequently equipped with several hand grenades.[1]

The surrender of 132 German soldiers would have left many weapons and equipment at the surrender site. In view of the amount of equipment and the distance to the nearest road, it is not surprising that some items escaped salvage. Items of German equipment located during the metal detector survey provide tangible evidence of the surrender of many soldiers. It is interesting to note that only the remains of one set of German cartridge pouches were recovered: that was a Model 87/88 pouch commonly issued to sappers. This pouch and the Gewehr 98b rifle bolt referred to later were probably associated with Thoma's Bavarian Sappers among the German troops (see Maps 38 & 38b).

Fig. 80: German gas mask recovered from the slope where the Germans surrendered. (Author)

Fig. 81: The same gas mask after conservation by the Lincolnshire Conservation Department, 2008. (Author)

Few weapons or weapon parts were recovered. Weapons–related artefacts consisted of two rifle bolts, three ersatz bayonets, the remains of several stick grenades, and a box of grenade detonators. One rifle bolt was from a Gewehr 98b carbine, carried by machine gunners and sappers. A total of seven empty bayonet scabbards or parts of scabbards and three bayonets were recovered. Fifteen entrenching tools and one entrenching tool scabbard were found.

It was surprising to recover more than forty-eight artefacts associated with German gas masks. Three complete gas masks and twenty filter canisters were

Fig. 81a: Doctor Tom Nolan, a light–hearted moment whilst registering finds on the GIS. (Author)

recovered. Considering the high concentration of gas referred to in official records, it is possible these belonged to German dead. A total of eighteen items associated with eating and drinking were recovered. This suggests that some of the Germans were eating and drinking when they were captured. A total of nineteen small metal cans, most containing weapon grease were recovered. The grease in one tin still bore the fingerprint of the last user.

Chapter 24

The Archaeologists and the Science

At the start of the third phase Tom Nolan was concerned that metal detecting in the first two sessions had been hurried and unsystematic, and that much material had been overlooked. This had been due in part to the bad weather, the lack of experienced metal detector operators, and the fact that the time spent on site had been insufficient because of work commitments.

As previously stated, the team wanted to repeat the metal detector survey of the site and expand its boundaries, uncovering material that had not been brought to light previously. Secondly, to locate evidence of the temporary burials of the six Americans in York's patrol. Five of the six burials were reasonably located in the U.S. graves registration records, and the earlier metal detecting had found artefacts probably related to the sixth individual (Murray Savage). The grave search would involve metal detecting, hand excavation, and mechanical stripping.

James B. Legg, the team archaeologist, states that the individual metal detector coverage continued throughout the project with as many as five experienced detector operators working at a time. The team strived for 100 per cent systematic coverage within the search areas, and conducted reconnaissance searches of adjacent landforms. The collection derived from the metal detecting was huge and, like the 2006 collections, its distribution fitted remarkably well with the events of 8 October 1918. Through most of the valley and on the hill slope to the north there was very little First World War material, confirming the team belief there was no other combat taking place in the immediate vicinity. In the area where it was thought the German prisoners were clustered there was a well-defined mass of German material including hundreds of unfired 7.92mm rifle cartridges, stick grenades, gas mask components, mess equipment, entrenching tools and personal items, etc. This was consistent with the prisoners abandoning their weapons and equipment, and it suggested the extent of the loose perimeter formed by their outnumbered American captors.

The first of the probable grave locations examined was likely that of Corporal Murray Savage, a friend of Alvin York, whom York saw riddled with machine gun bullets. His remains were removed in 1921. A 1919 photograph shows Savage's field grave cut into the base of a slope, and covered with equipment including his rifle, cartridge belt, and canteen cover (see Fig. 36). In 2006, metal detecting located artefacts including the remains of a U.S. cartridge belt and seventy unfired .30–.06 cartridges, canteen cover hardware, and a U.S. helmet at such a location, very near to where York was positioned during the action. Legg excavated a 2 × 2m unit at this spot in the hope of finding some evidence of the grave pit. He found additional web gear hardware, U.S. helmet liner parts and the sole of a U.S. hobnailed shoe (see Fig. 31), but no indication of a soil feature. Yves Desfossés then directed the stripping of a larger area using a backhoe, still without success. Yves and Jim Legg both agreed that the colour and character of the soil were such that a shallow backfilled excavation might be difficult or impossible to detect. Not far from the probable Savage grave, Legg found an 'American Railroad' pocket watch (see Figs 34 & 39). The opening of the watchcase that evening was attended with much excitement but it was, alas, not engraved with a name.

The other two grave locations appear to have been plotted accurately, including a row of four burials, [Privates Dymowski, Swanson, Wareing, and Weiler], and the isolated grave of Private Wine. Both localities are on the opposite [west] side of the American perimeter on the west side of the creek. The plotted vicinity of the four-man grave [removed in 1919] yielded a well-defined cluster of U.S. artefacts in both 2006 and 2009. These included a helmet, web equipment hardware, unfired rifle ammunition, mess utensils, a pocketknife, an opened bandage can, a uniform button, and a collar insignia of G Company, 328th Infantry Regiment.

A 1919 photograph of the four graves includes distant terrain details of the west slope of the valley, and this matches the view from the location of the U.S. artefact cluster. The photograph also shows that at least three of the graves are marked with helmets in addition to crosses. (See Fig. 17) A shallow depression is apparent at the probable grave location. Unfortunately, a large

Fig. 82: The Nolan Group after the discovery of the '328 G' Unit collar disc in 2006. From the left: Doctor Tom Nolan, Michael Kelly, Jim Deppen, Olivier Brun (archaeologist), Yves Desfossés, (Champagne-Ardenne regional archaeologist), Professor Michael Birdwell (Castier).

tree is centred in the depression, and with the limited time available the team did not undertake the difficult hand excavation that would have been required to investigate it. Yves Desfossés stripped the topsoil from several trenches around the depression, but no grave feature was detected.

Private Wine's solitary grave was not photographed by the Army photographer in 1919, but its location is well described in the records, and when Wine was removed in 1921 its depth was given as 1ft.

At the approximate location of Wine's grave, metal detecting had yielded the finds earlier described. Given the tree cover and the depth of the original grave, it is hardly surprising that the team did not detect a grave stain.

While the results of the various grave investigations were not as clear cut as the archaeologists would have wished for, James Legg was confident enough to state the following:

> I am firmly convinced that we have located the three documented burial sites. I should emphasise that the U.S. artefacts discussed in this context are not 'cherry-picked from a broad scatter of American material. With the exception of ammunition specimens, these 'grave' artefacts comprise the American collection, and they are indeed clustered in three tight locations. These locations fit well with the historical narrative of the York action, with the pattern of the general artefact distribution, and in two cases, with the locations recorded in 1919 and 1921. After some thirty-two years of working in historical archaeology, I am accustomed to seeing, at best, an ambiguous agreement between the historical record and the archaeological evidence on a site. In this case, the very detailed and well-supported participant narratives of the York action fit astonishingly well with the current landscape and the archaeological data.[1]

But what about the monument located on Hill 167 that informs all visitors that the firefight took place at that location? In fairness to the group that erected the monument, Legg wrote that their report:

> ... can be convincing material for the uninitiated. It is my opinion that the 'other' project was well intentioned, but amounted to an unsystematic, unprovenanced, and unauthorised relic hunt on the battlefield of the main 328th attack on October 8th, 1918 [where, of course, there were thousands of American and German artefacts].[2]

Legg is referring to the apparent absence of verifiable historical source documentation in Mastriano's report, other than lengthy lists of archival resources that are never actually quoted or presented. The report has little that can be fact-checked. As will be discovered later, the few quotes from German archival documents found in it are poorly translated; one entry seems to refer to events that occurred on another day. The maps found in the report are misconstrued, a result of the author's seeming misunderstanding of the correct position of the Humserburg, known to the Americans as the Cornay Ridge. The author continuously depicts Hill 167 as the Humserburg, despite the fact it can be clearly seen in the archival documents that the Humserburg is *not* this hill (see Map 41).

Both German and American accounts and narratives show that there is only one location where Alvin York's fight took place; that is in the ravine on the western side of the hill south-west of Hill 223. The American accounts are more revealing, but nevertheless the German accounts do enhance the understanding of the event and, importantly, corroborate the American narratives, in particular the location of the fight.

Yves Desfossés, the archaeologist responsible for the area around Châtel-Chéhéry, assisted the Nolan Group in their investigations. He too was interviewed later by Stephan van Meulebrouck about his thoughts on the Nolan versus Mastriano situation. He was surprised when he was told that he appeared on the SYDE report acknowledgements list, stating that he had never been invited to the unveiling of the monument. Yves told Stephan that the SYDE had never had permission to excavate; he states that it is not the police or the municipality that grant such permission but him and the property owner. He is the highest archaeological authority in the area and when asked why he had not issued a permit he said:

> Mastriano was already convinced that he had found the exact spot before he began digging and found those 21 casings. That was just too coincidental. Also, I think that he had a flaw in his methodology in thinking a fire fight should follow a set pattern.[3]

Desfossés continues, stating that Doctor Nolan did receive the necessary permits. He may have used a backhoe in his excavations, but he did with the assistance and backing of Desfossés himself. Archaeology is a disruptive science, and Nolan and his team documented all their finds and future archaeological investigation is still possible. Mons. Desfossés, in conclusion says:

> Mastriano ruined his research site ... they have destroyed a part of their own historical heritage ... as far as I know, the American army is not known for its archaeological expertise.[4]

In 2010, James Legg wrote a summary of the 2009 investigations:

> The 1 × 2m unit included numerous brass fittings from U.S. equipment, the German toothbrush, rubber pieces from a U.S. helmet, and much of a U.S. shoe. In 2006 Tom [Nolan] found the remains of a U.S. helmet, (See Fig. 42) nearly a full individual soldier's load of .30–06 cartridges, and numerous U.S. brass fittings, all in this immediate vicinity.
>
> Given the U.S. helmet parts, equipment hardware, and shoe that were recovered, I believe the grave was at or very near (within several metres) of the 1 × 2m unit. In most soils, a filled hole such as an emptied grave will show itself by discoloration or differences in texture – that was why I placed the 1 × 2m, in an effort to actually see the grave. I did not detect it, but there were artefacts buried under soil that was the same color as the soil color to be seen in all directions. In other words, even where I knew I was in disturbed soil, because there were artefacts down in it, I could see no difference. Yves and I saw the same problem (that is we saw nothing) when he did extensive trenching of the larger area, including the 1 × 2 location.
>
> There is one other location that might be the grave, two metres up the slope from where I found the pocket watch there was an unusual concavity on the slope, which was similar to the photo of Savage's grave (see Fig. 10). (There was also one of these concavities at the top of my 1 × 2). It is possible that this is the grave, and Savage's artefacts were thrown off to the side (to the area of the 1 × 2) when he was removed. The watch [pocket] could possibly be his ... The 4–man grave is the least understood of the three in terms of actual placement. It is generally clear where it is located from the photo, which matches the terrain in the foreground and background very well, and the description in the documents locating it relative to the stream and the path, agrees with the photo quite well. It is probably located at or near the U.S. helmet remains found by Eddie [Browne]. This is adjacent to two large trees which are growing out of a sunken area which may be the grave or perhaps a large shell hole if we are incorrect. Yves dug trenches near this feature in 2006 and 2009, but in neither case

actually explored the sunken area. (This would have been impractical with heavy equipment due to the tree roots involved) ... there were other U.S. artefacts, the 328/G disk, brass fittings, scattered toward the stream from this location.

The GRS documents place Wine's grave near that spot relative to the 4-man grave, the stream and the path, and the artefacts certainly suggest a U.S. casualty. As you may know, we have all three utensils, (knife, fork, spoon), knife with G/328, spoon with 328, fork not yet cleaned, as well as the fragments of U.S. helmet liner. These were in a very small area, perhaps 1.5 metres. Again, Yves and I were unable to detect a grave feature, but there is some reason for that collection of artefacts.

In general, I think we probably have true locations for the three graves, within a few metres in each case. I am not as interested as Tom [Nolan] in saying we know anything with certainty – in my business we deal with the evidence of silent objects and reasonable interpretations, and we can never be completely certain what we are looking at.

I will say that I am absolutely convinced that the York action took place in that ravine, in the vicinity of the earth dam. In many places in the Argonne it would always be impossible to confirm such a location, because the intensity of combat left far too much material to interpret, (Mastriano's site is in such an area). In that ravine, however, there was no general battle, and the artefacts indicate a minor, localised action with a German surrender and several U.S. casualties. Comparison of the various historical narratives with the distribution of artefacts, results in a remarkable agreement, the event exists now (for the very few who remember it at all) in the realm of national myth/legend, more the Gary Cooper version than anything else, but it is clear to me that it really happened much as it is described, and it happened in that ravine.[5]

Chapter 25

The SYDE Claims

Colonel Mastriano and his Sergeant York Discovery team made claim on their website report[1] to have discovered, with 100 per cent certainty, the site where Alvin C. York fought on 8 October 1918. The report was taken down during 2010 and a message was left telling of a new version to appear in May of that year. In the April 2008 report, the SYDE state that their biggest find occurred on Saturday, 21 October 2006 when they discovered nineteen of the twenty-one Colt .45 ACP cartridges fired by York. It was claimed to be the 'final piece of the puzzle'. And it was at that position where York fought off the German attack, continued the statement. These artefacts were spread over a 10ft wide area and were between 2–4in deep. Then came the following statement on the website report:

> This was followed by the discovery of the location where York used his .30-.06 calibre M1917 rifle to eliminate the German machine gun position. The find means that the search for the York spot is over.

They stated the discovery is verified by four pillars which are:

- **Primary source research in seven German and five American archives.**

The following is an extract from the 2008 website report relating to archival research:

> Understanding the strength of historical research meshed with battlefield archeology and military analysis we elected to employ a holistic multidiscipline approach to locating where York earned the Medal of Honor. This was made possible by over 700+ hours of

archival research in both the USA and Germany using hundreds of battlefield maps and documents. Herein lays the difference. Other American groups have attempted to identify where York earned the Medal of Honor, but shabbily relied upon only US based research. This put these groups in the wrong portion of the Argonne as they only had a portion of the story. We are the first research team to use both the American and German archives to research the York story.[2]

The report continues that archival study was a major part of the study; that one must avoid the one-sided approach of merely using the American data, which is the shortcoming of previous expeditions to find the 'York spot'. No team before the SYDE had used the German archives to gather the facts on York. The SYDE stated that the German reports provided an accurate picture of both terrain and the deployment of units. Several of the key German participants, they say, referred to a trench near the meadow where the fight took place. As far as the SYDE were concerned, there was only one trench in the ravine, which made the discovery of the area of search easy. The SYDE then relate to battlefield theory and intelligence preparation of the battlefields (IPB).

> … there is enough battlefield litter (remnants of war) for someone to mistakenly fabricate a story that they found the 'York Spot'. To avoid this pitfall, one must study the German and US archives and understand German 1918 military tactics (and use of terrain). These criteria can be developed to confirm the York location.[3]

After due examination of the report, the Nolan Group arrived at the conclusion that the SYDE used only four quotes from their list of German archival material. There are several quotes from the York diary; a quote from General Pershing, and a portion of York's Congressional Medal of Honor citation. The material in their report indicates they used only fractional quantities of the archival material they have in their list of references at the back of their report. The Nolan Group are of the opinion that this not only serves to confuse anyone trying to cross-reference their work, but it also conceals the lack of any real substance of historically accurate data, or interpretation. The SYDE state:

- **Classic Military Intelligence Terrain Analysis.**

Understanding how the Germans used key terrain is a key aspect of the search for the York Spot. After four-years of continuous warfare, the German Army was a master of using every terrain feature possible to bolster their defense.[4]

The Nolan Group believe that armies have been using terrain analysis for thousands of years; this is nothing new to 1918 German or American intelligence. In this specific engagement, there were a handful of American soldiers under the leadership of several junior non-commissioned officers, operating in a fast-paced and unplanned action to eliminate German machine guns threatening their unit's left flank. The Nolan Group believe American testimony has revealed that the patrol used the sound of the German machine guns to put the patrol directly behind the sound of gun fire, to launch a surprise attack from the rear. The site the SYDE claims to be the exact location of the York fight is directly in the front of the German machine gun positions, and in direct line of fire from their own unit, 2nd Battalion, 328th Infantry. The SYDE site is key terrain if it is considered that this was the hill being attacked by the main effort of 2nd Battalion, 328th Infantry.

- **Classic Military Intelligence Doctrinal Templating (using contemporary 1917 – 1918 doctrine).**

Under this section appears the statement that a school-trained U.S. Army theoretician who holds a Master's degree in Military Operations helped with this process, putting a perspective on the German and American operations, considering terrain and weather that are part of the IPB. The application of this doctrine by the SYDE considerably narrowed down where the York fight took place.

The Nolan Group believe that there were no new doctrinal intelligence methods used by either the Americans or Germans during this battle that are unique to this specific engagement. The use of high ground, flank protection and clearing fields of fire cannot be proclaimed as solid evidence to pinpoint the site of the York fight.

- **The Physical Artefact Evidence.**

The statement under this section says that the artefact evidence must match/complement the IPB military doctrine and terrain to confirm or deny the correct location. Based upon this consideration, the following criteria were developed to prove – or deny – the location of where York earned the Medal of Honor.

The SYDE state that there must be a 'yes' to all these points to be at the correct location of York's action.

a. Does it agree with historical facts about German units involved and unit defence locations?
b. Does the location make sense historically?
c. Is the location consistent with contemporary German and American tactics, techniques and procedures? (TTPs)?
d. Is it along the flank of the German 125th and 120th Regiments?
e. Does the terrain match the February 1919 photographs taken in 1919 during BG Lindsey's investigation of SGT York's combat action on 8 October 1918?
f. Is it supported by battlefield archaeology?
g. Is it close to the 1/120 regiment battlefront and within the 1/120th sector?
h. Is it logical from a tactical military perspective?
i. Does it agree with written German and American testimony?
j. Is it located where the machine guns are in the fight – engaging Americans in the valley?
k. Is it on terrain that dramatically impacted the outcome of the battle (decisive terrain)?
l. Does it agree with the battle progression/sequence as recorded by the 2nd Landwehr Division and the battle sequence as recorded by all of the American and German units involved in the action?
m. Is the location positioned where the German machine gunners were able to observe both the action of the American 328th Infantry Regiment trapped in the valley, and the meadow where York attacked the 120th?
n. Is it close to a trench (York and Vollmer's testimony)?
o. Is it near two roads that head east – out of the Argonne (York's testimony)?
p. Is it close to Vollmer's headquarters?

q. Is it on terrain that dramatically impacted the battle (decisive terrain) in which both the 120th and 125th would suffer sufficient damage that would cause the line of the German 2nd Landwehr Division (Württembergische) to collapse?

This is an extremely long list of criteria, much of which bears little relevance, but the Nolan Group responses will follow each of the SYDE question or claims.

Does it agree with historical facts about German units involved and unit defense locations?

The SYDE state:

> York took prisoners from the following four German Units. [An endnote here gives the source *as Gruppe Argonne unit deployment locations, 7 October 1918 (Nr. 47) (Generalkommando z.b.v. 58, Fifth German Army, German Imperial Army.]*

> 1. 120 Württembergische Landwehr Regiment, 2. Württ. Landwehr Division
> 2. 125 Württembergische Landwehr Regiment, 2. Württ. Landwehr Division
> 3. 210. Prussian Reserve Regiment, 45th Prussian Reserve Division
> 4. 7. Bayern Mineur Kompanie

> The location where York earned the Medal of Honor must be in an area that prisoners can be taken from each of the units mentioned above. In particular, the specific location must be along the 120th and 125th regimental borders. It was here that the 120th's Vollmer received the 210th Prussian soldiers and where he and the 210th were captured. It was also here that the 125th flanking machine guns wheeled about to engage the 17 Americans. [An endnote refers to '*Gruppe Argonne Attack plan/objectives between Fleville and Gesnes, la 6512, 7 October 1918 (Nr. 47a) Generalkommando z.b.v. 58, Fifth German Army, German Imperial* Army'.]

The German archives reveal that between 1914 and 1918, there is only one location in the entire Argonne where these units served together. [Depicted on a graph – not produced here.] A star on the graph indicates the 'only possible location' where York was fighting. The fact that York secured prisoners from each of the units depicted makes any and every other location impossible to achieve this task.

The Nolan Group state:

No. There appears to be little if no evidence to support the historical facts. The Group has not seen any archaeological evidence provided by the SYDE that supports the exact locations of ANY of the German regiments involved in this action. The German and American historical records do not confirm that York captured any soldiers from the 125th Landwehr and, according to the SYDE report, the 120th and 125th Landwehr boundaries are critical in determining this spot (see Map 42). German records show that the 4th Company of the 120th Landwehr was not located at their site, and was in fact further to the south-east, in and at the mouth of the wooded ravine. In addition, the German records show that the 210th RIR was in this same wooded ravine, 600m south-east of the SYDE York spot.[5]

The location must agree with historical facts about German units involved and unit defense locations, based upon archival data.

The SYDE state:

> The report of the 120th Regiment stated the following: 'The flank of 6th Company reported an enemy surprise attack. Next, the remnant of 4th Company and personnel from the 210th Regiment were caught by this surprise attack, where Lieutenant Endriss was killed. The company was shattered or was captured. Also, First Lieutenant Vollmer ended up in the enemy's hands. Now the situation was worse. Bad news followed more bad news from Chatel to the Schöne Aussicht a large enemy column moved towards the Schliesstal Mulda and the Boulassonbachs [up the valley into the Argonne]. By this, we knew the enemy was moving against the North–South Road.'

The German unit dispositions for October 1918 are very clear and precise in the various German archives. The following graphic [not shown here] illustrates with 100% accuracy the German lay down for 8 October. Exhaustive research in the battle chronology and chronicles in nearly twenty units (all written by different officers) verified this. See endnote for where this data was gathered. [The endnote referred to gives the source as '*General der Artillerie. Die 2. Württemberger im Weltkrieg 1914–1918. Berlag Berger's Literarisches, Stuttgart, Belser: 1920.'*]

The Nolan Group state:
There can be no possible link with any of the official records, be they German or American. The area the SYDE claims to be the site of the York fight is located west of Hill 223 and not 'directly south-west' as is reported almost unanimously by every American historical record and testimony. Furthermore, the SYDE site is located directly in front of the axis of 2nd Battalion, 328th Infantry's, attack.[6]

The German archives were visited by the Nolan Group, who found the quote from the 120th Regiment that the SYDE refer to in the above statement. It reads thus:

> Die Flankensicherung der 6. Kompagnie meldete feindlichen ueberraschenden Angriff. Bald kamen einzelene Leute der 4, Kompagnie, die berichten, ihre Kompagnie und die Leute vom Regiment 210 seien ueberraschend angegriffen worden, Leutnant Endress, de Kompagniefuehrer, sei gefallen, die Kompagnie versprengt oder gefangen. Auch Oberleutnant Vollmer geriet dem Amerikaner in die Haende. Nun war die Lage schlimmer als je, Hiobsbotschaft kam auf Hiobsbotschaft Von Chatel, von der Schoene Ausicht her drangen dichte feindliche Kolonnen, der Schiesstalmulde und dem Verlauf des Boulassonbachs folgend, durch den Wald gegen die Nordsuedstrasse vor.

This is an official translation of that document:

> The flank security element of the 6th Company reported an enemy surprise attack. Soon afterwards individual men from the 4th Company

came up and reported that their company and men from the 210th Regiment had been killed and that the company had been reduced to stragglers or captured. Lieutenant Vollmer also fell into the hands of the Americans. Now the situation was worse than ever, bad news followed more bad news. From Chatel and from Schoene Aussicht heavy enemy columns penetrated, following the course of the Schiesstalmulde and the Boulasson creek, through the woods towards the North – South Road.[7]

The reader may have noted the differences in the two German reports. In the official translation, Lieutenant Endriss is not mentioned by name, only Lieutenant Vollmer, and the references to the terrain and movements are misleading.

Is the location consistent with contemporary German and American tactics, techniques and procedures (TTPs)?

The Nolan Group state:

There seems to be an inference by the SYDE that the use of terrain was something new in 1918 German tactics. The use of the high ground to emplace machine guns is not new nor is it unique to this battle.

Is it along the flank of the German 125 and 120 regiments?

The Nolan Group state:

There appears to be *no* convincing evidence offered by the SYDE to confirm the exact location of the 120th and 125th regimental boundaries or artefacts found marked or in any other way that may be associated with a particular unit, other than a later announcement by the SYDE of the 125th Landwehr Infantry Regiment dog tag, found higher on their hill at the location where, according to the German records, this unit should have been located.[8]

Does the terrain match the February 1919 photographs taken during Brigadier-General Lindsey's investigation of Sergeant York's combat action on 8 October 1918?

The Nolan Group state:

The 1919 Signal Corps photographs of the graves of the American soldiers from York's patrol, shows terrain that appears to not be comparable to any land feature near the SYDE site.[9]

Is it supported by battlefield archaeology?
The Nolan Group state:

The SYDE did not seemingly conduct battlefield archaeology; they appear to have undertaken a relic hunt. Their methods as they have described would not hold up to any scrutiny from professional archaeologists or historians. It is believed that untrained boys (Boy Scouts) were used to excavate on a First World War battlefield that may still harbour unexploded ordnance. If this was the case, the results could have been catastrophic.

The Nolan Group have seen no archaeological evidence from the SYDE that will agree with any of the historical accounts of this fight. The twenty-one cartridge casings have no meaning on a battlefield where lots of soldiers were firing the same weapon. Many .45 calibre cartridges have been found around this area and alone cannot constitute conclusive evidence. There appears to be some confusion too with the exact number of .45 cartridges found at this site.[10] In order to prove categorically that a bullet was fired from a weapon belonging to York that weapon has to be presented for examination. Both York's pistol and his rifle have long ago disappeared.

Is it close to the 1/120 Regimental Battlefront and within the 1/120th Sector?
The SYDE state using the following quote:

Without any artillery preparation, the adversary launched a violent attack and there was heavy fighting, which lasted well into the evening. The enemy was repulsed almost everywhere. 1st Battalion absorbed the brunt of the enemy attack without wavering, due to its good defensive position. The endnote states: '*Dr. Gustave Strohm, Die Württembergischen Regimenter im Weltkrieg 1914–1918, Band 25, Das Württembergische Landwehr Infanterie Regiment nr. 120 Belser Verlasbuchhandklung, Stuttgart, 1922) translated by Sonja Gleichmann and Doug Mastriano, pp. 161–173.*'

The Nolan Group state:
Again, the Nolan Group can find no evidence to support this question. As shown in the previous observation, the SYDE offers no convincing evidence of the exact location of any of the German units involved, except for the 125th Landwehr dog tag, which was found west of their area, where a portion

of the 125th is reported to have been. Again, this find illustrates the 125th were where they were supposed to be.

This original German text was found in the archives by the Nolan Group:

> 5.30 Uhr abends erfolgt dann ohne besondere Artillerievorbereitung ein aeusertst heftiger Angriff mitt sehr starken Kraeften auf die ganze Hoehenstellung. Ein heftiger Infanterie kampt tobt bis Einbruch der Dunkelheit. Dann ist der Feind fast ueberall unter schwersten Verlusten abgewiesen. Die Hauptwucht des Angriffs hatte das I. Batallion ausgehalten, ohne zu wanken; ihm gebuehrt auch das Hauptverdienst an der Abwehr.[11]

Brad Posey obtained this official translation in English by a German court-appointed translator:

> Around 5:30 in the afternoon, without special artillery preparation, a very strong attack occurred against the entire positions along the heights. A fierce infantry battle rages until the onset of darkness. The enemy has been repelled almost everywhere, at the cost of terribly heavy casualties. The 1st Battalion bore the brunt of the attack without wavering; they deserve the primary credit for the defense.

The quote was taken from the 125th Landwehr Infantry history and refers to the 1st Battalion, 125th Landwehr Infantry defending the Champrocher Ridge on the afternoon of 8 October, *after* the York fight. It is *not* the 1st Battalion, 120th Landwehr Infantry.

Is it logical from a tactical military perspective?
The Nolan Group state:
No. For the SYDE to be correct, the patrol would have had to advance in front of their own front line.

Does it agree with written German and American Testimony?
The Nolan Group state:
The German testimony and records show that the German units were positioned differently from where the SYDE say they were. The American

accounts do not agree with the claims by the SYDE. There is no mention by Colonel Mastriano in his book *Alvin York* of the records of the American Grave Registration Services found by the Nolan Group. These are important records of historical, American evidence, which enabled the Nolan Group to locate the temporary American burials, 600m from the SYDE location.

Is it located where the machine guns are in the fight – engaging Americans in the valley?

The Nolan Group state:

As both groups discovered, there were machine guns in the fight at several locations on the hill west of Châtel-Chéhéry. The Nolan Group found the machine guns that were firing into the left flank of G Company, 328th Infantry, and the SYDE located machine guns that were firing into the front of the 2nd Battalion 328th Infantry's attack. The SYDE also discovered, but appear not to mention, the machine gun nest that was above and slightly to the north of their spot. These machine guns were reported by Major Tillman as being captured by E Company, 328th Infantry.

Is it on key terrain that dramatically impacted the outcome of the battle (Decisive Terrain)?

The Nolan Group state:

No. The German machine gun position the SYDE claim York defeated, is not located on decisive terrain in comparison to the large nest of machine guns that were located a few hundred metres north-west and up the hill from their York spot. In addition, the patrol was sent out to destroy the machine guns firing into their unit's left flank. It would be impossible for the SYDE machine guns to pose more of a threat than those German machine guns located on the hill directly south-west of Hill 223.

Does it agree with the battle progression/sequence as recorded by the 2nd Landwehr Division sequence as recorded by all the American and German units involved in the action?

The Nolan Group state:

No, as stated earlier, none of the German or American records appear to support the SYDE location of this fight. In addition, the SYDE claim the Nolan site was the scene of action between the 122nd LIR and the 28th Division at 1400 hours on 8 October, after the York fight. The 122nd LIR was at least 1km further to the south-west of here and never came anywhere close to this ravine. In addition, by 1400 hours, ALL German forces in the entire area had pulled back west of the Decauville railway and when the 28th Division finally did move forward from Hill 223 to the railway they met little, if any, resistance and reported no casualties in this area.

Is the location positioned where the German machine gunners could observe both the action of the American 328th Infantry Regiment trapped in the valley and the meadow where York attacked the 120th?

The Nolan Group state:

No, the fight occurred in an isolated ravine with German soldiers in the bottom of the ravine and on a western-facing slope with other machine guns located on the 'nose' of the hill or ridge, which fired down into the left flank of G Company, 328th Infantry. The SYDE German machine guns were situated in the direct front of the 2nd Battalion, 328th Infantry's, attack.

Is it close to a trench? (York and Vollmer's testimony)

The Nolan Group state:

There are no defined trenches in the area, however, there are old boundary ditches. The 'trench' the SYDE claims to have been used by [Lieutenant] Endriss, is a drainage ditch and runs east–west vs. north–south as it should be, against an attack coming from the east in a westerly direction. The Germans admit there were no trenches as a part of their defence.

Is it near two roads that head east – out of the Argonne? (York's testimony)

The SYDE state:

> Two Roads. York and Vollmer's testimony confirm that there were two roads available for York to march the German prisoners back to the American lines in the vicinity of Hill 223/Chatel-Chehery The SYDE designated location is adjacent to these two roads.

1. In a meadow. The first battalion, 120th Landwehr, under Leutenant Vollmer, *deployed below* [italics by author] Humser Hill, in the meadow valley west of Chatel-Chehery ... The men of the 210 regiment arrived west of Chatel Chehery and stopped in the meadow. [The endnote reference for this text is *'Das Württembergische Landwehr Infanterie Regiment nr. 120 im Weltkrieg 1914–1918.'*]

There is a further quote:

2. Vollmer, the former supply officer of the 125th, deployed along the southern edge of Humser Hill, in the meadow ... the Reserve Infantry Regiment 210 arrived in the meadow. [The endnote reference is *'Das Württembergische Landwehr Infanterie Regiment nr. 125 im Weltkrieg 1914–1918.'*]

The Nolan Group state:

There are many roads that lead east out of the Argonne; there is no document to their knowledge that indicates the presence of two roads heading east that played any serious role in determining the location of this fight.

These are the official translations by a German court-appointed translator of the two passages quoted above by the SYDE:

Waehrend diese Reserven im Anmarsch waren, war das I./L. 120 vom Humserberg ins tal westlich Chatel vorgezogen worden, um zusammem mit oertlichen Reserven des L.I.R. 125 un mit dem eben mit Kraftwagen herangefuehrten I.R. 210 (150 Gewehre) gegen Schoene Ausicht anzugreifen.[12]

While these reserves were approaching, the 1st Battalion, 120th Landwehr was *pulled forward from* [italics by author] the Humserberg into the valley west of Chatel, and together with local reserves of the 125th Landwehr, and with the 210th Infantry Regiment (150 rifles), which had just arrived by motor truck, were to attack Schoene Aussicht.

The 'pulled forward from' in the official translation is substantially different from the SYDE translation. Lieutenant Vollmer's unit was not positioned below the Humserberg, they had moved away from it, which leads us to a logical conclusion that the Humserberg is not where the SYDE believe it to be, but some distance away to the north-west. In addition, the quote describes the general situation on the evening of 7 October 1918, the day before York's action. And again, the German text followed by the official German translation:

2. Das I./L. 120 unter Oberleutnant Vollmer, dem frueheren Verpflegungsoffizier des II./L. 125, wird schon beim Ueberschreiten des Suedrandes des Humserberges vom feindlichen Artilleriefeuer zersprengt und findet sich erst teilweise am andern Morgen in de Mulde, dem sogenannten Schiesstal von Cornay, wieder zusammen, wo es dann dem weiteren Vorstoss der Amerikaner in der Mulde egliegt. Die Schoene Aussicht verbleibt in den Besitz der Amerikaner. Ja, diese sind auch noch im Lauf des Nachmittags weiter in die Mulde eingedrungen.[13]

The 1st Battalion, 120th Landwehr Infantry was led by First Lieutenant Vollmer, the former Supply Officer of the 2nd Battalion, 125th Landwehr Infantry, is dispersed by enemy artillery fire as soon as the troops cross the southern edge of the Humserberg, and is in part not able to regroup until the following morning, in the depression, the so-called Schiesstal of Cornay, where it then succumbs to the further advance of the Americans in the depression. The under-strength Reserve Infantry Regiment 210, which had just been arrived by motor trucks, remains in the meadows. Schoene Aussicht remains in the hands of the Americans. They even advanced further into the depression in the course of the afternoon.

It would seem the SYDE have combined the text from two separate German unit histories, the 120th and the 125th Landwehr Infantry regiments, both of whom are describing the events of 7 October 1918, the day *before* the York fight on 8 October.

What in effect has been repeatedly described as superb German archival research by the SYDE transpires to be nothing more than poorly translated regimental reports; some of the German regiments are not engaged in the specific action, nor are present on dates either prior to or after the York engagement.

Is it close to Vollmer's headquarters?

The Nolan Group state:

No, the headquarters for the 1st Battalion, 120th LIR (Vollmer), was in the ravine where the Nolan site is (see the 2nd LDW Division war diary and the German 1:25,000 topographical map from 1918).

Is it on terrain that dramatically impacted the battle (decisive terrain) in which both the 120th and 125th [Landwehr] would suffer sufficient damage that would cause the line of the German 2nd Landwehr Division (Wüerttembergische) to collapse?

The Nolan Group state:

The initial event that caused the German withdrawal when it did was when several men from the 210th RIR and the 7th Bavarian Mineur Company who had escaped capture reported to Captain von Sick, commander of the 3rd Battalion, 120th LIR, on Hill 244. They said that they had been attacked in the flank and rear. Not knowing this was the action of just a small American patrol and realising there was a huge gap in the German line on 'Hill 2' that a larger American force could easily slip through, von Sick reported the position no longer tenable, and the 2nd LDW Division ordered the withdrawal to positions that were west of the north–south road (see Map 25).

Simultaneously, other German positions were caving in to the 2/328 Infantry attack, and no doubt this too played a role in the time line for withdrawal. However, the capture of the 210th RIR and 7th Bavarian Mineur Company, and portions of the 4th Company, 120th LIR, is what convinced von Sick that his flank and rear was threatened and he risked being cut off and surrounded. The loss of the German machine guns at the SYDE location would play a minor role for the German commander in comparison to the value of the other crew-served weapon positions employed around the valley that day.

A group of Boy Scouts assisting the SYDE had been given permission to use metal detectors whilst helping to construct the York trail in the Argonne Forest. They were detecting on a hill behind the actual trail when they found artefacts associated with a dead German soldier, Private Wilhelm Härer of the 2nd Machinegun Company, 125th Landwehr Regiment. These consisted of the soldier's personal effects, his dog tags, which provided his identification, both of his shoes, his undergarment and uniform buttons, his gas mask and numerous assorted accoutrements.[14] A media report states that a commemoration was held in the soldier's village of Steinbach am Backnang on 28 April 2009.

In his book, Mastriano maintains that Härer's dog tag discovery was a major coup in the search for York. The soldier was assigned to Lieutenant Lipp's portion of Humserberg:

> who commanded the machine gun which Alvin York assaulted, and Lipp was captured by York.[15]

Lipp was captured on Hill 167 and not by York, simply because York was not at this location. The discovery of the dog tags and associated artefacts just serves to reinforce the fact that the 125th LIR were exactly where they should have been, on Hill 167 and nowhere near the York fight.

Chapter 26

The Dutch Investigative Journalist

Stephan van Meulebrouck is a freelance journalist who lives in the Netherlands. He has a long history of association with Alvin C. York having watched the movie as a teenager, although at the time he was of the impression that he was a fictional character. In 1998, he was walking with his wife in the Argonne when they came across the sleepy little village of Châtel-Chéhéry. He saw the statue of York outside the Mairie and realised the events from the film had actually happened. As it was, Stephan was looking for an investigative article to write. Here was the ideal story for him. He knew there was a new interest in the Netherlands for the Great War, and as it was approaching the ninetieth anniversary of York's feat this would be the ideal opportunity to write a piece. After some research, he realised there were two separate groups who were working on identifying the place where York had fought. He first spoke to Mastriano by telephone, after which he felt the man was plausible. After emailing Tom Nolan and talking to him, he thought that his case was even more cogent.

What really triggered him into action on the subject and the two different locations were the emails he received from Mastriano after their initial contact by telephone. These aroused his suspicions that all was not what it seemed, and so he embarked upon a fascinating period of investigative enquiry and research.

Stephan's excellent article, 'Hot on the York Trail', which was painstakingly researched, appeared in the British quarterly magazine of the Great War, *The Western Front Association*, Bulletin 84 in June/July 2009. In this van Meulebrouck wrote in detail about the SYDE and the Nolan Group. Not only that, but he spoke to most of the people who have been involved in both projects, including those in high places such as in the U.S. Army Center of Military History (CMH) who have had an input into this affair.

It is an unbiased article, well written and worthy of close examination. Much of the information van Meulebrouck gathered was from an article dated 2008 that appeared on the SYDE website (the same article much referred to in this book). It was removed later with the note that a new narrative was being written and would appear soon. Now, in 2017, the SYDE website does little to give satisfactory historical and archaeological explanation into their findings, and the 2008 report remains the one SYDE document containing any information that can be examined.

Van Meulebrouck's initial contact by email with Lieutenant-Colonel Mastriano resulted in the latter forwarding his so-called 'Four Pillars' that led to the discovery of the York site. (See Chapter 25). The email ended stating that the debate was over; Mastriano had found the site of York's action. There was nothing left to discuss. The French, the U.S. Army Center of Military History, local officials, the U.S. Army and the French Military concurred with their (SYDE) findings.[1] Another email from Mastriano attached 'the enthusiastic letter of support and endorsement from the U.S. Army Center of Military History', described as the 'Army's last word in history'. The email stated that not only did they (the CMH) endorse the work in the Argonne, but were so convinced that they were willing to allow the SYDE to operate using their name. There followed a ranting paragraph in the email that may be directed toward the Nolan Group and is not appropriate:

> At what point do detractors matter? What are their qualifications to second guess? What do they know about military history? How much and what type of military experience do they have? Who has endorsed their findings – beyond themselves? How complete and thorough was their research? These are the types of questions I imagine that you are asking about now. I am sure that you are beyond the base approach of striking controversy just for the sake of a good article ...[2]

A letter dated 27 March, 2007 from the Director of the Center of Military History, Doctor Jeffrey Clarke, expressed the Army's appreciation for all the fine work carried out by the SYDE. Clarke stated the CMH is:

> Pleased to offer your team encouragement and 'sponsor' your work as you proceed to Phase IV and beyond. While financial aid cannot be offered, you may use our name as one of the organizations that concur in your group's continued battlefield research.[3]

The letter ended with a contact name and phone number of the person at the Centre's museum who would receive any donated archaeological finds the SYDE would care to make.

Doctor Clarke retired in July 2010 and was succeeded by the deputy CMH Director, Colonel Peter Crean, who was less responsive to van Meulebrouck's questioning.

Stephan continued to research and in an email on 26 September 2008 to Mastriano he questioned his disapproval of the Nolan Group's use of a backhoe when Yves Desfossés had sanctioned the work. Van Meulebrouck suggested that the two letters Mastriano was sent were in fact Army documents and not 'third party endorsements' since the Army had its own interests. Stephan then asked if there were any independent publications supporting the SYDE claim and had there been any peer review, as was usual in scientific research?

In the response from Mastriano, the mood changed:

> I caution you against discounting the Army endorsements. The Army was NOT bound to endorse my findings – I do not work for the office of CMH in WASH DC and they have nothing to gain fro [sic] my find. They are THE [sic] experts in this field and if you discount them your article will fall under the logical fallacy of ad hoc ergo proter hoc. Your supposition is utterly ridiculous – who else should study the findings and decide? Who else is the expert? You have me quite flabbergasted. Ridiculous notion my dear friend.[4]

This email was followed by another from Mastriano on 26 September 2008 that included two photographs of the York Historic Trail, an orientation panel headed 'Corporal Alvin C. York', and the following note:

> Final note – as to the debate – do you know there are still people who believe the world is flat?[5]

After this, communication with the Army officer dried up.

After an introduction in his article that explains briefly the York action on 8 October 1918, van Meulebrouck describes Lieutenant-Colonel Mastriano's arrival on the scene. A serving U.S. Army officer, he was transferred to Germany in 2002, which allowed him to start his research in the German archives; in that same year, he paid his first visit to the Argonne Forest. His team, the SYDE, was formed in 2006. There were many discoveries of various artefacts but the lie of the land had to be examined and many questions had to be answered, for instance, did the logical location for the York spot pass examination from a military point of view? But the 'ace in the hole' as far as Mastriano was concerned were the German archives. The York spot had to be, it was said, along the border between two sections of the front, where the 120th and 125th Landwehr regiments had been on that day. Mastriano said that York had captured soldiers from both those regiments. In addition, the SYDE had discovered twenty-one cartridges that must have come from the Colt. 45 belonging to York himself. The conclusion, as we have read previously, was conclusive. The search was over. Mastriano and his team had located the spot where York had fought.

After talking with Doctor Tom Nolan of the Nolan Group, van Meulebrouck described the methodology used by the team, and, four months after the SYDE report was published in 2007, Doctor Nolan's dissertation became available. Nolan had told van Meulebrouck that the York spot was not where the SYDE had said it was and that Mastriano had based his work on the German archives, but they were unreliable. It was American sources, not German, that led the Nolan Group to uncover the unit collar disc marked 'G/328', an encouraging sign of York's unit being at that spot. Doctor Nolan had told the journalist that it was absurd to say that one was 'one-hundred percent sure of yourself. A scientist may never claim to know the absolute truth'. A comment was made later by the team archaeologist, James Legg, that to commit to be 100 per cent certain a bullet would have to be found with York's name on it.

Nolan told van Meulebrouck that his team had sought and obtained a permit to conduct an archaeological search using metal detectors. He knew that the SYDE had not gained permission from the French Department of Archaeology, adding that it could be said that their search was illegal and that all the artefacts recovered were obtained illegally. (Many of these were sent back to the U.S. to be displayed in places of interest.) Lieutenant-Colonel Beattie had been aware of the laws of the land for years before and had not employed the use of metal detectors during his searches, fearful of the consequences of such an offence. In answer to Nolan, Lieutenant-Colonel Mastriano told van Meulebrouck that the accusation by Nolan was 'silly':

A desperate statement by a desperate man. I asked for and received permission from everyone who mattered; the local mayor and the gendarmerie. Now that they've lost the debate, they've decided to switch to an ad hominem attack.[6]

Nolan was accused of being arrogant by his rival. Mastriano continued that Nolan had never even seen the German archives, and continued that Nolan's team didn't include any military experts. Away from the debate, the proof had to be with the results of the excavations and resultant finds, and a linking of the historical accounts that would present the most acceptable scenario.

Mastriano had said the best proof he had was that he played by the rules and that his version has been accepted; it was the willingness of *all* to accept the York Trail that had been constructed. Several kilometers long, this was a walking path following ostensibly in York's footsteps. If there had ever been any doubt the French would not have allowed that to take place. He continued that the CMH had endorsed his findings; they are the Army's last word in history.

We read earlier the comments made by Yves Desfossés, the regional archaeologist, that he is the only one authorised to issue a permit to conduct an archaeological survey using metal detectors, and he certainly did not issue one to the SYDE. He had also commented regarding the qualifications of the U.S. Army:

As far as I know, the American army is not known for its archaeological expertise.[7]

Van Meulebrouck interviewed some of the people in Châtel-Chéhéry, including the mayor Alain Rickal, who incidentally, appears in the acknowledgements in Mastriano's book, *Alvin York*, and, who 'took the bold step of endorsing our work'.[8] When Rickal spoke to van Meulebrouck, he said he was not interested in the conclusion to the whole discussion.

That is strictly between the two teams. I have no idea who is right.[9]

This can hardly be construed as a 'bold step'. Stephan, interested in the comments made by Mastriano regarding the Army CMH, contacted the Centre's director, Doctor Jeffrey Clarke, who:

had once wrote [sic] a letter expressing his admiration for the 'convincing and well-crafted record of the SYDE's efforts and findings.'[10]

That letter can still be found on the current Sergeant York Discovery Expedition website under a heading 'Endorsements'. Clarke told van Meulebrouck that he had been approached by Mastriano, who had explained his plans to search for the York site. He wished for official support from the CMH to show that he was a serious researcher and not some troublemaker. Clarke said that the trouble was there was no way to judge if the findings were correct. He was asked if he had read the SYDE report at the time. 'Probably not, I'm not interested that much,' as a manager of a large institute, he had too many other things on his mind. In that case, he was asked, why had he allowed Mastriano to use his letter on the SYDE website. Doctor Clarke said he was unaware of any such use, stating:

> He did what he wanted to do. Maybe I made a mistake. There's no real way to find the exact spot.[11]

In conclusion, the director said that the letter cannot be considered as evidence either, seeing as the CMH was not present during fieldwork, and describing research conclusions in terms of 100 per cent accuracy, as the SYDE has, is something he would never do.

Van Meulebrouck's article concludes with the following:

> Two reports, two different York spots, separated by a couple of hundred metres [600 metres – author's entry] of French soil. That may seem piddling when compared with a Front hundreds of kilometers long and a war that cost millions of lives.
>
> But not when one realises how lightly some of the players have dealt with the story of a national hero. Not when scientific principles are ignored and critical questions avoided.[12]

Chapter 27

Enter the Dutch Detectives

I n 2010, a group of battlefield detectives conducted their own investigations into the site of York's fight. They wrote a comprehensive report that appeared on their website stating they visited the area on 30 October 2010. They interviewed members of the Nolan Group, who gave the detectives the coordinates for the site on which they believed York was involved. They then went to the SYDE site in the forest, following the explanatory markers along the constructed footpaths leading to the monument. Whilst there, and looking at the various markers at the site, the objective of York's attack was explained on a marker, however, they could find no explanation as to the theory of the attack.

They did discover some laminated sheets of paper, with a text in English and French. This has been displayed on the battlefield detective website. It is anonymous, irrational and not easy to understand but it appears to be a person or persons who dispute York's 'heroic actions' against a group of thirty-eight 'exhausted dads'.[1]

Tom Timmerman interviewed the Dutch owner of the Argonne museum, Jean-Paul de Vries. He was asked if he had his theories on the work of the two teams:

> I am not going to come in between these groups and their theories. I run a museum with artefacts from Romagne and I observe a strict circle with a five-kilometre diameter around the village for their origins. The York spot is well outside this range. I understand that the relatives of Sgt York are content with the location where the monument is now. I have even heard of a new, a third investigation initiated by the ancestors of the other members of York's patrol. They seem to seek recognition for the heroism of their forefathers and are even trying to request posthumous military decorations for them.[2]

J.P. de Vries was interviewed at a different time about the SYDE by the Dutch investigative journalist van Meulebrouck:

> All the pieces of the puzzle fit together, but they could have fit just as well into another puzzle … they asked us to translate the finds, we were the field specialists … but the finds prove absolutely nothing, it was all too easy. When they found a door hinge, they concluded that it must have come from the headquarters of that German officer. That's when I pulled out of the project. They might have been right, but they should have been more thorough, but the press conference and the monument had already been arranged, so the spot had to become official.[3]

However, De Vries does not finish here. In a later statement to van Meulebrouck, he retracts his earlier comments; having now discussed the issue with the SYDE he has concluded they are right after all. There is no explanation from him as to his change of heart; instead he criticised the Nolan Group, stating that they did not know what troubles they were causing for the future.

The battlefield detectives, in their conclusions, asked the question, 'Which one is the right spot?'; their answer is straightforward. After explaining that they did not start with the intention of conducting an independent investigation to locate the spot, they say that after consideration, and taking into account the relevant publications and visiting the scene, they felt 'safe' to say the area designated by the Nolan Group was the most likely combat scene:

> Most convincing is the fact that the spot targeted by the Sergeant York Discovery Expedition is in the middle of the route of advance of the 2nd Battalion of the 328th Infantry. This unit was stopped in its progress by enemy machine gun positions which York's patrol was then tasked to eliminate. The patrol circled around these positions to do so. Therefore, the 'York Spot' can only be away from the route of advance of the main force, to be reached by a flanking manoeuvre.[4]

It is interesting to note the techniques the battlefield detectives used to determine the York area.

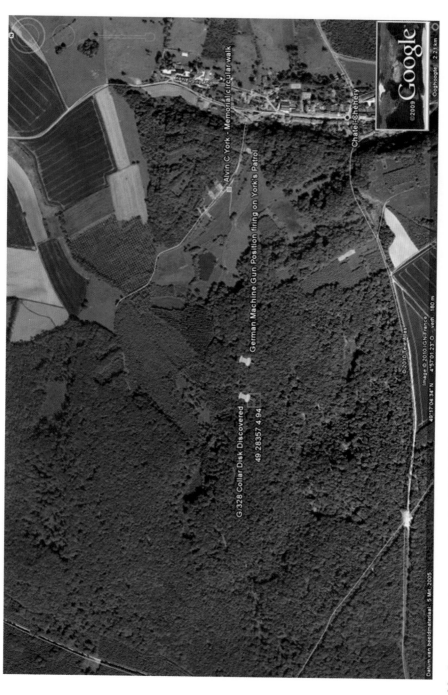

Map 39: Dutch Detectives map showing York Fight site on Google Earth. (Tom Timmerman)

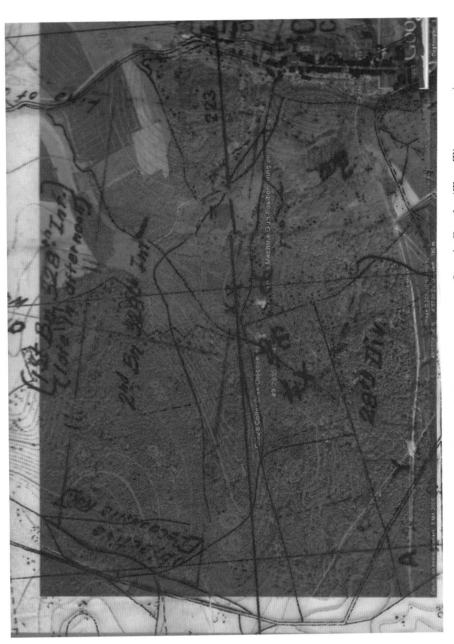

Map 40: Dutch Detectives cleverly overlay Danforth/Buxton map on to Google Earth. (Tom Timmerman)

… combining modern techniques and old-fashioned detective work. We pinpointed the exact (GPS) locations of the discovery of the G/328th collar disk and Dr. Nolan's research area on Google Earth and made a print of the screen. We then enlarged the map, annotated by Buxton and Danforth in 1929, to the size where still-existing terrain features (such as the forked main street of Châtel-Chéhéry and the course of the Argonnenbahn railway track) matched. We then copied it on a transparent sheet and put it on the Google Earth print as an overlay. The area of the York engagement as indicated by his commanding officers is consistent with the locations marked with yellow drawing pins on Google Earth. If nothing else, this was convincing enough to us for the likelihood of the right location.[5]

Chapter 28

The Analysis of the SYDE Claims

I t will be necessary during the summing up to repeat some information that has been disclosed earlier. This is a complex debate and the Nolan Group are of the opinion it has been made even more difficult to understand due mainly to inaccuracies that have served only to confuse.

We start at the beginning with the attack on the morning of 8 October 1918 by the 328th Infantry. The SYDE displayed a map on their website (no longer available) that showed the American attack to be almost in a north-westerly direction against the Champrocher Ridge (also called Cornay Ridge). Every historical account seen by the Nolan Group states that the actual direction of attack of the 2nd Battalion, 328th Infantry, was on a compass azimuth of 10 degrees north of west; in other words, 270 degrees. That would put the American attack a little more to the south than depicted by the SYDE and shows their site in a position where the Americans would be in the full face of German machine gun and artillery fire.

Confusion with the Terrain:

The SYDE appear confused with some terrain names. Where they believe the location of the Humserberg and the Bavarian Ridge to be seems inaccurate. The Humserberg is the Champrocher or Cornay Ridge and the Bavarian Ridge is so far to the south-east it is almost off the map.[1] The SYDE attach much importance to this high ground, stating that the German archives indicate the Humserberg to be the correct location where the York fight occurred.[2] There seems little explanation that can be found by the Nolan Group as to *why* that is the place. The German archives are so important that the SYDE include only four quotes from the German regimental reports, and they are from the 120th and 125th LIR. Posey has demonstrated after his time spent in the German archives that the quotes, after official translation, he believes

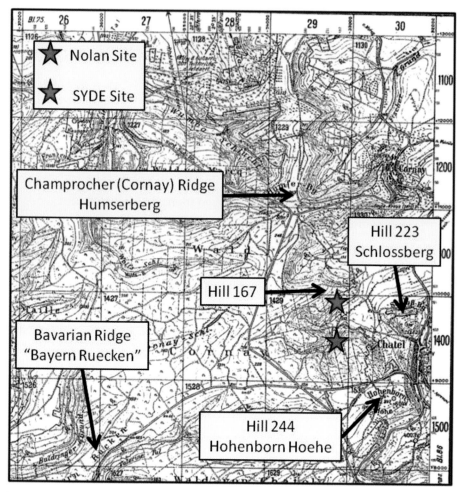

Map 41: German map showing topographical names. (Posey)

are incorrect, misleading, and have been seemingly used out of context from the original reports. One must make the point that although the SYDE have the Humserberg in the wrong place, they insist the fight *had* to take place here because it was key terrain. The Nolan Group have reiterated many, many times, that the York fight could not have been where the SYDE say it happened because if it were so it would have taken place in the full face of the 328th Infantry attack. The SYDE refer to the discovery of the German soldier, Willhelm Härer's, dog tag. There is a picture of Härer's personal effects in Colonel Mastriano's book displaying part of a gas mask, some buttons and the identification tag, amongst other artefacts. The description reads:

… Härer was involved in the 8 October fight and fell in action as the 125th Württemberg fell back after York broke its line. The discovery of Härer's personal effects was a major breakthrough in the search for the York site.[3]

In an article published by the German War Graves Commission in 2009 there was a report of a ceremony in Backnang, southern Germany, where descendants of the dead soldier gathered at his grave along with senior U.S. Army officials who received the identification tag on behalf of the U.S. Army Museum in Washington. The Commission reported that Härer had been killed on *10 October 1918* during heavy fighting at Humserberg.[4] With this information the 'connection' with York somewhat diminishes. Härer may very well have been on Hill 167 on 8 October, exactly where he should have been with the 125th.

Major Tillman, of the 328th Infantry, taking part in the battalion's main action, captured some German 77mm guns (see Figs 12, 13, & 14). The location of the guns is only metres from the SYDE site. This is corroborated by Brad Posey, who was present when Colonel Mastriano and his team discovered the gun site. It is extremely unlikely that a small patrol would endeavour to infiltrate such a position and then, finding a large group of German soldiers eating breakfast right on the main axis point for the 2nd Battalion, 328th Infantry, attack. There is no mention in the SYDE reports of the discovery of the German 77mm gun positions.

Grave Registration Service:

The SYDE state they have studied the U.S. archives and historical records, but there appear to be very few references to American material. Indeed, they make no reference to the GRS details that give the burial locations of the American dead from the patrol. The existence of such important research material is not mentioned anywhere in the SYDE reports, and indeed there is no recognition of the GRS.

METT-T and Similar Doctrines:

Military tactics and terrain analysis feature strongly in the SYDE case. (See a description of this doctrine in Chapter 12). These disciplines have no place in the York scenario. In these circumstances, where the action is fast moving, little attention can afford to be paid to such detail. Colonel Mastriano has said he visited the ravine where the Nolan Group say the fight took place and he dismissed it because he considered it did not fit with those military doctrines, together with his seeming reluctance to accept some facets of American and German testimony, which give a strong signal that this was the ravine where the fight took place. It is possible he followed the military tactics and terrain analysis principles for use in this project that were used during the earlier work of Lieutenant-Colonel Taylor Beattie.

Failure to Discover Machine Gun Components:

In his book, Colonel Mastriano dismissed the Nolan Group claim to have discovered the York site stating:

> The problem with the York Project [*Nolan Group*] was that it based its assessment of the location of the York fight on the discredited 1929 Danforth and Buxton map. This is the same map that Danforth warned the army against using, saying, 'I am afraid that no one, not even York himself, can give you a very accurate layout of the fight.' This placed them in a ravine about 650 yards south of where the York site was declared to be by credible American and German sources. This was compounded by premature claims of success. During their brief time in the Argonne they uncovered only 161 German 7.92 × 57mm casings, fifteen .30–06 live rounds, and three expended U.S. cartridges. This sort of evidence could be uncovered in nearly any ravine, hill, meadow, or valley in the Argonne. The presence of the 7.92 casings does not confirm that a machine gun was in the spot. In fact, German rifles used the same calibre rounds as the German MG 08/15 machine gun. To verify that an MG 08/15 was located in a specific position, one either needs parts of the MG recovered from the area or fragments of the 'patronengurt', the cloth belt used to feed the bullets into the gun. They found neither, and such a discovery would remain elusive to them in future trips.[5]

Why the Danforth and Buxton map was 'discredited' is not satisfactorily explained. The 'warning' from Danforth in his letter is hardly that, just an honest comment referring to the passage of time since the engagement. To all intents and purposes, the map served the 1929 re-enactment well. Both Buxton and Danforth were experienced officers who had annotated the map completely independently of each other. In addition, the map detail is corroborated by the descriptions as given in the American official histories and the GRS records. Finally, both Buxton and Danforth had spent a week with York in 1919 and visited the site of the fight, which had taken place just three months earlier, the next best thing to actual involvement at the scene. There was no one better qualified than these two officers to provide evidence to the 1929 investigation. As for the failure to find German machine gun components; the Nolan Group found a German machine gun water can, four machine gun drag hooks, a brass coupling from a water can and a water hose coupling, all from the York fight location in the ravine. These, like other artefacts, were catalogued and spatially recorded (see Fig. 67).

Spatial Analysis:

The SYDE claim that geospatial analysis played a part in their team.[6] Brad Posey spent some time with the SYDE assisting their exploration at no time did he ever see anyone in the team take any geospatial information, nor catalogue any coordinates to correspond with the location of the discovery of artefacts. This is corroborated by him seeing the participants returning to a central point with their finds and watching the lack of detail employed in their cataloguing. In addition, the Nolan Group has never seen linkage in any of the SYDE reports that spatially reference any of their artefacts and that could lead any future investigation back to the scene.

Positive Identification of Pistol Cartridges:

The SYDE discovered three U.S. pistol cartridges in the ground. They state that by using triangulation it enabled them to determine York's firing position, where they found a further twenty-four spent .45 calibre cartridges.

Colonel Mastriano requested the services of Doctor Douglas Scott, the world-acclaimed academic in his field of expertise specialising in forensic archaeology. Doctor Scott was sent forty-six .30-.06 cartridges, twenty-four

.45 calibre cartridges, and two .45 calibre projectiles, found near the 'Endriss Trench'. After examining the finds, Doctor Scott could determine that the:

> .30-.06 cases have strong extractor and ejector marks that are consistent with being fired and extracted from a Model 1917 Enfield rifle.[7]

Furthermore, he determined that they were consistent with being fired from the same M1917 rifle. Likewise, with the .45 ACP projectiles, there were clear 'land and groove impressions',[8] this together with firing pin impressions, determined that two .45 ACPs had been in action at that spot, one firing fifteen rounds and the other nine.[9] The forensic analysis, it was hoped, would support the SYDE claim that forty-six .30-.06 cartridges, three .45 calibre projectiles and twenty-four .45 calibre cartridges were from the York action. Indeed, Mastriano makes a statement that 'forensic analysis was used to verify this'.[10] As a result, according to the SYDE it resolved the ninety-year-old controversy surrounding the battle. But if there were two different pistols, only one of them could have been York's, so who was firing the other? Mastriano believes that Private Percy Beardsley is the only other member of the patrol who could have played this part. It is known that he was also armed with a Chauchat machine gun. The SYDE claim that forensic analysis shows that Beardsley resorted to using his sidearm after the Chauchat jammed.[11] This leads them to deduce that Beardsley fired nine of the rounds, whilst York fired the other fifteen.

The one positive result gained by the forensic examination proved that the same weapons fired those rounds. Two .45 calibre automatic pistols and one M1917 rifle. These types of weapons were being fired in abundance on the battlefield, particularly in this area, on the axis of the frontal assault. There is *no* evidence shown to support the SYDE conclusion that they discovered rounds that were fired by York or by Beardsley. Moreover, in his 26 January 1919 statement, Beardsley states he fired his pistol only two or three times.[12] A final word on this matter; Colonel Mastriano told Stephan van Meulebrouck that Nolan (the Nolan Group) had discovered French light Chauchat machine gun ammunition at his site, when later he declared that:

> None of the sixteen Americans with York on 8 October 1918 had this weapon.[13]

German Archival Records:

Much has been made by the SYDE about their many hours spent in the German archives and their reference to the Nolan Group failing to explore those archives. When the Nolan Group went to the German archives the results of the search presented another picture.

The later German records, those from 1918 are incomplete, with many units failing to draw up reports. The records are far from the accurate documentation that the SYDE and others would have us believe. At the time they were being written in 1918, no one from the German side had even heard of Sergeant York, so they could not have had any understanding of what transpired in the ravine on that October morning in 1918. It was not until 1929, during the German investigation, made because of the Swedish news account, that statements were obtained from some German officers, and even then there is only one document that mentions York by name. As has previously been stated, one should be wary when reading the 1929 accounts. There was reluctance amongst the Germans to admit that a small patrol had caused them so much of a problem. The narrative supplied by them reflects this reticence and, indeed, Vollmer's constant obstruction in submitting and retracting his account demonstrates his embarrassment of the whole incident. As for the 'X' they placed on the map they sent to the 1929 re-enactment, that was erroneous to hide the German embarrassment of the whole incident.

The SYDE place importance on the 125th LIR and refer to the capture by York of the German soldier Lieutenant Lipp from the 125th LIR. The German investigation did take statements from soldiers of this regiment but did not use any of them; this was because the 125th were not involved in the York action. There is no record available as to where Lieutenant Lipp was captured but it is safe to assume he was taken prisoner by E Company on Hill 167, not on the Humserberg as has been suggested and not by Alvin York. He was with the same group of prisoners who were sent back with York to Varennes. In the march back of 146 prisoners, which included York's 132, the majority were seen to wear the shoulder tags with the unit figure '120', which substantiates the Nolan Group claim.

The German statement of value was that written by Lieutenant Thoma of the Bavarian Sapper Company (7th Bavarian Mineur Company), who had given

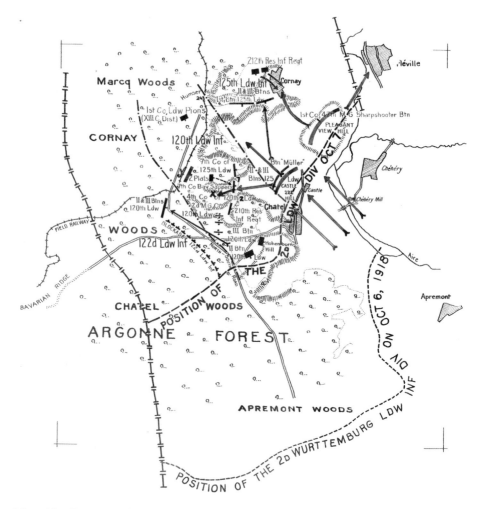

Map 42: German rebuttal map showing 'X' for the York fight – this is erroneous as the Germans were embarrassed by the fact that one man had taken so many prisoners. Note the location of the Humserburg.

it immediately after the war. He describes quite succinctly where he was and mentions the action to 'his right rear'. This could never have been on the hill to which the SYDE relate (see Figs 6 & 7). The Germans on that hill would only have heard or seen fire coming from their immediate front. Fire coming in from the right rear meant that Americans had infiltrated their lines and got in behind them.

Confirming the presence of the 7th Bavarian Mineur Company in the ravine, the Nolan Group unearthed a Bavarian button from the western-facing slope

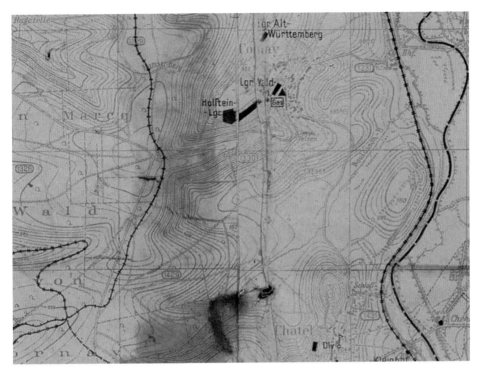

Map 43: Portion of the German Wirtschaftskarte of the Argonne map.

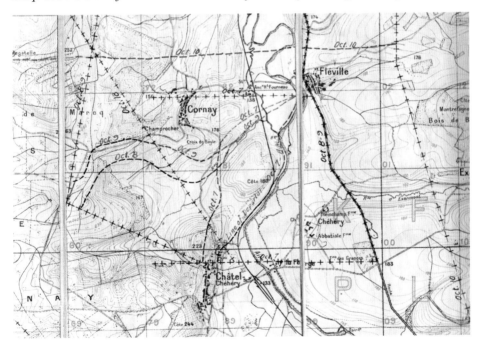

Map 44: French map – used by the Americans.

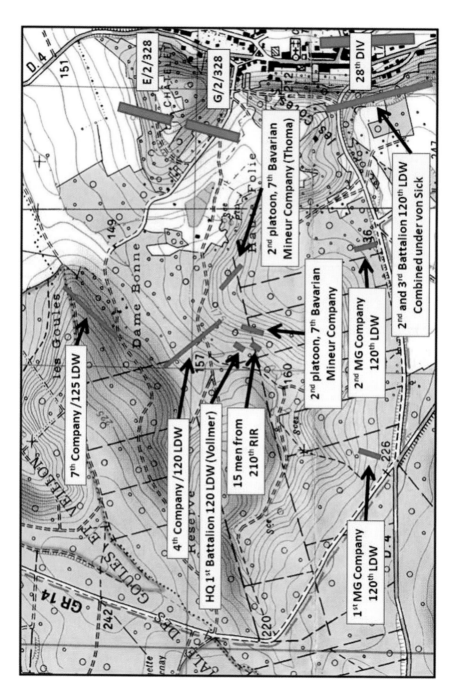

Map 45: German troop dispositions.

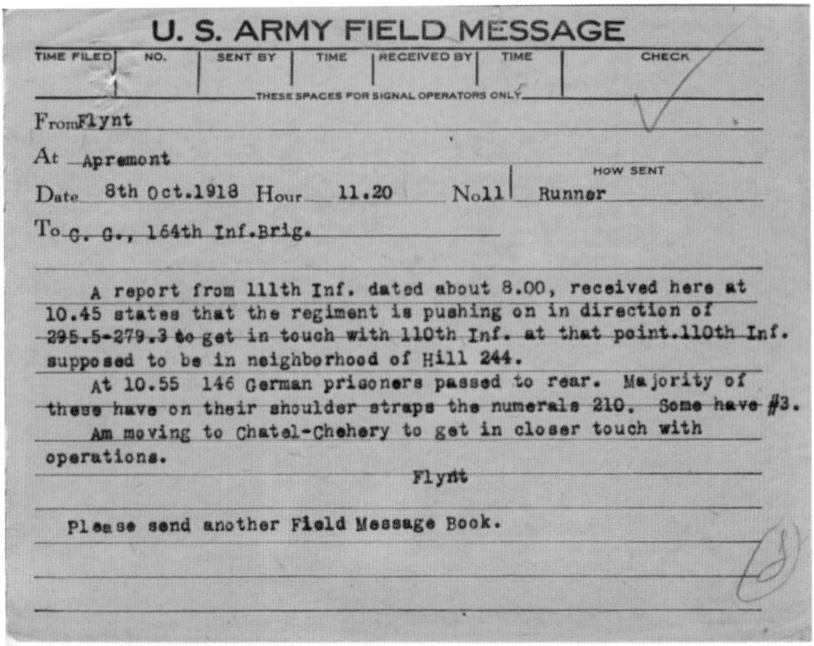

U. S. ARMY FIELD MESSAGE

TIME FILED	NO.	SENT BY	TIME	RECEIVED BY	TIME	CHECK

THESE SPACES FOR SIGNAL OPERATORS ONLY

From Flynt

At __Apremont__

Date 8th Oct.1918 Hour 11.20   No.11 Runner   HOW SENT

To G. G., 164th Inf.Brig.

A report from 111th Inf. dated about 8.00, received here at
10.45 states that the regiment is pushing on in direction of
295.5-279.3 to get in touch with 110th Inf. at that point.110th Inf.
supposed to be in neighborhood of Hill 244.
At 10.55 146 German prisoners passed to rear. Majority of
these have on their shoulder straps the numerals 210. Some have #3.
Am moving to Chatel-Chehery to get in closer touch with
operations.

Flynt

Please send another Field Message Book.

Fig. 83: Field message in which at 10:55 146 German prisoners were seen passing to the rear, the majority of whom were from the 120th LDW.

in the ravine. Nowhere else on the battlefield in question has such an artefact been recovered, and the 7th Bavarian Mineur Company were the only Bavarian unit present in that vicinity in that battle (see Fig. 68).

In short, the German testimony aligns with that of the American accounts.

SYDE Endorsements:

The current SYDE website (January 2017) displays several letters originating from notable people. There is a letter from Doctor Clarke, who was the director of the Center of Military History in the United States. The letter states:

(The CMH) … fully endorse SYDEs discovery as accurate. This endorsement includes CMH sponsorship of SYDE's work to preserve the SGT York discovery and artefacts.[14]

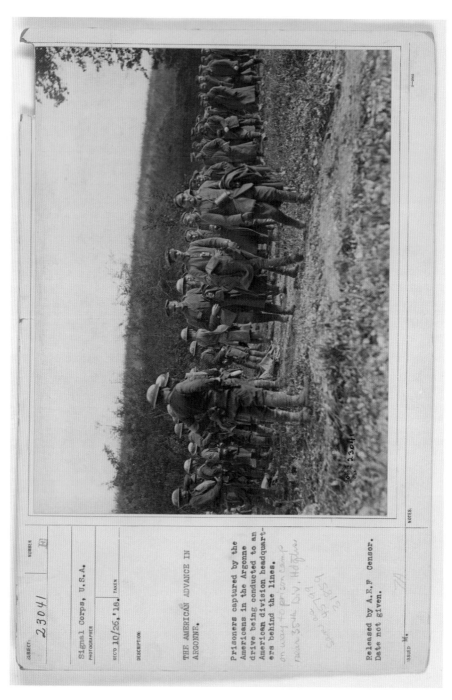

Fig. 83a: German prisoners near Boureuilles on 26 September 1918. Army War College. National Archives.

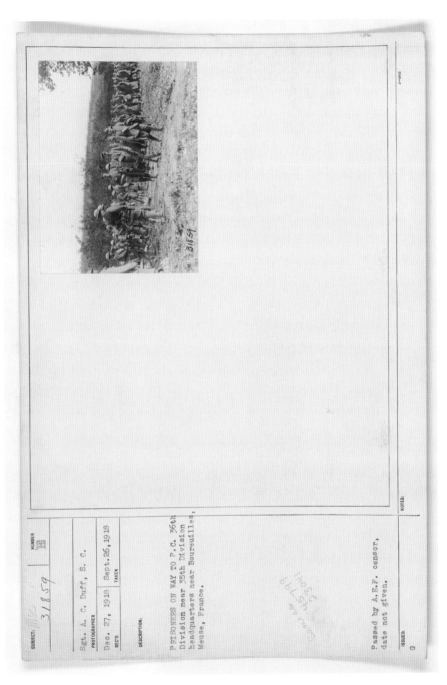

Fig. 83b: German Prisoners. 26 September 1918. Army War College. National Archives.

There is also a letter from Major-General Zabecki, described as one of the most senior U.S. Army historians and the U.S. Army expert on the First World War. He is extensively published on the Great War. Further letters appear, one from Alain Rickal, the Mayor of Châtel-Chéhéry at the time, endorsing the discovery by the SYDE of the York site and giving permission for the construction of the York Trail and the monument. The letter is dated 12 June 2009, more than eight months after the unveiling of the monument. It will be recalled that in Rickal's interview with van Meulebrouck he said he had no idea who (which research team) was right.

Major-General David Zabecki PhD, when interviewed by van Meulebrouck, said that there was a difference between academic historians and soldier historians. Military men had a much better understanding of tactics with which academics were not familiar. In his view, Mastriano was not approaching his undertaking as an historian per se, but as an intelligence officer, not striving for academic standards, but (basing the search) on his work on intelligence methods and by conducting a terrain analysis. He saw nothing unusual in the SYDE failure to publish GPS data in his report, stating Mastriano wanted to protect the site. (To date, no GPS or spatial data has ever been published by the SYDE.)

In answer to further questions, Zabecki made no comment about the temporary graves of the six patrol members killed in the York action. He had not heard of the burial files from the GRS that do not fit in with the SYDE location and to which no reference is made by them.[15]

Zabecki is reminded of the 82nd Division official history description of the 2nd Battalion, 328th Infantry, attack, along a compass bearing of 10 degrees north of west, meaning the SYDE location would be placed directly in the face of the frontal attack. Hardly the place for a large group of Germans to have breakfast! He admitted to not being aware of this and agreed to review the historic documents, which were sent to him by van Meulebrouck. No response was ever received.[16]

A letter from the French military mission to NATO is displayed on the SYDE website. According to the SYDE, the mission reviewed the SYDE findings and concluded they are 100 per cent correct. The letter is written in French and when translated it turns out to be merely an internal memo that relates to Colonel Mastriano's request to build the York Trail.[17]

Chapter 29

The Final Word

Sergeant Alvin York's heroics in the Argonne Forest were described by Marshal Ferdinand Foch as the greatest thing accomplished by any private soldier of all the armies of Europe. The feat of Sergeant York is still remembered in the United States, it is etched into the annals of history. It follows, therefore, that all due diligence should be applied to locate the site where it happened. It is hoped that within these pages the reader has arrived at a conclusion as to which of the two sites is the most likely.

There follows a precis of the facts that will assist the reader in their summation:

Forensic Examination of Projectiles and Cartridges:

The SYDE declared that they, with 100 per cent certainty, discovered the spot where York fought on 8 October 1918. Without categorical evidence this claim cannot be substantiated.

Rounds recovered from the Argonne Forest were sent to Douglas Scott, an archaeologist who specialises in forensic archaeology and who is the eminent authority on such matters. After examination, he stated that the rounds had come from three different weapons: two .45 ACPs, one firing fifteen rounds, the other nine, and a M1917 rifle. The forty-six .30-.06 cartridge cases came from the same M1917 rifle. Doctor Scott's interpretation can hardly quantify the SYDE claim to have discovered the York fight site. In the acknowledgements section on page 219 of Mastriano's book, *Alvin York*, there is this statement:

We are also honored to have the support of Dr. Doug. Scott, the nation's expert on historical ballistic analysis. His scientific analysis of the York bullets and cartridges confirmed our historical interpretation of these artifacts and at long last discredited the detractors.

There appears to be no corroborative evidence from Doctor Scott that substantiates the SYDE statement that these artefacts were York's or that they were fired by any other member of that patrol. They were found in an area that was subjected to a full-frontal and determined assault by the 2nd Battalion, an attack where many weapons of these types would have been used. It is not explained who the 'detractors' are.

German Archives:

The SYDE have repeatedly claimed that many of the answers lay within the German archives. After hundreds of hours spent searching, they concluded that they knew where the York patrol was involved on the morning of 8 October 1918. The SYDE have criticised the Nolan Group for failing to research the German archives. In the first instance they were correct however, it became possible when Brad Posey, who lived in Germany, joined the Nolan Group. He visited the German archives and he researched the same archival material that was viewed by the SYDE. He discovered new records that had not been previously seen by any of the investigators, one of the two Lieutenant Thoma statements was one example. It transpired the German documents were not as accurate as the SYDE and others had said they were. Nor did they appear to corroborate the SYDE story leading to the discovery of the York spot. The unit records from 1917 and 1918 were sketchy and poorly written, and a lot of 1918 material was missing. This was not an unusual occurrence by the end of the war, as the archive staff explained. Instead of the meticulous diaries the Germans had maintained before 1917, towards the end of the war just one entry might summarise several days' activities.

Posey had some of the German accounts translated by an official court-appointed translator, and he discovered differences in the SYDE translations that are difficult to explain.

Reading the SYDE webpage (now taken down), it is easy to be impressed by the vast number of references, particularly regarding German records. From the list of 356 or thereabouts source references at the end of the webpages, only a small portion were used; four to be precise. When the German archival records were translated by an official court-appointed translator, they were found to be unhelpful. There are several quotes from the York diary, a quote from General

Pershing and a part of York's Congressional Medal of Honor citation. It is believed that the long list of unused materials just serves to confuse people who may be trying to make cross-references to the work, and in effect, appears to conceal the lack of real sustenance of data or interpretation.

Clearly, others too may wish to revisit the facts. Taylor Beattie in his article 'Man, Myth, and Legend' stated:

> ...We clearly are biased in this debate. Mastriano's SYDE report is backstopped by superb German archival research and is in keeping with the military situation of the day. In other words, it is supportable from a military standpoint.

It appears obvious from all records, American and German, that the SYDE site was directly in line of the full weight of the 2nd Battalion, 328th Infantry, attack on 8 October 1918. The American accounts are clear when they say that the York incident took place on the *left flank* of the attack.

No more than 25m from the SYDE monument, Mastriano personally unearthed ammunition tube spacers that indicated the site of a German 77mm battery. At this time, Brad Posey was working with the SYDE and in 2009 he took Doctor Nolan to that location. It was one of the four 77mm gun positions that was captured by Major Tillman on 8 October and who described it in his report. Tillman was in action in the full-frontal assault. The discovery of and the positions of the guns are not mentioned anywhere in any of the SYDE material. There is seemingly no reference to them. It is unlikely that the York patrol engagement would have taken place so close to a battery of German artillery, furthermore, it is highly improbable that ninety or so German soldiers would have been sitting around eating breakfast in the face of a full-frontal assault, and next to an artillery battery (see Maps 28 & 29).

The American Accounts:

The American accounts agree that the York encounter took place in the ravine where the Nolan Group said it did. Paragraph sixty of the Official History of the 82nd Division states it took place on a western slope as has been described previously, while the proclaimed SYDE site is on an eastern-facing slope.

There are some discrepancies, as can be seen in some of the affidavits and accounts of patrol members and men from both sides. This is to be expected, not all things fit perfectly. The affidavits that attract attention are those of the patrol members that were taken just after the confrontation and into February 1919. They do tend to agree so much with each other that one might nearly think a blanket statement was signed by all.

American Artefacts in the Ravine:

Strong evidence has been shown that places G Company, 328th Infantry, and York's patrol in the ravine. They are the unit collar disc with the company markings, the knife and spoon bearing the same detail, the GRS records that led to the discovery of the many personal American soldier artefacts that were left behind by the exhumation parties, and the preponderance of discarded German equipment laying on the western slope indicating the surrender of many men. In addition, the picture that is painted from the scientific evidence, the spread of the ordnance within a controlled search area, leads one to conclude that the ravine is where the York confrontation took place. The Nolan Group cannot say outright that the bullets belonged to or were fired by any particular soldier in this fight, but the science, coupled with the documentary evidence, presents a strong picture of what took place in that ravine.

York's part in the action is not in question. There is little doubt that had he not taken the lead, there would have been more than six fatalities in the patrol, and they may well have been wiped out.

What is difficult to understand is why both Taylor-Beattie and Mastriano chose to ignore the Danforth/Buxton map, and why did the SYDE fail to discover or make reference to the existence of the Grave Registration Service records?

These two valuable sources alone indicate not only where the fight took place, but where the six casualties were buried.

Could it be possible that the SYDE may have chosen to ignore this material because it did not match up to where they said the York fight took place, or perhaps it was an oversight?

The SYDE believed York was engaging Germans from the 125th LIR. The Nolan Group could find no evidence in any of the German documents to prove this. The 1st Battalion, 120th LIR, and the 7th Bavarian Mineur records agree, and they are within 100m of the Nolan Group site (see Fig. 83).

In his book *Alvin York*, p. 114, Mastriano claims that the photograph is of York with his prisoners, Lieutenant Vollmer, Lieutenant Max Thoma and Lieutenant Paul Lipp, being led away after the 8 October action (see Figs 83a & 83b). York is allegedly walking behind the named Germans. However, the descriptive on the rear of the pictures clearly states the photograph to be of German prisoners near Boureilles, some 15km away and dated 26 September 1918, thirteen days before York's encounter.

The SYDE placement of the Humserberg and the Bavarian Ridge is incorrect. The Humserberg is the Champrocher or Cornay Ridge and the Bavarian Ridge is much further to the south-east and off the map. These appear to be fundamental issues and it begs the question; if the SYDE are seemingly confused with elemental topographical features, the value of their research has to be subject of scrutiny (see Map 41). The Humserberg was still in German possession on the evening of 8 October 1918.

GIS

Global positioning systems were not used by the SYDE, at least during Posey's time spent with them. He saw artefacts being bagged with no reference, geo-spatial or otherwise, as to where they were found other than 'top of hill', 'northern end of hill', or 'York spot', marked on the bags. Their claims to have conducted battlefield archaeology appear to be ill-founded and seem to be nothing more than an unsystematic relic hunt. Resultantly, the artefacts they claim to have come from the York site have no provenance. Any maps that have been seen produced by the SYDE offer no spatial information and consequently no provenance as to the location of their finds.

The SYDE display letters that have been sent to them by various official parties. They still adorn their website. When examined closely, these documents merely support the SYDE exploration but do not endorse in any way any proclaimed discovery of the York site.

There has been a distortion of history and it remains to be seen if any amendment will be made. There is no likelihood of the existing monument being relocated, and despite the haste undertaken to erect the monument, the

Nolan Group have no desire to request its relocation. The site determined by the Nolan Group investigation belongs to land owners who would resist any move to have a memorial erected there. However, it should be simplistically identified as being the place where Alvin C. York fought his heroic battle and where sixteen other brave men in the patrol took part, six of that number were killed and more than twenty Germans died.

Little is mentioned of the 'other sixteen' members of the patrol; in the appendices are details of what is known on a few of them. All but one of the six killed were reinterred in the U.S. Meuse-Argonne cemetery at Romagne. Of them, Private Fred Wareing was visited in 1930 by his mother and sister during a Gold Star Mother's pilgrimage. It is not known if any of the other graves have been seen by members of the family.

Whatever part the 'other sixteen' played in the firefight will never be certain. They were present in the action as it unfolded and they should all be remembered.

Fig. 84: Assistant Secretary for War Patrick J. Hurley congratulates Sgt Bernard Early after decorating him with his DSC at an Army Relief Carnival on 5 October 1929.

It may be true that the local French inhabitants care little about the intricacies of where exactly this action was fought 100 years ago. Memorials are abounding, both within the village and outside in the forest, and what does the York story bring to the village? Certainly, there are no droves of visitors eager to visit the site, and for those who do make the journey, they spend a little time and continue on their way. There are no shops, hotels or bars in this community to encourage the visitor to stay. The small village of Châtel-Chéhéry has escaped modernism, in many ways it has changed little from the grainy black and white photographs taken during the German occupation in the Great War.

However, I am certain that the people of Châtel-Chéhéry would join everyone in the remembrance of those who died on that autumnal morning in October 1918. No matter their race, or creed, the Americans fought for their beliefs and for the freedom of all free people. They were all heroes cast into a war waged on distant shores, far away from home.

Fig. 85: The Army Relief Carnival after Sgt Early received his DSC.

An Explanation of Ammunition

By Brad Posey

The Nolan Group think it extremely important to properly identify the following items of French ammunition. It was used in both the First and Second World Wars. There are differences and each 8mm cartridge should be examined individually under magnification. This includes fired 8mm projectiles.

In 1898 the French Army adopted the 8mm 'Balle D' cartridge for use in the Mle 1886 Lebel rifle. Balle D remained in service for the duration of the war.

In 1932 a replacement cartridge for Balle D was introduced and it was known as Cartouche Mle 1932, or 'Balle N'. It was designed for use in the Lebel and Berthier rifles marked 'N' on the receiver, meaning that they had been modified for the new cartridge. (Image 1)

Note the cupronickel jacket on the last cartridge on the right. It is another certainty that you are handling a post-First World War artefact if you see this. We found three variants of projectile jackets on the Balle N cartridges we discovered. They are: copper jacket, cupronickel jacket and a jacket that has a high ferrous content that causes the entire projectile jacket to rust – the core is made of lead on all three variants.

The head stamp is the first clue as to whether the 8mm cartridge in question is Balle D or Balle N. Here you can see the one on the left dated '17' for year of manufacture 1917 – this is Balle D. The one on the right is stamped '36' for production year 1936 – this is Balle N. (Image 2)

Here you see the base of both the Balle D on the left and Balle N on the right. (Image 3)

This is also very important as the entire battlefield west of Hill 233 is peppered with fired 8mm projectiles. Most are from the First Word War and are a result of the barrage fire laid down by American machine gun crews during

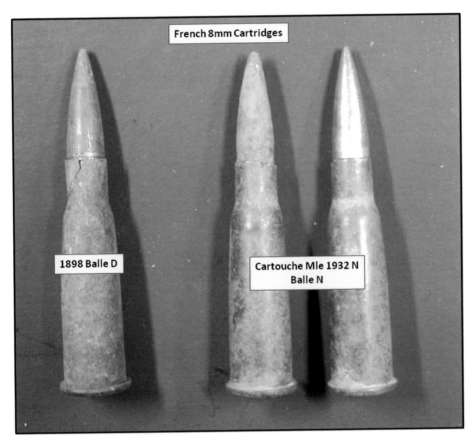

Image 1. Note the cupronickle jacket on the right cartridge, a sure certainty this is First World War era. The group found three variants of projectile jackets on the Balle N cartridges discovered. They were copper jacket cupronickle and a jacket with a high ferrous content that causes the entire projectile to rust. All cores are made of lead.

the initial phase of the attack on the morning of 8 October or from Chauchat squads in the infantry assault platoons.

However, the odd Second World War era fired 8mm projectile did turn up and were easily identified by looking at the base. On fired examples of Balle D the lettering on the base is often no longer visible, but they do not have a hole that exposes the lead core as all of the post-First World War Balle N examples have.

A photo of samples of several other types of ammunition found. Note: the rusted 8mm projectile jackets. We will show two rare German cartridges that

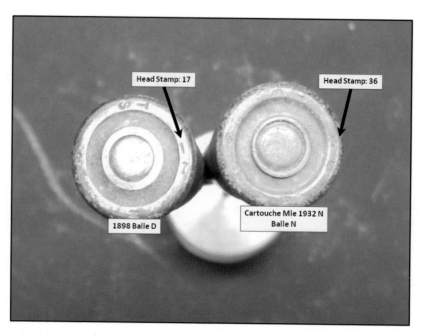

Image 2: The head stamp is the first clue as to whether the 8mm cartridge is Balle D or N. On the left it is dated 1917, the year of manufacture, and is Balle D. On the right is 1936, this is Balle N.

Image 3: The base of Balle D and N.

Image 4: Not to be mistaken for the German 7.92mm cartridge. These are the cartridge, projectile and five-round stripper clips for the French MAS-36 rifle known as the 7.5 mle 1924 Balle C (found in large numbers on the ridge).

Image 5: The base of 75mm Balle C

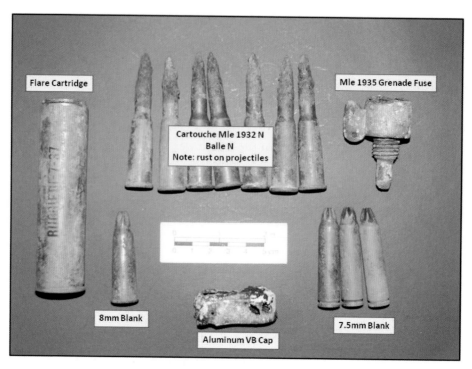

Image 6: Several types of ammunition found on the ridge. Note the rusted 8mm projectile jackets.

Image 7: This is the German 13.2mm Model 1918 anti-tank rifle (Tankgewehr 18) cartridge. The cartridge is marked '18' on the bottom and the projectile contains a tungsten core. The core you see in the photos came from one of the projectiles that fell apart disarming it.

were found on the east bank of the creek about 15 to 20m north of the old dam. The cartridges were not found together, they were separated by about 5m. In 2006 Doctor Nolan found one fired cartridge of this type in the same area. (Images 7 and 8)

Major Tillman in his report said that 2nd Battalion, 328th Infantry, captured several anti-tank rifles that morning, but he did not specify where. Obviously, there was at least one of these rare weapons available at some point during the battle.

Image 8: This is the tungsten core.

Appendix 2

The Dead

By Brad Posey

In the American affidavits and testimony section you may recall the statement given by Lieutenant Cox when he said that shortly before noon on 8 October 1918, he and a platoon from F Company, 328th Infantry, passed over the hill where the fight occurred and estimated that he saw about twenty German soldiers lying on the slope. What happened to the German casualties? York states that when he returned to the ravine the following day, both the American and German dead had been buried. We know now this is not the case as we have the record of the six American casualties being buried by Chaplain O'Farrelly on 24 October 1918. York was confusing this with a visit in February 1919.

From the records held by the GRS, we know that most other American casualties were buried by their own countrymen; some on the day of fighting or within a couple of days. Most of those who fell near Châtel-Chéhéry or on the slopes of Hill 223 were buried in the cemetery behind the church in the village, now a rather overgrown tennis court.

Those Americans who fell in the valley between Hill 223 and Hill 167, as well as the members of the patrol in the ravine, were buried where they fell by Chaplain O'Farrelly in October 1918.

The German dead more than likely remained unburied until the U.S. Army GRS teams, assisted by local French, helped exhume American remains, moving them to concentration cemeteries or to the American Meuse-Argonne cemetery at Romagne.

During the exhumations, German war dead were for the most part removed by the French and buried in one of several German military cemeteries. Little care was taken in identifying the remains, many of them being buried in common graves with countless numbers of other unknowns. So far, the Nolan

Fig. 86: American dead awaiting burial. (U.S. Army, 1918)

Fig. 87: The old tennis court at Châtel-Chéhéry. This served as a temporary American burial ground until they were disinterred and returned home or transferred to other U.S. cemeteries. (Author, 2016)

Fig. 87a: The village of Chátel-Chéhéry in the First World War during German occupation. (Courtesy Roland Destenay)

AMERICAN DEAD AWAITING BURIAL
Chatel Chehery, France.

Fig. 88: The village cemetery. Note the German Eagle – all that remains now is the base. (Army, 1918)

Group has been able to locate only one grave of one of the German soldiers killed in the York fight.

Lieutenant Endriss is credited by some as the leader of a failed bayonet charge against York, although this looks to be more of a reaction vs. a planned attack. Lieutenant Endriss, the commander of 4th Company, 120th LIR, was more than likely responding to the sound of firing coming from behind the old dam, and he rushed in that direction with several soldiers who were all killed by York's .45 automatic. Endriss received a mortal wound in the stomach.

After extensive research through the German War Graves Commission website, Volksbund Deutsche Kriefsgräberfürsorge e.V.[1] It was discovered that Lieutenant Fritz Endriss died on 8 October 1918 at a field hospital in Grandpré and was buried in the German military cemetery in Buzancy. This cannot be possible since Grandpré was in German hands on 8 October 1918. Endriss was in American hands when he died and there is no record of him or any other wounded German soldiers being transferred to German custody during this battle. Therefore, it is believed to be an error by the German War Graves Commission.

Fig. 88a: Buzancy German Cemetery. (Author, 2016)

Fig. 88b: Lieutenant Fritz Endriss. Buzancy communal grave. Shot by Alvin C. York, 8 October 1918. (Author, 2016)

Buzancy cemetery lies in a beautiful position on the heights above the small town. It was established by the French authorities after the war and German dead from forty-seven different communities and towns were brought here for final burial. Fritz Endriss is one of them. It is highly likely that it is the location of twenty or more Germans killed in the York fight, but for now, they remain unaccounted for.

At the end of the Great War, there were a high number of German cemeteries on the Western Front and it is understandable that the local populace appealed against them. They, after all, wished to return to their agricultural pre-war status, tilling the fields and managing their livestock.

Consequently, many of the dead from the smaller German cemeteries were exhumed and taken to highly concentrated cemeteries. Langemark German cemetery near Ypres has nearly 45,000 burials, 25,000 of whom are in a mass grave. Neuville St Vaast cemetery near Arras has 37,000 burials as well as more than 8,000 in a mass grave. Buzancy has 5,923 burials.

The Other Sixteen

L ittle has been published about the other members of the York patrol. Over the years there appears to have been some reticence in acknowledging them, the attention firmly centred upon York. There have been slights made against York from some of the patrol members, insisting that they too played a part and deserved recognition. From the very start Alvin York was the centre of attention in this action, the other patrol members were used merely to corroborate and enhance the case for his Congressional Medal of Honor. Within these pages there is no desire to divert any of the credit from York, he was well deserved of his awards, but the other sixteen members of that patrol deserved an endorsement, as General Lindsay acknowledged in his letter of 1930 (see Fig. 95). Both Bernard Early and Otis B. Merrithew, aka Private Cutting, spoke out loud after the war and both were awarded the Distinguished Service Cross in 1929. Merrithew was also to receive the Silver Star in 1965. Joe Konotski was awarded the Silver Star in May 1919. Most of the survivors did not receive any awards. A renewed appeal for recognition from relatives of the patrol in the early 2000s, went unheeded. This group are called 'The Other Sixteen'.

Sergeant Bernard Early

Bernard was born in County Leitrim, Ireland, on 15 November 1892. His family emigrated to the United States, where he lived first in New Haven, then in Hamden, Connecticut. Six years after his entry into America, he joined the Army. He led a seventeen-man squad into the Argonne Forest on 8 October 1918. During the battle Early was seriously wounded by machine gun fire. E. Loyd Ellis carried Early back on a stretcher and said that there was a hole in Early's back so large one could see a kidney. Six months later Early underwent a further operation to remove shrapnel. His recovery in France took one year to complete, by which time he was fit to return home.

Eleven years later he was presented the Distinguished Service Cross on 5 October 1929 by Assistant Secretary of War Patrick J. Hurley. He always told his friends that everyone aided in capturing the German prisoners. He said at his award ceremony, 'I feel all of us who took part in the exploit should share in the recognition.'

Early married and had four sons and a daughter.

www.theothersixteen.org

Private Fred Wareing

Nedwell 'Fred' Wareing was born in Lonsdale, Rhode Island, on 19 October 1894. He was the second of ten children (the eldest son) of Richard Wareing and

Fig. 88c: Private Fred Wareing. (Courtesy www.theothersixteen.org)

Flora, née Ainsworth, both of whom had emigrated from England and married in 1892. They sought work in the cotton mills in New Bedford, Massachusetts, and came to live there in 1903–04.

Fred and his younger brother Joseph earned a reputation as 'hellraisers' in the years leading up to the Great War. They were drafted into the United States Army in 1917. Fred was killed in the action in the Argonne on 8 October 1918, his brother Joe was seriously wounded but survived the war.

Fred was unmarried and without issue but his memory was kept alive by his family, particularly by his younger brother, Richard, who had idolised his other brother. Richard gave the name Frederick to his eldest son in honour of Fred and well into the 1980s frequently spoke of his brother having fought with Sergeant York.

Fred's death was particularly hard on his mother, Flora, who travelled to France with Fred's older sister, Elizabeth Wareing, as part of the Gold Star Mother's programme. They returned to the United States in 1932 having visited Fred's grave in the U.S. Meuse-Argonne cemetery and being photographed at Fred's grave.

On the night before she learned her son had been killed in action, Flora is said to have had a dream in which Fred appeared to her in uniform and said, 'It's alright Ma.'

www.theothersixteen.org

Private Ralph Weiler

No information is forthcoming nor can be found on this man.

Private Joseph Stephen Konotski

Joseph Konotski (Kornacki) was born on 15 August 1896 in Warsaw, Poland. He emigrated to the United States with his father and brother, both of whom returned to Europe prior to America joining the Great War. As a young man, he was employed as a blacksmith but at the age of twenty-three he enlisted in the United States Army as a means to expedite his status as an American citizen. He was inducted on 7 October 1917, and was ultimately assigned to the 164th Infantry Brigade, 2nd Division, 328th Battalion, Company G.

Fig. 88d: Private Joseph Konotski. (Courtesy www.theothersixteen.org)

Joe survived the action in the Argonne Forest and the war. He received a Brigade Citation for Gallantry in action, later converted to the Silver Star in May 1919 for his actions on 8 October 1918. He was given an honourable discharge from the Army on 27 May 1919 and returned to his home in Holyoke, Massachusetts.

www.theothersixteen.org

Private Carl Frederick Swanson

Carl Swanson was born on 3 April 1896 in Spring Creek township, Elk County, Pennsylvania. He was the third of seven children born to Amandus and Carrie Erickson Swanson. Amandus was killed in 1905 in an accident at the tannery where he worked. In 1913, the family moved to Jamestown, New York, to seek

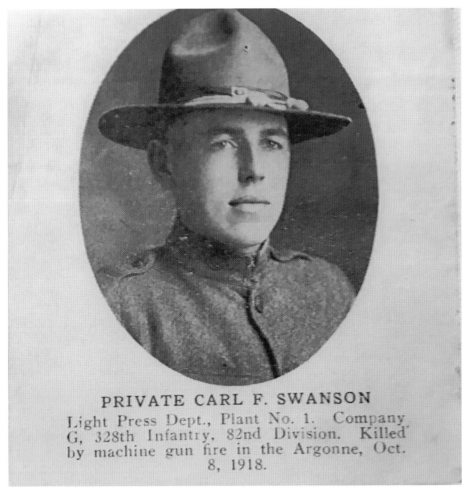

PRIVATE CARL F. SWANSON
Light Press Dept., Plant No. 1. Company
G, 328th Infantry, 82nd Division. Killed
by machine gun fire in the Argonne, Oct.
8, 1918.

Fig. 89: Carl Swanson. (Courtesy Karen Johnson)

better employment. It is believed that Carl went to work at Tillotson local furniture factory. On a date unknown, Carl joined the Army and was sent to the Light Press Department, Plant No. 1, G Company, 328th Infantry, 82nd Division. At this time he had a crooked left index finger and the word went around the family that if it had been on his right hand he would not have been accepted for the Army, this being his trigger finger.

Carl was a tall man, over 6ft, and he was sent overseas to France with his unit. Prophetically, his last letter home to his mother said that he would have to sign off as 'his candle was going out'.

On the same day the family were notified of Carl's death, daughter Ellen came home from school (not knowing of Carl's death) and started to play the hymn 'God Will Take Care of You' on the piano.

The family elected to have Carl's body returned to the U.S. when he was exhumed from the fight site. When he arrived in America two relatives went to view the remains; the only way they knew it was Carl was by his crooked left index finger. The flag that draped Carl's casket was in the possession of his niece, Karen Johnson, who has donated the flag to the Fenton History Centre.

Karen writes of Sergeant York paying a visit to Jamestown after the war and meeting with Carl's mother at the Hotel Jamestown. The conversation was not recorded but the visit was probably intended for York to offer her some sympathy.

Carl is resting in Lakeview cemetery, Jamestown.

Information courtesy of Karen Johnson.

Private Maryan Dymowski

Maryan Dymowski was born in Russia on 24 March 1890. He arrived in New York aged sixteen on 28 October 1906. He had arrived with his mother, older

Fig. 89a: Private Maryon Dymowski on the right of the picture. Probably at Camp Gordon. (Courtesy of Carol Schulties)

Fig. 90: French memorial certificate to the sacrifice of Maryan Dymowki. (Courtesy of Carol Schulthies)

Fig. 91: Maryan Dymowki (seated). His brother is on his left and a cousin on the right. (Courtesy of Carol Schulthies)

brother and younger sister. The USS *Umbria* ship's manifest reveals that he was a labourer, 5ft 2in tall, with a dark complexion, fair hair and blue eyes. He worked in the Crescent Pelting and Packaging Company in Trenton, New Jersey.

Private Percy Beardsley stated in his affidavit that Maryan and Fred Wareing were either side of him when the Germans opened fire with machine guns.

Both Fred and Maryan were riddled with bullets. Maryan rests in the Meuse-Argonne U.S. cemetery in France.

Information courtesy of Carol Schulties (Dymowski was her uncle).

Private Feodor Sok

Little is known of Feodor other than details from the ship's manifest of the *SS Dwinsk* in May 1914 that lists him as a twenty-one years old single male and his occupation a farm labourer. The ship had sailed to the United States from Libau in Latvia, the main emigration port from Russia to the West in the early twentieth century.

www.theothersixteen.org

Private Michael Saccina

Michael was born on 25 July 1888 in Rapone, Italy, a province of Potenza. He had two brothers, Joseph and Frank. Michael arrived in the United States in 1902 and became a naturalised citizen in 1908. The 1908 census revealed that Michael and Joseph lived as boarders in the home of their brother Frank on St Anne's avenue in the Bronx, New York City. He never married and after the war he lived in Manhattan, where he owned and operated the tobacco concession in the International Magazine Barber shop located in the Hearst Building on West 57th Street. He was a quiet, unassuming man who rarely spoke of his experience during the war.

www.theothersixteen.org

Private Mario Muzzi

He was born on 8 October 1888 in Civita di Bagnoregio in the province of Rome, Italy. He emigrated to the United States in 1910. It was his thirtieth birthday on the day of the fight in the Argonne Forest and he was the only survivor of Corporal Murray Savage's squad, being seriously wounded in the shoulder.

He returned to the United States and married. He worked as a baker for the National Biscuit Company (later Nabisco) at the bakery on West 15th Street,

New York City (now the Chelsea Market). He lived with his wife, Concetta, at 302 East 48th Street in New York, becoming a United States citizen on 12 January 1923.

Mario retired to his homeland and the town of Civita di Bagnoregio, dying there in April 1978 at the age of ninety. Civita, which had been known as the 'Dying City', has become a tourist attraction, located on the top of a hill and accessible only by a narrow footbridge. Mario was the last to die of the other sixteen members of the patrol.

www.theothersixteen.org

Private Thomas Gibb Johnson

Born on 5 June 1895 in Lynchburg, Vancouver. More is known of the previous generations of Thomas's family than there is about him. They originated from Virginia and his elder brother had been a mate on the Packet Boat *Marshall* as it bore the body of Civil War General 'Stonewall' Jackson from Richmond to Lexington for burial in May 1863. On Thomas's twenty-second birthday he registered for the draft along with his elder brother, John Gray Johnson.

In June 1918 Johnson was drafted overseas and became part of the 'York' patrol in the Argonne Forest. After the war, both brothers returned to Lynchburg, Thomas working as a stock clerk in wholesale shoes. In the late 1920s the brothers moved to Denison in Texas. It is not known the reason for this great migration.

Elder brother John died in 1939 and Thomas continued to live his life in the shadows. His invitation to the 1929 ceremony was returned unopened. It wasn't until the release of the 1941 movie *Sergeant York* that Johnson was connected to the fight. The newspaper in Denison reported that it had found Johnson 'living quietly … nursing nerves shattered by the war'.

In September 1961 Johnson died from a heart attack and he was buried in Fairview Cemetery in Denison. The local newspaper carried a small story and photograph showing six First World War veterans carrying the casket. It was not until an article appeared in *The Lynchburg News & Advance*, in a 4th July package of 2008, that Johnson descendants in Virginia knew that a war hero was part of their family.

www.theothersixteen.org

Corporal William Cutting (real name Otis B. Merrithew)

Otis B. Merrithew was born in Boston, Massachusetts, on 26 May 1896. The family had an absentee father, which resulted in Otis dropping out of school to assume a variety of jobs in the area. He did what he could to help his mother and four siblings. At the start of the Great War his mother did not want him to enlist but he was determined he would, and there was a conflict of interest

Fig. 91a: Private Cutting, whose real name was Otis Merrithew. (Courtesy www. theothersixteen.org)

between the two that resulted in him running away to join up. He enlisted on 3 October 1917, just over a year away from the fight in the forest that was to become an important part of his life after the war. He passed a store in North Adams, Massachusetts, and noticed the name 'William B. Cutting', deciding to use this name as an alias as he was worried that his mother might find out that he had enlisted.

His decision to take another name was to prove a temporary obstacle. Both his commander, George Edward Buxton, and Sergeant Bernard Early were unable to locate Otis shortly after the war. Both men wanted to talk to him to discuss the events that took place on 8 October 1918. It is known that Bernard Early felt that York deserved all due accolades but he felt that some sort of recognition should be given to the other members of the patrol.

It was Otis's mother who persuaded him to correct his enlistment papers, changing his name from Cutting to Otis B. Merrithew. He then embarked on a mission after reading newspaper reports of York's action. He wanted to put over his story as to the events on 8 October 1918.

Otis was invited to and attended the re-enactment in 1929 at the Army War College in Washington. His arrival was met with great enthusiasm by the other members, who thought that 'Cutting' had been killed.

Over the next three decades Otis tried to gather support from many people including other members of the patrol, some of whom changed their original affidavits. There were many letters written between him and George Edward Buxton, his old commanding officer. Indeed, this was a letter exchange that continued until 1935, during which Merrithew appealed for recognition for the other patrol members. Although gracious in his response to Merrithew, Buxton may have been reticent to follow this course of action. Perhaps these were delaying tactics as he did not wish to divert any attention from York. This is despite a letter written by the Brigade commander, General Lindsay, in 1930 in which he recommended recognition be awarded to other members of the patrol (see Fig. 95).

Many years later, in September 1965, Merrithew was awarded the Silver Star. The ceremony was attended by his family. Afterwards he turned to his son-in-law, Chuck Gaffney, and said, 'You know Chuck, I feel sorry for York. His grandchildren did not see him receive any of his medals, but my three daughters and eleven grandchildren did.'

On 13 October 1977, the town of Brookline erected a sign at the corner of Whitney Street and Meadowbrook Road (the street where Otis lived for forty-two years). It read 'Otis B. Merrithew Square' and each Memorial Day there is a dedication at this site.

This excerpt is taken from a passage on Otis B. Merrithew at www.theothersixteen.org

Private Patrick Donohue

Born in Ireland, Donohue arrived in the United States when he was about seventeen years old. He had two brothers, Ned and Timothy, and a sister, Jane. At the outbreak of the First World War he was attending night school and was employed by the E. Frank Lewis plant in Lawrence, Massachusetts. He joined the Army on 5 October 1917 and was sent to Devens, where he was assigned

Fig. 91b: Private Donohue. (Courtesy www.theothersixteen.org)

to Company G of the 328th Infantry, 82nd Division. He was discharged from the Army on 4 June 1919. Little is known of him after this period, and he was unwilling to speak about the part he played in the events of 8 October 1918. Donohue returned to being a mill worker in Lawrence.

Corporal Murray L. Savage

Little is known of the antecedents of Murray Savage. A newspaper called the *Daily Messenger* reported on Friday, 11 October 1974 from East Bloomfield,

Fig. 92: Corporal Murray Savage. (Courtesy, The Sergeant York Foundation)

Ontario County, New York, giving a brief biography. He had joined the Army from the town of Bristol in the United States. The article reported that Savage was remembered in the Bloomfield Savage Post of the American Legion. On the following day, 12 October, the Legion was hosting a dedication and open house of its new home in the town of East Bloomfield. Among the many guests were the niece and nephew of Murray Savage, Mrs Erwin Moranda of Bristol Centre and Glen McPherson of Bristol. Sadly, this Post closed down in 2006 due to decreasing membership and the buildings and 18 acres of land were passed over to the town of East Bloomfield.

Corporal Savage was a friend of Alvin York and they held similar religious beliefs. He is buried in the Meuse-Argonne cemetery.

Corporal Percy Beardsley

There is little information on the whereabouts of Percy Beardsley after the war, although it is known he returned to his father's farm near Roxbury,

PERCY BEARDSLEY rests on stone fence near his Roxbury farmhouse. It was from this farm that he left in 1917 to join Army.

IN UNIFORM of World War I doughboy, Beardsley served in 82nd Division with Sgts. Alvin York and Bernard Early of New Haven.

Fig. 92a: Corporal Percy Beardsley in 1964. (The New Haven Register, Connecticut, 8 November 1964.) (Courtesy www.theothersixteen.com)

Connecticut. His father was 'Nate' Beardsley, a champion Devonshire cattle breeder. It is known that Percy attended the re-enactment in 1929, at which time he was unmarried.

Private George W. Wills

George Wills returned to the United States after the war. He lived with his wife and two boys in a frame house near the dumps in South Philadelphia. He worked as a teamster, driving a feed wagon every day from 6 am till 7 pm. It was reported that none of his customers were aware of his wartime connections or exploits.

Information from *The Niagara Falls Gazette*, Monday, 11 November 1929.

The Niagara Falls Gazette

The *Niagara Falls Gazette* of Monday, 11 November 1929, published an article entitled 'Controversy Still On Between Members of Heroic Band of Soldiers in Argonne Fight'.

The controversy reportedly originated with George Wills informing the newspaper that all the fellows in the squad made the capture (of the German soldiers) and should have been credited alike, 'York seems to have got all the glory,' he had said.

Sergeant Harry Parsons

Before the war Harry Parsons had been an actor who had worked in vaudeville. He was a natural born leader and was present when York brought in his 132 prisoners, hardly believing what he was witnessing. It was Harry who had ordered Bernard Early to take out the patrol and he must have felt that it was unlikely he would ever see its members again. Harry disagreed with Private Wills, stating that York deserved all the credit, 'His was the greatest achievement of the war.'

After the war, Parsons returned to work in an auto and accessory store in his native Brooklyn.

Here they are as they are today, 11 years after: No. 1, Private Patrick Donahue; No. 2, Corporal Otis B. Merrithew and his family; No. 3, Private Mario Muzzi; No. 4, Private George W. Willis; No. 5, Private Michael Sacina; No. 6, Sergeant Bernard Early and Mrs. Early; No. 7, Sergeant Harry M. Parsons.

Fig. 93: Seven of the patrol survivors as depicted in The Niagara Falls Gazette, 11 November 1929.

Fig. 94: The 328th Infantry Company G, the date and location is unknown. Sergeant Bernard Early is believed to be the ninth in the rear rank, right to left. (Courtesy www.theothersixteen.org)

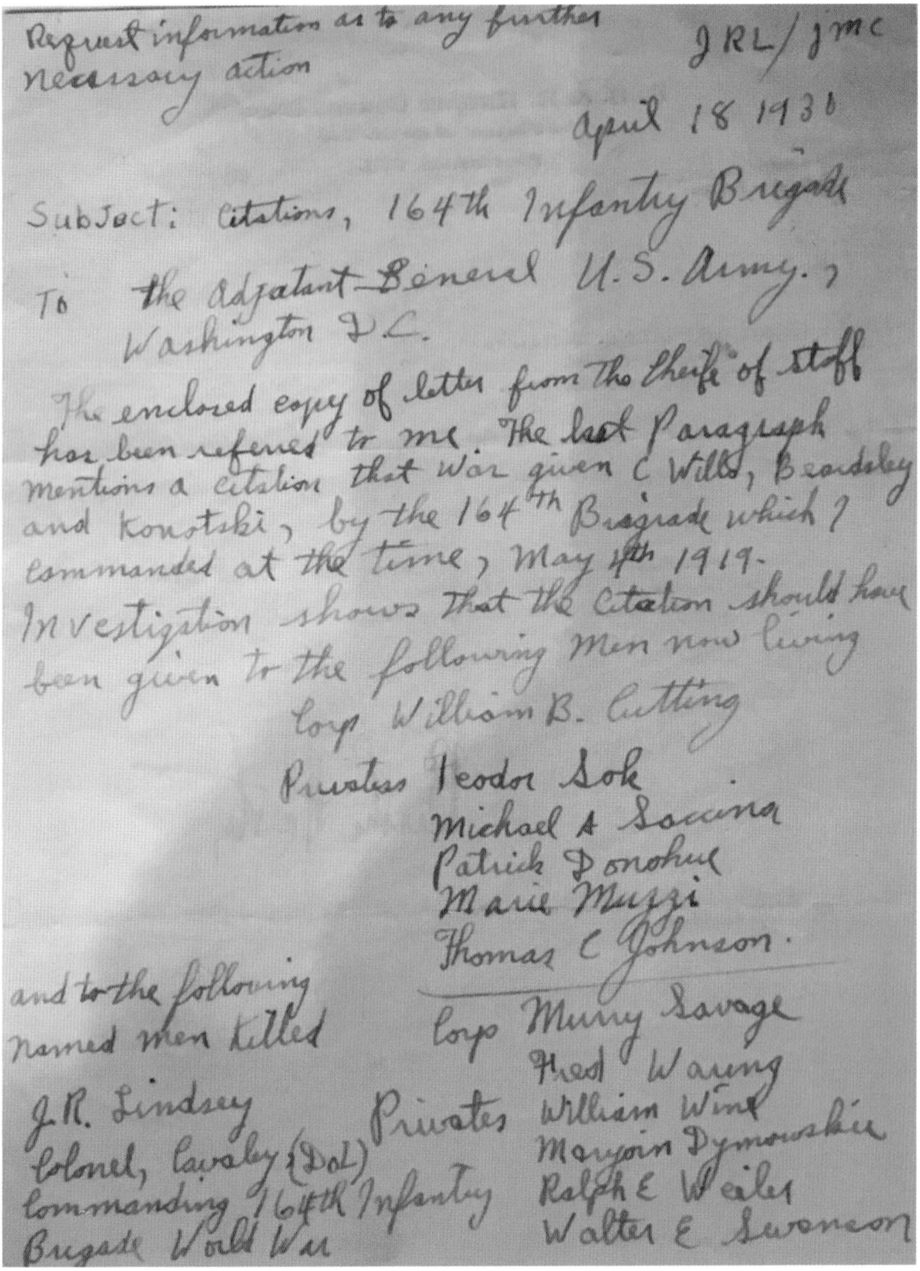

Request information as to any further
necessary action

JRL/Jmc

April 18 1930

Subject: Citations, 164th Infantry Brigade

To   the Adjutant-General U.S. Army.,
Washington D.C.

The enclosed copy of letter from the Chief of staff
has been referred to me. The last paragraph
mentions a citation that was given C Wills, Beardsley
and Konotski, by the 164th Brigade which I
commanded at the time, May 4th 1919.
Investigation shows that the citation should have
been given to the following men now living

Corp. William B. Cutting

Privates Teodor Sok .
    Michael A Sacina
    Patrick Donohue
    Marie Muzzi
    Thomas C Johnson .

and to the following
named men killed

J.R. Lindsey
Colonel, Cavalry (DoL)
Commanding 164th Infantry
Brigade World War

Corp Murry Savage
    Fred Waring
Privates William Wine
    Maryoin Dymowskie
    Ralph E Weiler
    Walter E Swenson

---

*Fig. 95: A letter from General Lindsay to the Adjutant General in Washington,
dated 18 April 1930, in which he writes that all members of the patrol should have
received a citation. (Courtesy www.theothersixteen.org)*

Fig. 96: Flora Wareing, Private Fred Wareing's mother, at the Meuse-Argonne American cemetery, France, during the Gold Star Mother's Pilgrimage in 1930. (Courtesy Greg Stevens)

Fig. 97: Fred's sister, Elizabeth, paying her respects to her brother (Courtesy Greg Stevens)

I have a rendezvous with Death,
At some disputed barricade,
When Spring comes back with rustling shade
And apple-blossoms fill the air –
I have a rendezvous with Death
When Spring brings back blue days and fair.

It may be he shall take my hand
And lead me into his dark land
And close my eyes and quench my breath –
It may be I shall pass him still.
I have a rendezvous with Death
On some scarred slope of a battered hill,
When Spring comes round again this year
And the first meadow-flowers appear.

God knows 'twere better to be deep
Pillowed in silk and scented down,
Where love throbs out in blissful sleep,
Pulse nigh to pulse, and breath to breath,
Where hushed awakenings are dear …
But I've a rendezvous with Death
At midnight in some flaming town,
When Spring trips north again this year,
And I to my pledged word am true,
I shall not fail that rendezvous.

Alan Seeger

(An American fighting with the French Foreign Legion
Killed in action, 1916)

Endnotes

Foreword

1. Thomas Justus Nolan, PhD Dissertation, San Marcos, Texas, 2007.
2. Van Meulebrouck, Email to Doctor Jeffrey Clarke, CMH by permission. Held by the author.

Chapter 1: The Hero

1. Lee, *Sergeant York, an American Hero*, p. 17.
2. Unpublished biography, Gladys Williams. Held by the York Institute.
3. York maintained he was not a conscientious objector but a 'soul in doubt'. When this conflict was resolved in his mind, he never again voiced objection to fighting. Gladys Williams.
4. www.army.mil/cmh

Chapter 2: Welcome Home Alvin

1. Birdwell, *Celluloid Soldiers*, p. 101.
2. Mead, *The Doughboys*, p. 404.
3. Birdwell, p. 129.
4. Lee, p. 134–5.
5. His real name was Otis B. Merrithew. He and Sergeant Bernard Early were the only two survivors of the patrol to receive any recognition, in this case the Distinguished Service Cross in 1927.
6. Birdwell Biographical paper. www.alvincyork.org/AlvinCullomYork.htm
7. Ibid.

Chapter 3: The Meuse-Argonne Offensive

1. Mead, p. 286. A final agreement was reached between Foch and Pershing after a stormy period where the former had desired to split the U.S. Army. Pershing

stuck to his guns, telling Foch that he would not allow the U.S. Army to be anything else than a concentrated force working together. Compromise was reached allowing the attack to commence at 5 am.

2. *American Armies and Battlefields in Europe.* Center of Military History, United States Army, p. 173.

3. *To Conquer Hell.* Meuse Argonne, 1918. Edward G. Lengel, p. 58.

4. Ibid, p. 58.

5. Ibid, p. 299. The problems that this attack presented on such a short front were enormous. There were just three narrow roads and three railway lines. The logistics of moving 600,000 men and their equipment into such a small area, hampered by bad weather, troops and dead horses in the roads, proved horrendous.

6. Terraine. *White Heat. The New Warfare* 1914–18, p 68.

Chapter 4: The Americans at Châtel-Chéhéry

1. 82nd Division, Summary of Operations, p. 12.

2. Thomas, *The History of the A.E.F*, p. 289.

3. Buxton, *Official History of the 82nd Division*, p. 57–8.

4. Ibid, p. 57–8.

5. *History of the Three Hundred & Twenty Eighth Regiment of Infantry*, p. 45.

6. Ibid, p. 43.

7. Skeyhill, *Sergeant York, His Own Life Story and War Diary.* Ed. Tom Skeyhill. Sergeant York Foundation, Pall Mall, Tennessee, p. 237–8.

8. The Champrocher Ridge was the American name given to the feature south and west of Cornay, probably taken from the French 'Les Champs Crochet'.

9. Skeyhill, pp. 237–8.

10. *History of the Three Hundred & Twenty Eighth Regiment of Infantry*, p. 45.

Chapter 5: A Man for All Seasons

1. To date, the official statement has not been found in Washington.

2. Skeyhill, p. 223.

3. Ibid, p. 262.

4. Ibid, p. 223.

5. Ibid, pp. 262–3.

6. This is the same stream the patrol had crossed upon meeting the two German Red Cross soldiers.

7. It is not known why York thought Vollmer was a major, he had little trouble in identifying Endriss as a German lieutenant.

8. Skeyhill, p. 225.

9. Ibid, p. 263. The 'east bank of the stream' thus the steep slope, the area where the fight would take place, was west facing.

10. Ibid, p. 226.

11. Firing a weapon unsupported.

12. Skeyhill, p. 227–8.

13. Ibid, p. 264–5.

14. Ibid, p. 230.

15. Ibid, p. 266.

16. Ibid, p. 267.

17. Ibid, p. 268–8.

18. Ibid, p. 235.

19. Salvage of battlefield equipment was well organised in 1918 in the A.E.F. General orders were issued stating that 'all abandoned equipment and material will be collected for salvage however worthless it may appear' ... *U.S. Army Center of Military History* 1992, p. 169.

20. Those who surrendered were mainly from the 120th Landwehr Regiment, who were made up of draftees, both young and older men.

21. Skeyhill, p. 237–8.

22. Ibid, p. 240.

Chapter 6: The Official History of the 82nd Division

1. Buxton, *The Official History of the 82nd Division*, p. 3.

2. The 'runner' was a soldier designated to carry messages. It was an effective but dangerous method of communication, his lifespan measured in hours. The underground telegraph wires were easily destroyed by artillery.

3. *The Official History of the 82nd Division*. Section, p. 58.

4. Ibid, Section p. 59.

5. Ibid, Section p. 59.

6. Ibid, Section p. 60.

7. Ibid, Section p. 61.

Chapter 7: The York Diary, Sergeant York and his Own Life Story

1. On 21 February 1929, a letter from Buxton to Otis Merrithew (aka Private Cutting) states that it was Sergeant Major Stafferman who typed the statements that were read to the entire group afterwards. The survivors all agreed that the statements fully covered the facts that related to their participation in the fight. Brad Posey explains that this was the way things were done, particularly when many of the men were illiterate or could hardly read or write.
2. Skeyhill, pp. 260–7.
3. Ibid, p.1.
4. Tom Skeyhill was killed in a flying accident in the United States in 1933.
5. Ibid, p. 24.
6. Ibid, p. 27.
7. Ibid, p. 29.
8. Ibid, p. 31.
9. Ibid, p. 32.

Chapter 8: American Statements and Affidavits

1. Ibid, pp. 249–51.
2. Ibid, pp. 245–7.
3. The adjutant is an officer who assists the commanding officer, attending to correspondence, orders and secretarial duties.
4. Skeyhill, p. 247–9.
5. Ibid, p. 255–7.
6. Ibid, p. 258.
7. Pattullo's article mentions target shooting by Tillman and York where the latter demonstrated his prowess with a gun. As we will see, some of the artefacts discovered by the Nolan Group were subjected to target practice, and this visit to the scene would have been the ideal opportunity for York and Tillman to target shoot.
8. Lieutenant Stewart was first shot in the legs, rallying his men. He bravely got to his feet but then was killed by a shot to the head.
9. Skeyhill, pp. 240–2.
10. Ibid, pp. 243–4.

Chapter 9: The Saturday Evening Post

1. This is believed to be a medieval boundary ditch that is referred to later. See Lieutenant Glass reference.
2. Pattullo. *The Second Elder Gives Battle. Saturday Evening Post*, 26 April 1919.
3. Ibid. This version differs greatly from York's diary in which he states … 'we first saw two Germans with Red Cross band on their arms. Some one [sic] of the boys shot at them and they ran back to our right.'
4. PC, Post of Command.
5. *Saturday Evening Post.*
6. Ibid.
7. Ibid.
8. Ibid.
9. Ibid.

Chapter 10: A Summary of the American Accounts

1. Murray Savage was buried on his own. Private Wine was also buried separately, Privates Weiler, Dymowski, Swanson and Wareing were together in the third plot.

Chapter 11: The German Accounts

1. Lee, p. 40.
2. Gilbert, *First World War*. P. 451–2.
3. Testimony of German Officers, College Park, Maryland, National Archives and Records Administration, Record Group 165, Entry 310b, 'Thomas File'.
4. Ibid.
5. Captain – Cavalry.
6. Testimony of German officers.
7. Command Post.
8. Testimony of German officers.
9. Ibid.
10. Ibid.
11. Testimony of German officers.
12. Das wuerttembergischen Regimenter im Weltkrieg 1914–1918, Band 25 Das Wuerttembergische Landwehr Infanterie Regiment Nr. 120.

13. National Archives and Records Administration, College Park, Maryland Record Group 165, Folder II 864 – 33.5.

14. 2nd LDW Division war diary; 45th Reserve Infantry Brigade (of which the 210th RIR was a part); 120th LDW Regiment – history and war diary; 1st Machine Gun Company, 120th LDW Regiment war diary; 2nd Machine Gun Company, 120th LDW Regiment, war diary; 122nd LDW Regiment history and war diary; 125th LDW Regiment history and war diary; 7th Bavarian Mineur Company – unit roster with all casualties listed. No war diary exists for 1918; Lieutenant Thoma – personal folder/files.

15. Hauptstaatsarchive Stuttgart, M411 382/2700 Pages 22–23. Regimental Staff, 120th LDW.

16. 2nd Battalion Landwehr Regiment war diary, Hauptstaatsarchiv, Stuttgart, M411 386/2723, two pages concerning 7–8 October 1918.

17. 3rd Battalion, 120th Landwehr Regiment, war diary. Hauptstaatsarchiv, Stuttgart. M411 388/2733, three pages concerning 7–8 October 1918,

18. 1st Machine Gun Company war diary. Hauptstaatsarchiv Stuttgart, M411 388a/1389. One page concerning 7–8 October 1918.

19. *Saturday Evening Post*.

Chapter 12: The Beattie/Bowman Field Study

1. *Army History*, The Professional Bulletin of Army History. Summer–Fall 2000. *'In Search of Man, Myth & Legend'* by Taylor V. Beattie with Ronald Bowman. p. 13.

2. Ibid, p. 4.

3. Ibid, p. 13.

4. *Army History*, The Professional Bulletin of Army History. Winter 2008. *'Continuing the Search for York'* by Taylor V. Beattie. p. 23–4.

5. M.A. Snell, *'Unknown Soldiers. The American Expeditionary Forces in Memory and Remembrance'*. An article by Taylor V. Beattie, *Man, Myth and Legend*, 2008.

6. Brigadier, (Retd) Ray McNab. Australian Army. Email quote. 5 December 2016.

7. Army History, 2008, p. 27.

8. Stephan van Meulebrouck, unpublished paper, 'A Spot of Bother – Looking for Sergeant York', p. 8.

9. Ibid, p. 9.

Chapter 13: The Nolan Group Objectives

1. Van Meulebrouck, 'A Spot of Bother'.
2. Nolan and Justus, T. (2007) 'Battlefield Landscapes: Geographic information science as a method of integrating history and archaeology for battlefield interpretation'. Dissertation for PhD. T. Nolan. p. 2.

Chapter 15: Phase II of Field Study, 14–24 November 2006

1. James M. Tillman, '82nd Division Field Orders and Memos, History of Operations', from 82nd Airborne Division War Memorial Museum Archives, (Fort Bragg, N.C., 1918).

Chapter 18: The 1929 Re-enactment

1. G.E. Buxton, Letter to Captain Henry Swindler, 23 July 1929, College Park, Maryland, National Archives and Records Administration, Record Group 165, Entry 310C, 'Thomas File'.
2. Letter to Captain Henry Swindler, E.C.B. Danforth, College Park, Maryland, National Archives and Records Administration, Record Group 165, Entry 310C, 'Thomas File'.

Chapter 19: The Graves Registration Service

1. The body of Private Swanson was repatriated to the United States. He is buried in Lakeview cemetery, Jamestown, New York.

Chapter 21: The Site of Engagement

1. Buxton, *Official History of 82nd Division American Expeditionary Forces*, 1919.
2. Merten, 'Testimony of German Officers and Men'.
3. Personal Akten von Lt. Thoma, Personal records of Lieutenant Thoma. München, Bayerische Hauptstaatsarchiv, Abteilung IV Kriegsarchive, OP 14800. This is the most important statement of all the German accounts. It offers the only first-hand German account of what happened *before* the York incident was known to the Germans. He was describing the circumstances of his capture as he perceived them. He made it in 1919, almost one year after his capture.
4. Testimony of German Officers, College Park, Maryland, National Archives and Records Administration Record Group 165, Entry 310b, 'Thomas File'.
5. Mastriano, *Alvin York*, p. 197.

Chapter 22: Individual Firing Positions

1. Thomas Justus Nolan, doctoral dissertation.
2. Buxton, Letter to Captain Henry Swindler.
3. Pattullo, *The Second Elder Gives Battle*.
4. Ibid.
5. Skeyhill, p. 262,
6. Buxton letter to Captain Swindler.

Chapter 23: German Equipment Items

1. Thomas Justus Nolan, doctoral dissertation.

Chapter 24: The Archaeologists and the Science

1. University of South Carolina, Scholar Commons. *Legacy*. Vol. 14, No. 1. 2010. '*Finding Sergeant York*.' James B. Legg.
2. Ibid.
3. Ibid, p. 4.
4. Ibid, p. 4.
5. Legg, Report for Nolan Group team and University of South Carolina. Scholar Commons. *Legacy*. Vol. 14, No. 1. 2010. 'Finding Sergeant York'.

Chapter 25: The SYDE Claims

1. Dated April 2008. No longer available online at www.sergeantyorkdiscovery.com. There was a message saying the report would undergo a thorough review and update. A copy is held by the author.
2. Ibid, under the section *Research Methodology*.
3. Ibid, under the section *The Condition of the Battlefield – Today*.
4. Ibid.
5. B. Posey, report, after visiting German archives.
6. Ibid.
7. *Das wuerttembergische Landwehr Infanterie Regiment Nr. 120 im Weltkrieg 1914–1918*, p. 164.
8. Ibid. The dog tag was that of Schütze Wilhelm Härer, a gunner private with the 2nd Machine gun Company, Landwehr Regiment 125.
9. Brad Posey report. He was totally familiar with the ground where the SYDE claim York fought.

10. Ibid. Posey did not see any attempts by the SYDE to mark, or record locations where artefacts had been recovered. He saw no usage by them of spatial technology or GPS.
11. *Das wuerttembergische Landwehr Infanterie Regiment Nr. 125 im Weltkrieg 1914–1918*, p. 172.
12. *Das wuerttembergische Landwehr Infanterie Regiment Nr. 120 im Weltkrieg 1914–1918*, p.164.
13. *Das wuerttembergische Landwehr Infanterie Regiment Nr. 125 im Weltkrieg 1914–1918*, p. 171.
14. Mastriano, *Alvin York*, p. 205.
15. Ibid, p.205.

Chapter 26: The Dutch Investigative Journalist

1. Email. Mastriano to van Meulebrouck. Thursday, 25 September 2008. 10:29:30.
2. Email. Mastriano to van Meulebrouck. Thursday, 25 September 2008 10:33.00.
3. Letter attachment sent to van Meulebrouck in email of 25 September 2008 10:33 by Mastriano. A copy of this letter appears on the current SYDE website.
4. Email. Mastriano to van Meulebrouck. Friday, 26 September 2008 02:53.
5. Email. Mastriano to van Meulebrouck. Friday, 26 September 2008 03:27.
6. Stephan van Meulebrouck, *The Western Front Association*, Bulletin 84. June/July 2009 'Hot on the York Trail', p. 29
7. Van Meulebrouck, 'A Spot of Bother', p. 7.
8. Mastriano, *Alvin York*, p. 217.
9. Van Meulebrouck, *The Western Front Association*, Bulletin 84. June/July 2009. 'Hot on the York Trail', p. 30.
10. Ibid, p. 31.
11. Ibid, p. 31.
12. Ibid, p. 31.

Chapter 27: Enter the Dutch Detectives

1. www.battledetective.com/battlestudy19.html
2. Ibid.
3. Van Meulebrouck, 'A Spot of Bother', p. 3.
4. www.battledetective.com/battlestudy19.html
5. Ibid.

Chapter 28: The Analysis of the SYDE claims

1. The author holds a copy of the SYDE report together with their annotated maps.
2. Van Meulebrouck, 'A Spot of Bother'.
3. Mastriano, *Alvin York*, p. 206.
4. Stimme & Weg. Arbeit für den Frieden. 4/2009, p. 17. Translation by Kim Hassel.
5. Mastriano, *Alvin York*, p. 197
6. Ibid, p. 196.
7. Ibid, p. 211.
8. Ibid, p. 212–3.
9. Ibid, p. 214.
10. Ibid, p. 210.
11. Ibid, p. 107.
12. Skeyhill, *Sergeant York, His Own Life Story and War Diary*, p. 249–51.
13. Van Meulebrouck, 'A Spot of Bother'.
14. www.sgtyorkdiscovery.com/SYDE_NEWS.php
15. Van Meulebrouck, 'A Spot of Bother'.
16. Ibid.
17. Ibid

Appendix 2: The Dead

1. Link to the Buzancy cemetery on the German war graves commission website: www.volksbund.de/kgs/stadt.asp?stadt=634

References

1st Machine Gun Company. (1918). [War Diary] Hauptstaatsarchiv, M411 388a/1389. Stuttgart.

2nd Battalion, Landwehr Regiment War Diary. (1918). [Diary] Hauptstaatsarchiv, M411 386/2723. Stuttgart.

2nd Landwehr Division War Diary and Annexes. 1–10 October 1918. (1918). [War Diary] National Archives and Record Administration, College Park, MD, Record Group 165.

3rd Battalion 120th Landwehr Regiment. (1918). [War Diary] Hauptstaatsarchiv, M411 388/2733. Stuttgart.

7th Bavarian Mineur Company Unit Roster. (1918). [Record] Hauptstaatsarchiv, Casualty Records. Stuttgart.

82D Division Summary of Operations in the World War. (n.d.). United States Government Printing Office 1944: American Battlefields Monuments Commission.

Stimme & Weg. 'A Unique Act of Reconciliation.' (2009). (German War Graves Commission), 4/2009 (October Edition) p. 17.

American Armies and Battlefields in Europe: A History, Guide, and Reference Book. (1995) United States Government Printing.

Anon, (1911). Sergeant York biography by Gladys Williams. [online] Available at www.sgtyork.org/gwilliamsbiography.html [Accessed 28 August 2016].

Beattie, T. (2008). 'In Search of York. Man, Myth and Legend.' Edited by Mark A. Snell.

'Unknown Soldiers. The American Expeditionary Forces in Memory and Remembrance.' 2008. The Kent State University Press.

Birdwell, M. (1999). *Celluloid Soldiers: Warner Brothers' Campaign Against Nazism*. New York, NY, United States: New York University Press.

Buxton, G. (1929). Letter to Captain Henry Swindler 23 July 1929. [Letter] National Archives and Records Administration, College Park, MD., Entry 310C, 'Thomas File'.

Buxton, G. (2000). *Official History of the 82nd Division: American Expeditionary Forces, 'All American' Division.* Reprint of 1919 text. Nashville, TN: Battery Press.

Cowan, S. (n.d.). *Sergeant York.* New York, United States. 1922: Grosset & Dunlap.

Danforth, E. (1929). Letter to Captain Henry Swindler. 5 August 1929. [Letter] National Archives and Records Administration, College Park, MD., Entry 310C 'Thomas File.'.

Das wuerttembergische Landwehr Infanterie Regiment Nr. 120 im Weltkriege 1914–1918. (1918). [War Diary] Hauptstaatsarchiv., Band 25. Stuttgart.

Das wuerttembergische Landwehr Infanterie Regiment Nr. 125 im Weltkrieg 1914–1918. (1918). [War Diary] Hauptstaatsarchiv, Stuttgart.

Das wuerttembergischen Regimenter im Weltkrieg 1914–1918. (n.d.). [Regimental History] Hauptstaatsarchive, EIIe 101/25P, 163–165, Das Wuerttembergische Landwehr Infanterie Regiment No. 120. Stuttgart.

Drive, D. (n.d.). Welcome to New River Notes. [online] Available at www.newrivernotes.com [Accessed 27 August 2016].

Eisenhower, J.S.D. (2002) *Yanks. The Epic Story of the American Army in World War 1.* New York: Simon & Schulster Adult Publishing Group.

Gilbert, M. (1995). *First World War.* London: Harper Collins Publishers.

Graves Registration Services. (n.d.). [Records] National Archives and Records Administration, Graves Registration Service Office of the Quartermaster General. College Park, Maryland, U.S.A.

Hart, B.L.H. (1992) *History of the First World War.* London: Macmillan paperback.

Hastings, M. and Hastings, S.M. (2013) *Catastophe 1914: Europe goes to War.* London, U.K: Harper Collins Publishing.

Hauptstaatsarchiv, Stuttgart (n.d.). 2nd Battalion Landwehr Regiment War Diary. M411 386/2723.

History of Three Hundred and Twenty-Eight Regiment of Infantry. (n.d.). ed. Allen County Public Library Gen 940.410.

History of the Eight Hundred and Fifth Pioneer Infantry American Expeditionary Forces. Major Paul S. Bliss, 1919 St Paul, Minn.

Keegan, J. (2000). *The First World War*. 1st ed. London: Hutchinson, pp. 401–403.

Kelly, M. (2008). *Sergeant York of the Argonne: Tour Guide*. London, United Kingdom: Ennogra Forest Publications.

Knowles Ed., A. and Harris, T. (2002). GIS in Archaeology. *Past Time, Past Place*.

Lee, D. (1985). *Sergeant York: An American Hero*. United States: The University Press of Kentucky.

Legg, J. (2010). 'Finding Sergeant York.' University of South Carolina. Scholar Commons, *Legacy*. Vol. 14 (No. 1 2010).

Lengel, E. (2009). *To Conquer Hell, The Meuse-Argonne, 1918*. Henry Holt & Co., New York.

Lowe, D. (2002). 'Telling Civil War Battlefield Stories with GIS.' Ed. Anne Knowles. Past Time, Past Places.

Mastriano, D. (2014). *Alvin York: A New Biography of the Hero of the Argonne*. 1st ed. Boulder, CO, United States: The University Press of Kentucky.

Mead, G. (2000). *The Doughboys: America and the First World War (*Allen Lane. London, United Kingdom: Allen Lane.

Merten, F. (1936). 'Testimony of German Officers and Men.' Anent Sergeant York. National Archives and Records Administration, College Park, MD., Entry 310B, 'Thomas File'.

Nolan, T. (2007). 'Battlefield Landscapes:' Geographic Information Science as A Method of Integrating History and Archaeology For Battlefield Interpretation. Ph.D. San Marcos, Texas. U.S.A.

Pattullo, G. (1919). 'The Second Elder Gives Battle.' *The Saturday Evening Post*.

Regimental Staff, 120th Landwehr Regiment. (n.d.). [Document] Hauptstaatsarchive, M411 382/2700. pp. 22–23. Stuttgart.

Scott, D. (1989). *Archaeological Perspectives on the Battle of the Little Bighorn*. 1st ed. Norman: University of Oklahoma Press.

Skeyhill, T. (1928). 'Sergeant York. His Own Life Story & War Diary.' 1st ed. New York: DoubleDay Doran, The pre-publication manuscript by Skeyhill. Held by the Sergeant York Foundation.

Swindler, H. (1929*)*. Letter to Colonel G. Edward Buxton. [Letter] National Archives, Entry 310C 'Thomas File'.

Swindler, H. (1929). Letter to Colonel G. Edward Buxton, 17 July 1929. [Letter] National Archives and Records Administration, College Park, MD., Entry 310C 'Thomas File'.

Swindler, H. (1929). Letter to Major E. C. B. Danforth, 29 July 1929. [Letter] National Archives and Records Administration, College Park, MD., Entry 310C 'Thomas File'.

Tallet, R. (1929). 'Controversy Still on Between Members of Heroic Band of Soldiers in Argonne Fight.' *The Niagara Falls Gazette*, [online] Page 4. Available at http://Fulton.history.com. (Item 0228 November 1929) [Accessed 26 April 2017].

Terraine, J. (1982). *White heat: The New Warfare, 1914–18*. London: Sidgwick & Jackson.

The Sergeant York Discovery Expedition. (2017). Home Page. [online] Available at www.sgtyorkdiscovery.com [Accessed 8 Nov. 2016].

Thoma, L. (1919). Personal Akten von Lt. Thoma (Personal Records of Lieutenant Thoma). [Statement by Thoma] Munchen, Bayerische Hauptstaatsarchiv, Abteilung IV, Kriegsarchiv, OP 14800, Thoma Personal Records. Munchen.

Thomas, S. (2000). *The History of the A.E.F.* Nashville, TN: Battery Press.

Tillman (1918), J. (1918). 82nd Division Field Orders and Memos. History of Operations. 1st ed. 82nd Airborne Division War Memorial Museum Archives, Fort Bragg, North Carolina.

Timmerman, T. (2017). Battle Detective Battle Studies. [online] Battledetective. com. Available at www.battledetective.com/battlestudy19.html [Accessed 10 March 2017].

United States Army Airborne Division, (2008). *Official History of 82nd Division American Expeditionary Forces: All American Division, 1917–1919* (1919). New York, NY, United States: Kessinger Publishing.

Van Meulebrouck, S. (2009). 'Hot on the York Trail.' The Western Front Association Bulletin, 84 (June/July 2009).

Van Meulebrouck, S. (2010). 'A Spot of Bother.' Unpublished Article. pp. 8–9.

Volksbund.de. (2017). Kriegsgräberstätte Buzancy, Volksbund.de (German War Graves – cemetery at Buzancy). [online] Available at www.volksbund. de/kriegsgraeberstaette/buzancy.html [Accessed 24 April 2017].

Wood, R. and Fox, R. (1997). *Archaeology, History, and Custer's Last Battle: The Little Big Horn Reexamined*. Norman: University of Oklahoma Press.

Index